The Devil's Advocates

Exposing the Counterfeits

Volume 1

The Devil's Advocates

Exposing the Counterfeits

Volume 1

Dr. A.J. Handy, Ph.D.

The Devil's Advocates
Exposing the Counterfeits
Volume 1

© Dr. A.J. Handy, Ph.D. 2023

All rights reserved. Without limiting the rights under copyright reserved above, no part of this publication may be reproduced, stored in a retrieval system, or transmitted, in any form or by any means (electronic, mechanical, photocopying, recording or otherwise), without the prior written permission of the copyright owner of this book.

Published by
Lighthouse Christian Publishing
SAN 257-4330
5531 Dufferin Drive
Savage, Minnesota, 55378
United States of America

www.lighthousechristianpublishing.com

Dr. A.J. Handy, Ph.D.

Foreword

It gives me great pleasure to write this foreword (The Devil's Advocates, Exposing the Counterfeits) for my friend and fellow brother in the Lord, Evangelist (Dr.) A. J. Handy. We met while stationed at Hickam Air Force Base, Hawaii in the mid-1970s. I was a member of St. Paul Church of God In Christ in Honolulu. The Pastor at that time was Bishop W. H. Reed. Brother Handy came seeking the gift of the Holy Ghost. His was an appetite that only God could assuage. Brother Handy's determination to be filled with the Holy Ghost was somewhat analogous to that which the Apostle Paul pontificated: "I follow after, if that I may apprehend that for which also I am apprehended of Christ Jesus." The would-be evangelist kept pressing his way seeking for, seemingly, an elusive prize. However, God lets us know that if we thirst and hunger for righteousness we shall be filled. And, as I recall, the author was filled with the Holy Ghost during one of Bishop Reed's Forth-night revivals, during the mmid-1970s I am told by many that he has won many souls for Christ since his experience.

Ensuing, we would both be reassigned to the mainland; I'm not exactly sure who left Hickam A.F.B first, Evangelist Handy or myself. But it has been more than forty years since we've spoken to one another. To hear from him, after such an extended period, was absolutely wonderful. We have a mutual friend, Minister James Davis of Palestine, Texas (who was also stationed with us at Hickam A.F. B). It was he which facilitated our reconnection. I am absolutely thrilled to endorse Dr.

Handy's work (The Devil's Advocates, Exposing the Counterfeits). The information is excellent, well researched, and extremely necessary for such a time as this. The Author has investigated twelve cults/sects and compared and contrasted their philosophies and liturgies to that of orthodox Christianity. The Scriptures says, "ye shall know the truth, and the truth shall make you free" (Jn. 8: 32). Well this corpus, and the invaluable information which it encapsulates, (if adhered to) will certainly do just that, make you free. God informed the Prophet Hosea that his (God's) people were destroyed because of a lack of knowledge. Evangelist Handy however has answered God's concern with this wealth of information; the scholar has also facilitated the acquisition of biblical knowledge by identifying, and punctuating, his narratives with Scripture references throughout the text. In his prose the author allegorically takes the readers by the hand and leads them through the labyrinth of the sects which he investigates. Moreover, within this book the scholar has presented us with an exhilarating, and research-based account of the possible existential effects presented by many of the most prominent cults and sects of today. Somewhat akin to a physician which makes a diagnosis, the writer not only enlightens his readers to the many nefarious montages exuded by several cults he also, proverbially, leaves the reader with a prescription, faith in Jesus Christ. The evangelist's detailed analysis, and graphic depiction of Protestantism's dismal failure in the county of Haiti is absolutely impeccable, as well as thought provoking.

The avid reader will notice that to captivate his readers Dr. Handy transitions his prose meticulously, and quite subtly, from the more obscure and least threatening

Abakua Cult, to the more profound and controversial ones. Even though each topic has its own apogee, the crescendo of the text superbly arises at the end, with Santeria and Voodoo. The scholar's review of the circumstances surrounding the deaths of Joseph Smith, Jr. and his sibling Hiram, the litigation procedures of Charles T. Russell and Judge Rutherford, and the Catholic's unwitting advancement of Santeria and Voodoo will, no doubt, raise lots of eyebrows while engendering much controversy. The author's denouncement of the United Pentecostal's positions of Forfeiture of Salvation, Speaking with Tongues as a requirement for salvation, and Jesus' Name only Baptism will, perhaps, prompt many within the movement to, at least, re-examine the concepts. Although the writer has obviously put aside any preconceived ideas, notions, and misconceptions concerning religious groups, the evangelist's narratives concerning - and asking the question - who are the "true Muhammadians" of Islam? will colloquially leave a bad taste in the mouths of many extremists. Nonetheless, readers will be enthralled and captivated throughout this riveting, illuminating, and thought-provoking text.

Elder Harold R. McDonald
Pastor: Temple of Prayer COGIC
Superintendent: Greater Greensboro (NC.) District
M/Sgt. USAF (Retired)

It is my utmost pleasure to give my friend and colleague, Dr. Adam J. Handy permission to include this foreword in his book titled: The Devil's Advocates, Exposing the Counterfeits.

Harold R. McDonald

About This Book

In this volume I have attempted to identify, expose, and carefully denude much of the erroneous and existential doctrine espoused by many major cults and sects. Doctrines and concepts which have lead many people astray for centuries, if not millennia. In or around the year 90 C.E. the Apostle John, reiterating the warning (1Jn. 4:1) which the Apostle Paul enunciated to the churches of Galatia some thirty years prior (Gal. 1: 8-9, 3: 1), pontificated that the Church (which is to say, the Body of Christ) should not accept the legitimacy of every spirit, spirits which purport to be sent from God, without validating their concepts by the Scriptures. Subsequently, *The Devil's Advocates, Exposing the Counterfeits* reveal to us, in the current age, many of the charlatans, false teachers/prophets, and much of the disturbing liturgy (which espouses unscriptural doctrine) which seek to deceive. Moreover, as noted within this corpus, a superfluity of those false teachers and charlatans will ostensibly display a "form of godliness" (See 2 Tim. 3:5); viz., practices which prima facie appear as biblical. However, in the run of their literature, and liturgy they harbor a proclivity for ignoring the power of the true and living God, Jehovah. Lastly, and perhaps more importantly, this book explains why the narratives promulgated by John and Paul (See 1 Jn. 4: 1, Gal. 1: 8-9,

3: 1), although announced over one thousand nine-hundred and thirty years ago, must be particularly adhered to during today's globally capricious social environment, and pantheistic ethos.

{Adam James Handy, Ph.D., Oct.15, 2021}

An Autobiographical Note

I was born on December 03, 1951 in the quaint, frontier town of Greenwood, Louisiana (USA), not far from the Texas border. Growing up I was the ninth child of Mary and Adam Handy; both are deceased. There were nine siblings. My father was an employee of the Kansas City Railroad Company; however, to supplement the household income he employed the Mule, plow, and harnesses to till the soil, preparing it for sharecropping. Mother (whom was colloquially referred to by my siblings and me as *Madear*) worked tirelessly – as a domestic - for the "social elites" of the cities of Greenwood, and Shreveport, Louisiana. I pitched in by mowing lawns in those cities where *Madear* was employed.

Ours was a Christian mileau; in fact, we were engaged in some aspect of church activity three to four days per week. Not unlike other extensions of the Jim Crow South schools, restaurants, and access to health care were the subjects of racial segregation. For I recall that the text books which were "handed down" to us, at Walnut Hill

High School (an institution for students whom were phenotypically Black), from C. E. Byrd High School, and Woodlawn High (institutions for students whom were predominately Anglo) were conspicuously scribbled with the "N-word" on several pages. Demeaning caricatures depicting stereotypical images of African phenotypes were also displayed among the contents. Gaining access to quality health care was a challenge for the family during the epoch of the Jim Crown experiment. I, in particular, suffered with asthma throughout childhood.

To finance my tertiary, and graduate level education - while simultaneously contributing to the war effort, in Vietnam – I enlisted in Dec. of 1969, two days short of my eighteenth birthday. Quite decorated and hurried through the ranks, after twenty years of distinguished service, I would don the dress-blues for the final time on May 31, 1990. Now, back in the States I matriculated at Chapman University, in Orange, Ca. It was at Chapman that I would make the acquaintance of the premier, prolific author, and highly sought after Professor Wilburn. Wilburn, after grading and extolling (before a class of many) one of my Term Papers encouraged me - as classmates applauded - to expand upon my topic, delve deeper into the subject matter, and possibly publish my findings. Those findings were published, not long thereafter, in my *Ethnocentrism and Black Students with Disabilities, Bridging the Cultural Gap*. That encouragement prompted me to author two other books:

Dr. A.J. Handy, Ph.D.

Comprehending the Pauline Epistles, a Study Guide, and *The Devil's Advocates, Exposing the Counterfeits.*

I have been involved in Christian Ministry, and evangelism, for well over forty years. During which time I've had the privilege of evangelizing throughout the U.S. (including Alaska & Hawaii), Latin and Central America (including Panama & Peru), the U.K. (to include Bedfordshire, Cardiff, Liverpool, Manchester, and London. My journeys have taken me through many other western destination of the United Kingdom as well; viz., from the southernmost Lands' End/Cornwall, to the most northern John O' Groats. I also served as Chaplain (in 1989) at Taegu Air Base (Republic of Korea) for a period. Finding no better place in which to retire I now reside in N. W. Louisiana, not far from the quaint, unassuming, frontier town where I grew up.

My Alma maters are:

Chapman University, Orange, CA.
The University of Nebraska, Lincoln
Louisiana State University, Baton Rouge
The University of Metaphysics, Studio City, CA.
Northwestern State University, Natchitoches, LA.
The University of Maryland, College Park

Acknowledgment

I have embarked upon my sixty-eighth year; my sixty-ninth is rapidly encroaching, and seventy lies not far beyond the horizon. It seems fitting, therefore, that I should narrate this acknowledgment of the Stranger before my twilight; before the synapses, the myelin sheath, and the dendrites seek to abrogate their duties; before age robs me of clarity; before the hemispheres capitulate and succumb to atrophy; before cognition begins to schedule her holidays; before the cornea and glaucoma embark upon their inevitable courtship; before stamina eludes; and, above all, before memory flees, hiding its face in betrayal of me.

The Stranger

When reading this acknowledgment of the Stranger, please note that the misspellings are not mere cacography or orthography but satiric, employed to more accurately script the colloquial lexicon of those I have referred to as hooligans.

In this work, I must acknowledge the brave, courageous Stranger who came to my rescue when, as a thirteen-year-old, I—after manicuring several lawns in a sweltering and completely unforgiving Louisiana summer and prevented by frugality from exchanging the fifteen cents required for the bliss of a refreshing Nehi—hastily decided to assuage my palate by repairing to an "off-limits" water fountain. This took place in the summer of 1964 in the northwest Louisiana frontier town of Greenwood. That day is one that will live in infamy, for I learned from that blunder that the uncompromising, systemic, and institutionalized laws of Jim Crow were not to be ignored.

It was as though the ghost of Bobby Lee himself had summoned Beauregard, Jackson's Virginians, Pickett's charge, and the entire Confederacy upon me! The very thought of the possibility of being carted off to the infamous, bloodthirsty Caddo Parish Penal Farm—reminiscent of the camps of Auschwitz or Dachau—was a crucible in and of itself. The scene, which I have kept quiet about since that day, has been indelibly etched within my hemispheres. Given the whirlwind of commotion, one would have thought that simply touching the handle of the fountain was a crime worthy of the gallows.

As the four bellicose eighteen to twenty-year-olds (reeking of alcohol) approached me, a young lady, after exiting one of the businesses, came to investigate. She was not hostile nor malevolent; rather, she was my protector. For, while engaging in a brief verbal exchange with the de facto justices of the peace, she demonstratively flung her right arm around me and, amazingly, shielded me ever so close against her back. Although momentarily discombobulated by my perfusion and the wallops of the heroine's long, dancing red locks (for as she whirled to face the apoplectic combatants, the tresses presented quite an erratic performance), I noticed that one of the ruffians—as he exited the green two-tone '57 Chevy—was carved with the insignia of the Confederacy on one of his shoulders. One of his taller, more vociferous, mates wore the swastika near the sternum. I have lost the memory of which shoulder featured the Confederacy, for I was thirteen then; I am sixty-eight now. Much of the minutiae has escaped me.

The more salient details, however, remain indelible. Nonetheless, during his (that is to say, the villain displaying the emblem of the secessionists) encroachment, several cigarettes escaped the package (labeled Kool) that was cuffed in his soiled short sleeve. One of his mates preferred Camel but not nearly as much as the alcohol of which he reeked. With her left arm straightened at approximately one hundred and eighty degrees, palm firmly facing outward (similar to that of a traffic police officer), the heroine curtailed the nefarious purposes of the Hitler youths.

However, one of the hooligans colloquially spewed, "Dat nigga ain't got no business putting his filthy mouth on our watta fountain!"

The Stranger replied, "He's a kid, leave him alone; can't you see he's thirsty?"

One of the hooligans: "I don't give a damn! Next thang you know, dem niggas gonna wanna use the same toilets as us and eat at the same lunch counters as us!"

Another one of the hooligans: "Hell, it's too late for dat; they done already took over Woolworth; we can't even get a dam seat in dare no mo!"

The Stranger: "Well, it's not this kid's fault."

The castigation continued, for one of the villains insisted, "Hell, there's a watta fountain round the back just for them; let him use dat one!"

One of the hooligans: "I don't know where you from, but round here we don't allow dat. That son of a bitch know his place."

Adam J. Handy (age twelve) A drawing of the Stranger
(A year prior to the encounter) (By Victoria Skye English)

GREEN MOOR ELEM.
1962–63

Along the periphery of my vision, I spied a truck that had pulled up; it was laden with pulpwood. Two men exited; wiping the sweat from their brows and brushing debris from their heads and clothing, they ambled unassumingly toward the fountain (the exact same one that I had tasted from) and refreshed themselves. *What temerity!* I thought. The two had the physique of a twenty-five-year-old Arnold Schwarzenegger, although they were somewhat heavier. The shortest must have been around 6'9", the mate three or four inches taller. Both were at least sixteen stone. The two were not harassed; they appeared to be Mandingo (Mandinka). Why was I singled out for such anathema as a persona non grata, I wondered. *Must I have the physique of those guys in order to get by?* I surmised. Nonetheless, I had never heard such language before, nor had I ever encountered anyone so enraged and apoplectic. Suddenly, a scantily clad, bodacious blonde exited the front passenger's side.

Adjusting her halter top, she shouted, "Knock it off, guys! Leave that boy alone!" Momentarily she was ignored; however, she would continue to shout, "Come on! It's hot out here; we're late guys. We gotta be in Tyler at two!"

The ringleader (the villain flaunting the Stars and Bars of the Confederacy) took one last dig; leaning forward, he slowly and deliberately exhaled a cloud upon me. The irritant, albeit a sweet-smelling tobacco (combined with oppressive humidity, the stench of alcohol, and temperatures exceeding ninety-eight degrees Fahrenheit), entering and annoying the olfactory system, exacerbated my asthmatic predisposition. Albuterol Sulfate, Advair HFA, or Proair/Rescue inhalers (medicines used to treat asthmatics) were not very prevalent, as I recall, in many disadvantaged communities. At any rate, there was no time to let on, for the ordeal before me was much too daunting. Methodically, the young man squashed the remains of his cigarette with the ball of his right foot. Finally, there was relief, for as the scoundrels (absolutely devoid of compunction) retired to their '57 Chevy, fear reluctantly made its escape and was supplanted by a modicum of comfort, which slowly began to entertain me. From neutral to first gear, one last proverbial shot across the bow was volleyed: "NIGGA LOVER!" To the lyrics of Patsy Cline's "I Fall to Pieces" (Cochran and Howard, 1961), the four-on-the-floor, burning rubber and oil and relinquishing one of its hubcaps as it fishtailed seemingly out of control, screeched vociferously toward Waskom and Harrison County. Ensuing obnoxious Quaker State, along with light-blue smoke, lingered along Highway 80 in its wake. Simultaneously, we gasped.

It was extremely unique and quite daring on the Stranger's part (demonstratively coming to the aid of an African-American), considering the ethos of that period. After depositing the handsome sum of four bits (the equivalent of fifty cents in US currency at that time and, indeed, quite a handsome, gratuitous amount, particularly in the mind of an exhausted thirteen-year-old) in my sweat-exuding palm and deliberately enfolding my trembling fingers around the coins, she advised me to run along. The heroine did not have to tell me twice! Although relieved, anxiety would not summarily abandon me; however, I was able to rally enough composure to amble from the scene. With the four bits in hand, I was not only able to purchase that refreshing drink but a succulent Honey Bun as well. As I recall, there was change to spare. Most things simply were not very expensive during the early to mid-sixties. Indeed, five or six dollars were enough to allow the entrance of two people into the ShowTown Drive-in Theater in Shreveport with enough left over for a couple of sodas and hot dogs.

Throughout the years (somehow disguising the pain of that dreadful scene), I have often thought of the Stranger, replaying the archived, indelible scene quite often, wondering how I would have fared if she had not intervened. Some, if so accosted, would've no doubt branded her an angel—perhaps so. However, at that time, I was only interested in escaping the crucible. Nevertheless, whether providence or simply arbitrary, hers—it seemed—was a philosophy of dissonance, very egalitarian. She appeared to be devoid of any ethnocentric predispositions; her position on class structure and the superiority or inferiority of phenotypes simply did not resonate with that of the status quo.

    The idea of lodging a complaint against the hooligans was only briefly entertained, for even if I had known the correct procedures or could have rallied enough courage to seek the redress of my grievances, justice would simply have "changed its robe" and hidden its face while inequality, case law, and discrimination—instigated by decades-old unfavorable legislation—conspired against me. Ethos, no doubt, would have corroborated their testimony. Nonetheless, such an action would have been fruitless, for the infamous George W. D'Artois, Sr. was public safety commissioner at that time, and during that epoch, the Shreveport (a much larger city contiguous to the hamlet of Greenwood, LA) public safety commissioner was not obliged to answer to the mayor. Not that it would have made any difference.

    At any rate, D'Artois was left to invent his own "neo-Draconian" form of law and order. D'Artois thought of Caddo Parish and every town or hamlet therein as his own fiefdom. And when it came to the control of certain phenotypes, his form of law and order was an architecture that was all but despotic. The former Shreveport public safety commissioner, a surrogate for Nathan Bedford Forrest and an admirer of the ethnocentric Alabama Governor George Wallace, was an ardent segregationist.

Dr. A.J. Handy, Ph.D.

D'Artois made it his proverbial badge of honor to prolong the "reign of terror" espoused by *Plessy v. Ferguson*. For under his watch, there would be little, if any, deviation from the Plessy experiment, the "Brown legislation" (striking down Plessy) notwithstanding. To D'Artois, egalitarianism was a foreign concept, a cogitation that unfortunately never found its way into his repertoire. But I cannot judge; I do remain, however, keenly aware— even after these many years—of the facts, and it is quite factual that "separate and unequal" was his mantra. If not for the grace of God and the divinely authorized in loco parentis of the Stranger, I would have, quite possibly, gone the way of Emmitt Till, Medgar Evers, James Meredith, or perhaps Harper Lee's character Tom in the classic *To Kill a Mockingbird* (1960).

None of what I have chronicled in this narrative concerning George W. D'Artois is hyperbole. Rather, all that has been revealed concerning Mr. D'Artois are facts, archived, well documented, and unfortunately well experienced by the minority population of that era. These facts must be made known, not by outsiders whose only intentions are to profit at book signings or, as in the case of many untenured professors, to publish prolifically in order to facilitate the obtainment of tenure. When scripted by such motives, accuracy, attention to detail, and objectivity will be severely compromised. It must be told by those who were actually there at the time. Subsequently, it is incumbent upon me, one of the few minorities that are still around from D'Artois's heyday, to, albeit briefly, illustrate some of the malicious and nefarious actions of George D'Artois.

Three books addressing the exploits of D'Artois have already been published; that triumvirate (e.g., J.

Joiner, 2013; G. Joiner, 2016; Brock, 2001), focusing primarily on the former public safety commissioner's alleged malfeasance and the hit that was put out on D'Artois's former campaign manager, Jim Leslie, does not present a totally accurate rendition of the minority population's experience during D'Artois's "reign of terror." Two of the sources leave it as a proverbial footnote. J. Joiner, however, paints a decent portrait of the African-American experience, but the background and foreground, allegorically, could do with a bit more contrast along with some retouching. A much different perspective, however, is presented when viewed through and written from the lenses of a minority scholar, particularly one who actually experienced D'Artois's despotic and draconian measures.

     As for the Stranger, never once did I see her smile, even when danger had been abated. Perhaps she had realized that she, too, had broken the "rules" of Jim Crow. Within Mr. D'Artois's kingdom and tributaries far afield, no one (e.g., J. Leslie, J. Joiner), even those in his inner circle, was totally secure, for fear of the former Shreveport public safety commissioner was even harbored by those with whom Mr. D'Artois was closely connected. As concerning the Stranger, perhaps it was I who was simply oblivious to her smile. As a product (although not fully assembled) of the Jim Crow/Plessy experiment, I had learned vicariously during my thirteen years that it was unlawful for a "colored" man (at least in D'Artois's fiefdom) to stare at or look directly into the eyes of a Caucasian woman. That was the law, solidly Jim Crow. It was colloquially termed "intentional eyebrowing," an accusation that could have caused one to—at the very least—receive a prison sentence. For more on D'Artois's reign of terror and exploits, (including his alleged murder-for-hire plot, malfeasance and bribery charges, his racial injustices, and the brutal beating by D'Artois's deputies of a prominent preacher/civil rights leader), the reader is advised to acquire a copy of *Badge of Dishonor: A True Story of Police Racism, Brutality, and Murder in a Deep South City* (Jere Joiner, 2013). Gary D. Joiner's work, *Legendary Locals of Shreveport*, coauthored by Prime (2016, pg. 99), while corroborating my testimony, reveals a grim exposé of a dejected, demoralized D'Artois, essentially relegating memories of him to the repositories of the forgotten relics of the past. Brock (2001, pg. 43), in his corpus *Images of America, Shreveport Faces of the Past*, although failing to treat much of the minutiae of the de facto despot, substantiates many of the allegations against D'Artois brought forth in this text.

Moreover, much of D'Artois's alleged exploits are also archived at the East Baton Rouge (Louisiana) Clerk of Court's repository. To retrieve this information, one should contact the East Baton Rouge Clerk of Court/19th Judicial District Court Criminal Records Department. As of the date of this composition, their web address is ebrclerkofcourt.org. Upon inquiring, the researcher should reference case numbers 04-77-0635, and 04-77-0491. The texts mentioned above, coupled with the information formally archived concerning D'Artois at the East Baton Rouge's Clerk of Court office, will corroborate most of which has been mentioned concerning the former Shreveport public safety commissioner. However, as concerning the havoc and brutality wreaked upon the Black citizens by the lieutenants of D'Artois fiefdom, only a few of us are left to tell.

Nonetheless, perhaps that brave lady, garbed as

though she would have been more comfortable at a Led Zeppelin, Grateful Dead, Hendrix, or Woodstock concert than in our sleepy little town, is still among us. It is quite possible, for she was in her early to mid-twenties in 1964. Succinctly put, the Stranger was one who, metaphorically, "marched to the beat of a different drum." Nevertheless, she is afforded this acknowledgement, for while she did little that would affect the modus operandi within the proverbial feudal domain, she displayed a wonderful paradigm of cross-cultural awareness. The Stranger vicariously taught me that "true Christianity," the brand by which I had been nourished, was still extant. Following that, the implications were that no group is completely monolithic; therefore, no preconceived ideas or notions should be harbored against any phenotype, ethnicity, or group. Those vicarious lessons have not evaporated. The Stranger taught me well on that sweltering summer's day.

A. J. Handy, PhD, March 16, 2020

Dr. A.J. Handy, Ph.D.

Dedication

I would like to thank my wife, Beverly, for lending me her set of lenses and keeping the research afloat for three weeks while my pair recovered from LASIK eye surgery. She is also credited with ensuring the accuracy, harmony, and relevance of scriptures as they relate to this manuscript. Samantha, my daughter, also insisted that I not tax my lenses until such time as recovery was complete. Thank you, Beverly and Samantha, for—even though my research has been severely stymied by the predatorial and indiscriminating coronavirus pandemic and three surgical procedures (Jan. through Sept. '20)—without your contributions and advice, this work would've been much further delayed. My gratitude is also extended to the professors at Louisiana State University, the University of Metaphysics in the Golden State, Chapman University (also in southern California), the University of Maryland, the University of Nebraska, and Northwestern State University (Louisiana), for it was they who provided me with the skillset necessary to endure such an eclectic and rigorous assignment. Many librarians and the East Baton Rouge Clerk of Court opened their repositories to me; I'm immensely grateful! I would be remiss if I did not posthumously thank Mary Blackshire Handy and Adam Handy (my parents), who braved the draconian social elements (that is to say, sharecropping, intimidation at the ballot box, poll taxes, literacy exams, etc.) of Plessy and Jim Crow so that life for me and their subsequent progeny would be better than they had known it.

Mary B. Handy　　　　　　**Adam Handy**
(9/21/1919–10/6/2004)　　　(8/22/1902–8/30/1980)

My mother's parents, of whom I have no recollection, were Bessie Waynes McKnight and Elisha Blackshire. I've no record of my father's parents, only that his father's name was Dan. To all of them and those who came before, I and many others shall always be immensely indebted. Of course, I must thank God, Jesus, and the Holy Ghost, the triumvirate upon which I ultimately rely, for strengthening and reassuring me, for there were occasions when I considered (after three rounds of surgery) it might be best to shelve this work, walk away, and forgo it. However, God continued to prod, constantly reiterating that his grace is sufficient for me.

　　　　　　　　　　　Dr. A. J. Handy, PhD

Table of Contents

Introduction--22

Abakua/Naniguismo------------------------------------33

Buddhism--45

Christian Identity Groups-------------------------------65

Confucianism---79

Hinduism--99

Islam---117

Jehovah's Witnesses/Watchtower Bible and Tract Society---138

Mormonism---168

Oneness Pentecostals-----------------------------------195

Rastafarianism---207

Santeria---217

Voodoo (Vodou)---243

Summary and Avoiding the Lure of the Devil's Advocates--258

Suggested Churches/Denominations-----------------266

References--272

Further Suggested Literature--------------------------280

Introduction

From the lesser-known skull cults of Gobekli Tepe, Turkey, that practiced nearly eleven thousand years ago to the mesmerizing Voodoo practices of Marie Laveau (who perfected her alchemy in what was once known as Congo Square, now identified as Louis Armstrong Park, New Orleans, Louisiana, in the U.S.), to the more widely known concepts of Mormonism and the more recent practices of the Rastafarians (who are soundly convinced that the late Emperor Haile Selassie I, a mere mortal, is the Messiah), occultism and the paranormal have victimized and disillusioned the psyche of mankind since the dawn of time. This research involves the investigation of twelve cults; some (e.g., Mormonism, Buddhism) the reader will recognize on their face but might not be aware of their agendas; others (e.g., Abakua, Santeria) the reader may, perhaps, find totally foreign.

Moreover, while many aspects of the occult will be addressed in this inquiry, this text is not designed to disclose the features of all religious cults or sects, for such a volume would invariably be severely betrayed; rather, the focus of this inquiry is primarily on the exposure of those sects/cults that, while disguising themselves under the banner of Christianity (i.e., Mormons, Oneness Pentecostals, Jehovah's Witnesses, etc.), not only employ the tactics of brainwashing to ensure the adherence of their proselytes but also vigorously promulgate Satan's deceit. This the author has termed "orthodoxy dissonance." The concepts and rituals of Eastern and African-connected cults—that is to say, Hinduism, Santeria, Abakua, and their appendages—will also be addressed in this corpus. Also, please note that for the purposes of this investigation, unless otherwise noted, all biblical references cited in this text are to be interpreted in the language of the classical King James Version. At this juncture, it is appropriate to examine the features that are characteristic of cults.

Criteria Associated with Cults

(1) The use of methodologies, dogmas, or liturgy along with, or that do not comport with, biblical scriptures.
(2) Unquestioned loyalty to the founder(s) or current leader.
(3) The leaders dictate the outside activities and attire of the members.
(4) Mind-altering or behavior modification practices.
(5) The leader, or founder, is viewed as deified or closer to God than anyone or anything else.
(6) Only the group's practices and concepts are correct; all others are entirely false.
(7) Ridicule/peer pressure resulting from noncompliance or from questioning the group's motives or activities.
(8) Members fear being outcast or banished.[1]

Of the criteria listed above, arguably the most

---

[1] *International Cultic Studies Association (ICSA) Today*, *Vol. 6, No. 3*, 2015, 10.

telling are criterion one, two, and five, for they provide the elixir necessary for the confluence of all others. Moreover, perhaps the most dangerous of the cults—for those wishing to pursue Christianity—are those that feature the Bible in their liturgy (i.e., Santeria, Christian Identity Groups, Latter-Day Saints, Jehovah's Witnesses). Because the Bible, and in some instances even Jesus himself, is lauded among the principals of these congregants, the unsuspecting worshippers—and in many instances, neophytes—assume that they will be properly taught concerning Jesus and God's plan of salvation. They are instead lured further and more insidiously into the occult's entrapment. If fabricated or ostensibly inexplicable events should occur in such gatherings, invariably and without a modicum of doubt or skepticism, such occurrences are immediately attributed to the actions of a god. Furthermore, when the authenticity of such events is questioned, the principals are offended; dissidents are subjected to derision; they're soon maligned, ridiculed, and marginalized. Others, to avoid such sanctions, will assimilate the deceit. Hence the onset of brainwashing.

From this point on, few doubts or suspicions are harbored, for the converts are constantly reminded, albeit subtly, that to question the veracity of the cult's practices would result in the foreclosure and subsequent forfeiture of their salvation. In their attempts to lure and capture their prey, counterfeit religious leaders will initially appear quite charming and benevolent. However, as soon as the converts are ripe, the leaders will suddenly begin to exude a demeanor that's more dictatorial and malevolent. They're shrewd. Many of these iniquitous groups will purport the premise that there is, somehow, a type of symbiosis or nexus between their dogmas and that of orthodox Christianity. Be warned, for that's not at all true. While there are some similarities between, let's say, Mormonism and orthodox Christianity, when the two are juxtaposed, it is basically dichotomies and contradictions that rise to the fore.

Therefore, if the newly converted Christian is to thrive in the knowledge of Jesus Christ, such groups must be vigilantly surveilled and avoided. The neophyte must also be warned to never dabble in the theology of such sects nor attempt to convert the adherents. One will find that many among these groups are well aware of the life and legacy of Jesus Christ. Moreover, the overzealous abecedarian can be completely overwhelmed by the Devil's surrogates. Many rituals, particularly those metastasized by the ancient African arts (that is to say, Santeria, Voodoo, Abakua) and allowed to distill across the globe, are apt to result in feats that are quite mesmerizing—the pathology and epitome of evil! This mesmerizing can nowhere be better exemplified in the Bible than in Acts 19:13–16.

However, efforts must be put forth to bring the good news of the gospel to everyone. Nowhere other than the gospels is there a better paradigm of this than in Acts 10:9–15, where the Apostle Peter harbors prejudice toward the Gentiles, coupled with his obedience in Acts 10:25–35, and his pronouncement in 2 Peter 3:9, during which the apostle proclaims, "The Lord is not slack concerning his promise…but is longsuffering toward us, *not willing that any should perish*" (emphasis added). Nevertheless, only the most adept evangelists should tread here, and extreme caution should be taken. The tactics of the occult are very subtle, cunning, and witty. For it does not distinguish its prey; its prize is the pauper as well as the elite; the illiterate is not second to the Rhodes or Fulbright Scholar. The occult has an insatiable appetite for the minds of all; the Cambridge University dean, the Juilliard graduate, and the Ivy League presidents are not exempted. Cults are not intimidated by, nor are they partisan to, any social or political divisions. To all but a few, phenotypes are of little concern. That is to say, the Mormons, up until 1978, believed that those of the African diaspora were cursed; subsequently, the Latter-Day Saints did not bother to proselytize among them. Also, the Abakua, and Santeria cults, deeply rooted in ancient African rituals, were once reluctant to initiate those of non-African progeny into their orders.

Even the most theologically advanced are quite often no match for those who practice under the auspices and direction of satanic forces. Consider, for example, the renowned reformation father Martin Luther. With perhaps the exception of St. Augustine or John Wycliffe, Luther was arguably the most prolific theologian of post-biblical times (St. Thomas Aquinas, Jerome, John Huss, or LeFevre notwithstanding); yet he proved to be an inferior opponent for the decadent and bellicose papal authorities of his day. For demonic forces aroused Pope Leo X to use the power of the corrupted papacy as leverage to excommunicate Luther in 1521 CE. Approximately one hundred and thirty-five years earlier, diabolical forces would move upon Pope Gregory XI to cause John Wycliffe to experience similar engagements as those hatched against Luther, though he was not excommunicated (White, 1911). The papacy wielded great satanic powers and authority during the pre-Reformation and well into the post-Reformation periods.

The papacy has, of course, since evolved; it is unfortunate, however, that many Protestant theologians, as well as other biblical scholastics, continue to view the system through fourteenth-, fifteenth-, and sixteenth-century lenses. The popes, as of the seventeenth century, abandoned much of the debauchery and excessive opulence maintained and flaunted by the pejorative old guard (e.g., Leo VIII, Benedict V, Leo IX, Leo X, Gregory VI, Gregory XI, Gregory XIII, Benedict I).

Nonetheless, the occult knows no boundaries, for control of the mind is what it seeks. Moreover, it does appear that an inordinate number of the occult's followers are those who are seeking religious acceptance and a sense of belonging. They have been betrayed and subsequently disillusioned by the mendacious deeds of charlatans (who have misrepresented Christianity) of legitimate orthodox Christian groups (i.e., Baptist, Methodist, Lutheran, Episcopal, Presbyterian, Pentecostals, etc.). Subsequently, the disenchanted become prime targets of the Devil's advocates and their deceitfulness.

Many of these cults, in order to advance their initiatives, have even indicted and sought to impeach not only Jerome's Vulgate but the Septuagint as well. The Jehovah's Witnesses, for example, have published their own version of the Bible (The New World Translation/NWT), the veracity of which must be held suspect. Their text must be called into question, for many verses—the reconstruction of which the novice might be oblivious of—are clearly satanic in their transliterations, as can be observed by theologians. Those verses seek to supplant and betray many of the basic (theological) tenets of orthodox Christianity. Why is it important, one will ask, to steer clear of the NWT? It's necessary because, for instance, the King James or authorized version (KJV) was translated from Greek via the aforementioned Vulgate, which the Witnesses have misconstrued. Therefore one will not garner from reading the NWT the true concepts that the KJV (and most others) wishes to communicate. One must remain cognizant of the fact that the New World Translation was written by Jehovah's Witnesses specifically to promote their viewpoints and theirs alone. Discrepancies of this sort will be discussed under the appropriate headings elsewhere in this volume.

Since the downfall of Adam and Eve (Gen. 3), man has struggled with and agonized over the void within that, if he is to find true peace and happiness, must be filled. He seeks the truth and the corollary results of finding it. However, the occult's mission is to ensnare, arrest, and darken the mind and soul of the individual. Neither salvation nor eternal life can be found in its repertoire, for all cults advocate on behalf of Satan and function pursuant to his auspices.

Conversely, Jesus Christ is the harbinger of legitimate salvation and eternal life. Matt. 4:16 reveals, "The people which sat in darkness saw great light; and to them which sat in the region and shadow of death light is sprung up." Many centuries prior to and during the entirety of the four-hundred-year Silent Period (from the writings of the prophets to the advent of the New Covenant, or coming of Christ), the people of Yahweh (another name for God or Jehovah) were primarily idolatrous and, to put it mildly, hedonistic. They were in search of fulfillment, an enigma with which the unregenerated will continues to struggle. To fill the emptiness and the void within, they crafted their own gods (see Ex. 32:1–6, 1 Kings 18:17–39, 1 Cor. 10:7. They couldn't fathom the premise that following Jehovah could be as simple as approaching him through faith; therefore, they went in search of what they thought was the truth (see Deut. 18:10–12, Lev. 19:31, 1 Sam. 28:7–13, 1 Chr. 10:13–14, 2 Chr. 33:1–7).

During his three and one-half years' ministry, Jesus proclaimed, "Ye shall know the truth, and the truth shall make you free" (John 8:32). The actions of the occult, in some affiliations, (i.e., Voodoo, Witchcraft, Abakua) can often mimic those practices revealed in the Bible (see Ex. 7:10–12, 20–22, 8:6–7, Acts 8:9–24); however, as it was with the false prophets in the days of pharaoh and the Apostle Paul, so it is with the cults of today. They always keep their date with doom. Note the prose of Ps. 55:23: "Bloody and deceitful men shall not live out half their days." The Devil employs many weapons when mobilizing and rallying his lieutenants. Among these lieutenants' most trusted, dependable, and reliable charades are to masquerade as demonstrative, magnanimous, and more intellectual than other more orthodox Christian groups. Perhaps it was not mere nugatory verbiage when the legendary Apostle Paul penned, "We wrestle not against flesh and blood, but against principalities, against powers, against the rulers of the darkness of this world, against spiritual wickedness in high places" (Ephesians 6:12). Furthermore, the truly born again can take comfort in the prophecy of the former captive Isaiah, for he proclaimed, "No weapon that is formed against thee shall prosper" (note Isaiah 54:17).

An in-depth analysis of biblical scripture and a sincere desire to be led by the Spirit of God will allow one to avoid the pitfalls, deceit, and entanglements of the

Devil's disingenuous advocates. Jesus put it succinctly when he said, "Beware of false prophets, which come to you in sheep's clothing, but inwardly they are ravening wolves" (see Matt. 7:15). This volume will illuminate the deceit of many of those false prophets, which Jesus (and the venerable Apostle Paul; Rom. 16:17–18, 1 Tim. 4:1, 2 Tim. 3:1–5) predicted would arrive. I shall attempt to accomplish this by exposing theological malpractices where discovered while extolling those doctrines that harmonize with orthodox Protestantism.

Those who are familiar with my works, however, have come to expect that when referencing religions, stylistically, my narratives are invariably devoid of polemics, derisions, and orientalism. This volume also is without exception, for, as with any evangelistic endeavor, it is important to bring unbelievers into the ethos of Christendom. Ridicule or satire are to be avoided, for those only serve to further alienate. Sincere pathos and compassion (their antithesis), however, are the qualities that the author would like to prescribe. God, when warning Israel about future events, announced through the Prophet Jeremiah, "With lovingkindness have I drawn thee" (Jer. 31:3). Therefore, those who would evangelize or otherwise lead others to accept Christ must never become conflicted between orthodoxy (adhering to a set of beliefs) and orthopraxy (correct conduct and behavior while adhering to those beliefs). The two are never mutually exclusive. Nowhere is such a confliction better exemplified than in the hypocritical behavior of Jesus's nemeses, the Pharisees, and the scribes. Even though they were well versed in Moses's orthodoxy, their orthopraxy was egregiously wanting; they would often "say, and do not" (Matt. 23:3).

While maintaining scholastic and academic integrity, the author has formatted the topics in a clear and concise motif. This formula will allow the readers to easily grasp the information without resorting to painstakingly muddling through rigid, much too academic, and intimidating sources. Moreover, the author has assiduously identified, arrested, and euthanized any personal preconceptions, and biases of the sects that are being investigated. Objectivity is paramount in a work of this genre, for only by employing it can accurate accounts and portrayals be realized.

Each chapter will begin with an investigation of the history of the cult/sect in question. The brief history will be followed by a look at the basic beliefs and rituals of the cult. Following that, I have attempted, where possible, to illuminate the parallels shared by the cult and orthodox Christianity. Next, the reader will notice my endeavor to reveal the contrasts or dichotomies between the religion under review and orthodox Christianity. I am also compelled to elaborate upon the soteriological views (how salvation is obtained) of each dogma. Of course, the reader will want to know what the cult promulgates about the apocalyptic age or the end times; this will, of course, be discussed under the heading of Eschatological Perspectives. Afterward, the author has explained the concerns and implications that the orthodox Christian should be aware of. For more in-depth study, each section will be followed by a carefully composed list of suggested readings. The section titled "Summary and Avoiding the Lure of the Devil's Advocates" will amalgamate the contents of this corpus. That topic also introduces the reader to measures and paradigms that can be employed to properly evangelize and sever ties with the occult.

Lastly, one will notice a presentation of a list of suggested churches/denominations.

Dr. A.J. Handy, Ph.D.

Section One

Abakua/Naniguismo

Founding/Brief History

The dawn of the mid-nineteenth century was followed by the continuance of the transatlantic slave trade to Cuba. Whereas slavery in the United States (U.S.) and its territories had long been abolished by the passage of the Thirteenth Amendment during the early 1860s, it would be another twenty years or more (1886) before Spain suspended its Cuban ports of call. The authorities, by royal decree, would end involuntary servitude. This decree, however, was only a formality; it would not make life much better for the enslaved people. They were still considered inferior and were forced to accept their deplorable conditions. Moreover, Velez (2000) reveals that 85 percent of all slaves brought to Cuba arrived there far into the 1800s. Spain appeared to have had a proclivity for and was primarily interested in capturing the peoples of Nigeria along with Nigeria's western neighbor Benin and perhaps those as far east as Cameroon. These populations (i.e., Nigerians, Cameroonians, and Beninese) commanded the Yoruba and Bantu dialects. They were rounded up, shackled, and crammed into awaiting vessels. At this juncture it is important to be clear. For, although Britain did not officially sanction the arrival and involuntary servitude of captured Africans - via the Transatlantic Slave Trade – into its United Kingdom (e.g., Wales, Scotland, Northern Ireland, England) She would of course employ that trade to practice chattel slavery far abroad, within her tributaries. Barbados, Jamaica,

Trinidad and Tobago, Saint Vincent, and Montserrat were only a smidgen of her fiefdoms. Alexander Campbell's 1852 phrase still rings true; the sun never sets on the British Empire. Spain's ports of call, now that the U.S. and Great Britain had banned slavery, were almost invariably Brazil, Cuba, and Haiti. Life was harsh. However, the enslaved peoples were deeply rooted and predisposed to cultic and ritual fervor. Abakua, a religion that is widely practiced in Cuba by the progenies of the Yorubas and Bantu peoples of West Africa, had its impetus in, and was heavily influenced by, the Leopard Society. This community appears to have been located along the Cross River section of southeastern Nigeria and portions of Cameroon. The captives, although completely subjugated, did not abandon their customs. Rather, to disguise them, they amalgamated their rituals with those presented to them by their overlords and Spanish priests.

These religious syncretism primarily evolved into Voodum (Vodou) in Haiti, Candomblé in Brazil, and Santeria in Cuba. However, there were smaller, lesser-known cults brewing in Cuba (i.e., Abakua, Paleros) that would eventually percolate and satiate the cultural and religious appetites of many. Abakua, or Naniguismo, which is the focus of my investigation in this section, was, according to Nichols, Mather, and Schmidt, founded in Cuba in 1834 by one who shares the cult's name, Abakua (2006). Although Abakua is a cult in its own right and is stylistically unique, research leads one to conclude that, invariably, the Nanges (often referred to as Nanigos) are not exclusively involved in Abakua. They have a proclivity for dabbling in other West Indian and Caribbean cultic arts (e.g., Santeria, Voodum) as well. Santeria and Voodum will be given their places and discussed at length elsewhere in this volume. However, because Santeria, Abakua, Voodum, and Rastafarianism—the four Afrocentric cults that I've investigated—are closely related, they will at times be juxtaposed to reveal dichotomies and similarities under one another's headings.

Basic Beliefs and Rituals

Despite being dwarfed by larger, more preeminent cults (i.e., Santeria, Voodum, and Rastafarianism), primarily located within the Caribbean or West Indies region, this secretive, all-male dance troupe/cult known as Abakua or Naniguismo has weathered the storm and managed to survive. The initiates are known as Nanigos and often referred to as Nanges. Abakua somewhat resembles Santeria in that it is syncretic with Catholicism, rooted in West African, Cuban, and Christian traditions, and employs divination.

Although there are ideological and philosophical similarities between Abakua and Santeria as mentioned in the previous paragraph, the two are stylistically quite different. They must be treated as such. Abakua is ideologically and philosophically similar to Santeria in that the converts are initiated into one of the orders of the Orishas, or seven main African gods. The Orishas will be discussed in more detail in section eleven, wherein the author addresses the subject of Santeria. There are two main orders of the Abakua Society: the Efo and the Efi. Initially, and for quite a number of years, those who were not phenotypically African weren't allowed initiation into either of the branches. However, due to the assertive proselytizing efforts of competing religions (that is to say,

Christianity, Mormonism, Rastafarianism, and various island-born Cuban and Creole cults) and financial constraints, both groups reluctantly amended their prerequisites. Brown (2003) maintains that there were Whites initiated into the Efo's branch in Havana (Cuba) of the Abakua cult as early as 1863, some twenty-nine years or so after the cult's founding.

Unlike Christianity, which insists upon baptism in water only, those who desire initiation into the Abakua cult have a choice of either having what amounts to dirt poured over them or having water from a hollowed gourd emptied over them, along with being showered with basil leaves. Afterward, an African name is adopted, and the neophyte, as it is with the converts to Santeria, pledges to one of the Orishas, or seven main African gods. Not unlike all other aspects of Abakua (which are shrouded in secrecy), the convert's new name is his secret identity. The esoteric practices of this sect are, from the drumming to the maneuvering of the Iremes (those— although it's usually one person—who are allegedly delivering and mimicking the instructions of one or more of the gods), very secretive and not to be leaked. Hence, outsiders—if allowed to attend rituals—are viewed with suspicion and cautiously observed.

Worship focuses upon Abasi (the supreme god of the Abakua theology), the Okobio (the priest), drumming, dances, the Famba or temple/altar, and, of course, the Iremes or little devils. The purpose of the liturgy and ceremony is to conjure up or invoke a familiar spirit called Diablito, or better known among the Nanigos (the faithful) as Ireme(s). During the invocation, the priest holds one maraca or carved-out gourd (often filled with the leaves of plants, beans, or even pebbles) in each hand.

The more violently and profoundly he dances and shakes the maracas, the more likely the Iremes are to appear. The Nanigos insist that the drums are sacred and must be consecrated and given sacrificial blood periodically. The drumming is also believed to provide an avenue to animate Abasi and serves as a pivotal and necessary part of the Abakua modus operandi. Abakua rituals must always begin and end with drumming. As the four drums are played, the drummers are allegedly drumming to the interpretations of what the Iremes, which are always silent, are relating to the congregants. The Iremes are invoked to provide guidance, advice, and warnings concerning future malevolent or benevolent events and dangers. An Ireme, in masquerade attire, will always appear during the sessions and supposedly mimic the interpretations and revelations of the gods. Paradoxically, the Iremes, or "little devils," are supposed to protect against evil spirits.

Parallels to Orthodox Christianity

Although Abakua presents an altar adorned with pictures of Christ and the Virgin Mary along with the rosary, a crucifix, and pictures of Catholic saints, one must not be deceived. Alongside these can also be seen maracas or gourds filled with dried plant leaves, rooster feathers, perhaps a model of a rooster, and other esoteric objects as well. These are designed to appease and facilitate the propitiation of one or more of the gods of the Abakua pantheon. This is what the Apostle Paul had to say about such practices: "Ye cannot be partakers of the Lord's table, and of the table of devils" (1 Cor. 10:21). The Abakua cult, therefore, shares no symbiosis with, nor does it in any way resemble, orthodox Christianity. Nonetheless, to the unsuspecting, it prima facie, or on its face, might appear to be a form of Catholicism. It's not. As explained elsewhere in this text, Abakua is a fusion or syncretism of Catholicism with other preconceived religious beliefs and rituals.

Contrasts to Orthodox Christianity
Pantheon

The dichotomy between orthodox Christianity and Abakua, not unlike the contrast between Christianity and other Afrocentric cults, is quite salient and extremely fluid. For example, antithetical to Abakua and many other polytheistic cult religions, Christianity does not subscribe to, nor do the adherents recognize, a pantheon of gods. The book of Leviticus teaches us that "The Lord our God is one Lord" (Deut. 6:4; see also Mark 12:29). Subsequently, the orthodox Christian's allegiance is *soli deo gloria*, or glory to God only, in the embodiment of the Father, the Son, and the Holy Ghost. Moreover, within the Christian's construct of God and Christology, there aren't any subsidiaries or auspices.

Initiation Process

Contrary to the practices and tenets of cult religions, there aren't any initiation processes or propitiations required of Christians. No blood sacrifices, works of righteousness (Titus 3:5–7), or anything of the sort are offered to appease or propitiate God. Motifs, props, sacrifices, and mantras are unnecessary. Faith, or *solae fide* (second only to love, 1 Cor. 13:13)—the second most important term within the Christian's repertoire—is the avenue by which the Christian is to approach God (Mark 11:22, Heb. 11:1, 6). We (Christians) believe that Jesus Christ's atonement, or the blood that he spewed while agonizing on the cross at Calvary, has already and forever propitiated for us (see 1 Jn. 2:2).

Patriarchal

A religion that subscribes exclusively to the needs of a particular segment of society (in the case of Abakua with its males-only dogma) cannot be given a modicum of credence, let alone be taken seriously. Contrastingly, in Christianity, we believe that a religion should extend to all and not be limited to one's stripe, phenotype, social or economic circumstances, and certainly not limited to one's gender. Concerning this matter, the ubiquitous Apostle Paul expressed the following: "If one died for all, then were all dead...he died for all" (2 Cor. 5:14–15) and "There is neither bond nor free, there is neither male nor female" (Gal. 3:28). The Apostle Peter, after reluctantly entering a Gentile setting, pontificated, "God is no respecter of persons. But...he that...worketh righteousness, is accepted with him" (Acts 10:34–35).

Religious Syncretism

Orthodox Christianity, as opposed to occult religions, does not borrow from nor share symbiotic relationships with other sects. For because of its construct, its faith requirement (*Sola Fide*) in particular, it simply cannot be adapted to the confluence of other dogmas. This can best be exemplified by the Bible (*sola scriptura*) itself. The

Bible reveals to us, for example, that Judaism and Christianity, vis-à-vis their close relationship, can never amalgamate even though they are included within the same text. Rather, it appears to have been God's intention to present Christianity, the outcome of the New Covenant, as the very antithesis of Judaism, which—four hundred and thirty years after Abraham's justification by faith (See Rom. 4:13-14, Gal. 3:17-18, Ex. 12:40, Gen. 15:6)—was placed under the auspices of the Levitical law. Subsequently, there can be no confluence or accommodations made between Judaism and Christianity. Why not? Succinctly, one, Christianity, is based on *sola fide*, or faith alone (Rom. 3:24–25, Gal. 3:7–9, 11, Eph. 2:8); the other, Levitical law, is based on the works or practices (Rom. 3:20, 11:6, Gal. 2:16, 3:2, 10, 12, Eph. 2:9) of individuals. It's labor-intensive only, as the legendary Apostle Paul pontificated: "the law is not of faith" (Gal. 3:12).

Soteriological Views

Soteriologic. Greek: *Soterion*, denoting deliverance or the means of salvation.

The initiates into this hermetic cult, while recognizing a higher power, do not entertain the thought of a heaven or hell. Rather, they simply pledge to fulfill their duties as a mutual aid society along with being loyal and good members of their households and communities. They also take an oath to never reveal the secrets of their order. Therefore little is known by the outsider (unless properly vetted and befriended) of the cult's intricacies. This premise of salvation, however, does not resonate with the orthodox Christian's motif. While theirs (that is to say, the adherents of the Abakua sect) is a salvation predicated upon human effort or works, the Christian concept of salvation is, of course, based solely upon *sola fide*, or by faith alone (Eph. 2:8–9).

Eschatological Perspectives

Eschatology. Greek: *Eschatos*. It connotes the question of what is to be expected at the end of
life or at the end of an epoch.

Commensurate with other cults deeply rooted in archival African rituals and folklore (i.e., Santeria, Voodum/Vodou, Candomblé, Paleros/Palo), the adherents to the Abakua cult have imagined and maintain that there is no heaven above nor a hell below us. They insist that while there is a supreme being or God, there is no heaven to look forward to, nor is there a hell to fear. Rather, their belief is that, at death, reincarnation will occur until the individual has fulfilled his destiny or predetermined duties on Earth. This belief is, of course, unconscionable in the realm of Christianity, the orthodox version or otherwise, for the scriptures inform us that "it is appointed unto men once to die" (Heb. 9:27).

Concerns and Implications for the Orthodox Christian

The Abakua cult does not, at this juncture, present an existential threat to the more towering, assertive, and ubiquitous Christianity. Its hermetic and secretive ethos, compounded by the progressive spread of Christianity, Islam, and Catholicism, will eventually lead to its demise or its absorption by other Afrocentric cults. It will fit well with Santeria, Candomblé, or Paleros. To remain viable, a religion must promote proselytism; there must be a well-disciplined cadre who are willing to recruit and instruct others. The Abakua cultists insist upon secrecy nonetheless.

Moreover, as will be explored in further detail in sections ten (under the topic of Rastafarianism) and eleven (where the subject of Santeria will be treated), many across the African diaspora mistakenly believe that Afrocentric religions are their panaceas. These tend to be, almost invariably, those who have been disillusioned by the deceitfulness of charlatans who have, in some ways, betrayed the gospel that they've preached or espoused. The unsuspecting, then, seeks refuge within the confines of the proverbial outstretched deleterious arms of the occult.

The revered Swiss psychoanalyst Carl G. Jung (1961), in his most notable and brilliant work in manuscript form *Memories, Dreams, Reflections*, asserted that everyone at some point experiences religious ideations (1955). The scholar also maintained that the human psyche has a religious aspect. Moreover, Jung vociferously espoused that we humans are born with an archetype (that is to say, a preconceived idea of the image and personality) of God. If indeed true, this might help to explain why some, even at the expense of impending deception, are willing to seek spiritual guidance from cult leaders while others with different archetypes lean toward their idea of God. Jung's premise should be given at least a modicum of credence and not summarily dismissed as mere conjecture or speculation. Unlike Sigmund Freud, from whom the scholar, after their 1907 confrontation in Vienna, eventually dissociated, Jung viewed human psychology through the proverbial lenses of Christianity.

He didn't view his practice merely from a clinical or analytical perspective (Butler-Bowdown, 2006). Freud, on the other hand (despite his Jewish upbringing), in his enlightening *Civilization and Its Discontents*, intimated at creating a religion pursuant to his brand of psychoanalysis (1961).

Suggested Readings:

(1) Aimes, Hubert H. S. 1907, 1967. *A History of Slavery in Cuba: 1511–1868*. Octagon Books: New York.

(2) Finnegan, Ruth. 1970. *Oral Literature in Africa*. Oxford: Clarendon Press.

(3) Jung, Carl G. 1958. *The Undiscovered Self*. Penguin Publishing.

(4) Jung, Carl G. 1964. *Man and His Symbols*. Random House.

(5) Klein, Herbert S. 1986. *African Slavery in Latin America and the Caribbean*. New York, London. Oxford University Press.

(6) Moore, Carlos. 1988. *Castro, the Blacks and Africa*. Los Angeles: University of California Press.

Dr. A.J. Handy, Ph.D.

Section Two
Buddhism

Founding/Brief History

In order to grasp the structure of Buddhism, it is important to understand the milieu and historical context from which it precipitated. After the Aryans/Indo-Europeans (Germanic peoples) established hegemony over what is presently known as northwest India some three millenniums ago, Brahmanism, a reconstruction of India's former caste system, was established. The institution of Brahmanism allowed the Aryans to perpetuate and maintain their supremacy over the indigenous people. Moreover, according to the allegations of Martin, the caste system invariably allowed the Aryans to maintain the purity of their race (2003).

Over time, reforms would be made; Brahmanism would be transformed into today's Hinduism. These reformative measures, however, did not significantly alter the caste system. Over 65 percent of the populous (i.e., the peasantry who despairingly robbed the affluent Indus of its chordate and other vital resources; the marginalized outcasts/Untouchables, many of whom were plagued by incurable diseases; and those who eked out a meager living by tilling the soil) continued to languish at the lowest levels of the socioeconomic strata in abject poverty. This was the India into which one Siddhartha Gautama (Buddha), during or around 495–412 BCE, was born. Subsequently, Buddhism would splinter from Hinduism; and even though the two—Buddhism and Hinduism—are cousins and often confluent, the dichotomy between the two is very pronounced. For example, whereas Hinduism perpetuated class struggle (e.g., the bourgeoisie vs. the proletariat) and socioeconomic distinction, Buddhism, contrastingly, took a more egalitarian approach, for it to some degree denuded the distinction between the haves and the have-nots.

Ironically, the ethos of India during that epoch was not stylistically different from that of pre-Islamic Saudi Arabia, in which Abu al-Qasim Muhammad had his infancy. Siddhartha's and Muhammad's reactions to the deplorable conditions of the masses were also eerily similar. Reminiscent of Muhammad, Siddhartha Gautama would venture onto a spiritual journey. His, like Muhammad's, would be a cause to eliminate sufferings and despair. Their resolve to rescue the masses, however, could not have been more divergent. Sources varies widely—some as much as seventy to eighty years—concerning the actual date that Buddhism was founded. Molloy (2002) is quite vague; Martin (2003) did not entertain the topic; Nichols, et al. (2006), however, puts it (the founding) at sometime between 563–483 BCE.

While there are two major schools of Buddhism (Theravada, initiated in southern India, and Mahayana, with origins in the northern sector) and much dogma that has been trafficked and rebranded in other regions (e.g., Vajrayana, a Tibetan sect of Buddhism), it is the intention of this narrative to reveal Buddhism from the perspective of its embellished Western cloak, Zen. Zen Buddhism is a derivative and Chinese import of the Mahayana order of Buddhism. It has been assimilated far beyond the borders of its Asian origins and has great appeal to both Americans and western Europeans regardless of ethnic origins.

Dr. A.J. Handy, Ph.D.

Basic Beliefs and Rituals

If one is to appreciate, laude, or place themselves in a position to objectively scrutinize the teachings of the Buddha, the layers of indelible misconceptions accumulated throughout the years will have to be eliminated. This can be a tall order. It's difficult to let go of negative ideas, thoughts, and opinions, and remain receptive of their antitheses. These might fly in the face of or be an affront to our long-held prejudices, prejudices, and pejoratives that, even when completely denuded, portray one's concepts as being more plausible than those of others.

All that anyone knows about the teachings of the mendicant are those which were orally passed down and compiled in what is called the Pali Canon or the Tipitaka. The Buddha, who quietly abandoned his wife, family, and his life of opulence and ventured off into the twilight, allegedly never penned his thoughts. His teachings and beliefs are believed to have not been written down until some three hundred or more years after his death. Consequently, over time, word meanings were etymologically lost in translation, especially when imported by several diverse populations and cultures. Hence, a completely accurate exegesis will continue to elude. Remaining cognizant of this, we must rely upon the veracity of the five hundred amanuensis who penned what they believed to have been the oral teachings (the Tipitaka) of the Buddha.

The adherents to this cult insist that everyone should mimic the personality, demeanor, and meditative practices of Siddhartha Gautama (Buddha). The faithful also allege that the Buddha is not dead nor nebulous, but peacefully resting in the outer galaxies. The followers of Theravada Buddhism and its branches rely heavily upon the Dhammapada (other sayings of the Buddha), which purport to explain how populations, societies, and individuals should behave toward one another, toward the earth, and toward all life forms.

The monastic (Sangha) lifestyle is fundamental and quite essential to classical Buddhism's modus operandi. Moreover, regardless of the brand of Buddhism, the Dhammapada (the text that is alleged to be the actual teaching of the Buddha) and Sangha are ubiquitous concepts among Buddhists. The Westernized Zen meditative practices, however, have a massive appeal to Westerners. It basically requires one to sit on the floor with legs crossed, the back of hands resting on the inner femur (palms up), and eyes slightly ajar while picturing an object within the mind. If that position is too difficult to employ and maintain, Westerners are told to just sit up straight (reminiscent of Siddhartha's posture) in a chair with feet flat on the floor or even just sit on a couch with feet flat on the floor. The eyes and palms, of course, should be held in the same position as if meditating while sitting on the floor. Zen has made great progress in its courtship of the West, for it appeals to the Westerner's perfunctory and cursory lifestyle.

Nonetheless, the Buddha promulgated that, in order to obtain nirvana (enlightenment), one must be released from rebirths/sufferings (i.e., karma or the result of Samsara, the cycles of life/reincarnation). The Buddha taught that there is an eight-fold avenue, or path, that, if adhered to, will release man from sufferings. He allegedly insisted that if one practiced those procedures, karma will be eradicated, rebirths (reincarnation) will cease, and, ultimately, the stage of nirvana (that is to say, total enlightenment) will be acquired; hence the end of suffering.

The eight procedural etiquettes that the Buddha is said to have championed are (1) the right motives, (2) the proper speech, (3) the correct understanding, (4) the right actions, (5) the right profession, (6) the right effort, (7) the correct thoughts, and (8) the proper meditative technique. If those paths are not followed, the Buddha asserted, when a person dies, a return to another life—on Earth or within the universe—is inevitable. This reincarnation could be in the form of, let's say, a tree, dog, horse, another person, a flower, etc. Molloy argued that these cycles of deaths (Samsara), or reincarnations, are said to continue until the desires of the individual, which are the causality of man's sufferings, is finally stymied by nirvana, which purges the person of karma (2002).

It may require several lifetimes for man to relinquish his wrong attributes, his lusts, and his desires; however, once, and if, they are eliminated, reincarnation is no longer necessary. Nirvana is obtained, and, subsequently, the person is enlightened. These concepts (i.e., nirvana, reincarnation, and karma) will, of course, be reiterated under the heading Contrasts to Orthodox Christianity.

Parallels to Orthodox Christianity Meditative Practices

All the major orthodox religions of the world (e.g., Judaism, Christianity, Buddhism, Islam, Hinduism) tend to have a proclivity for leaning toward some form of meditation. Easterners, who primarily practice Eastern religions regardless of persuasion (i.e., polytheism, monotheism, pantheism, or henotheism), however, focus almost invariably upon what they perceive to have been the behavior of the religion's founder during meditation, that is to say, for example, upon the universe as a whole or upon an object (i.e., a lotus flower or perhaps something as mundane as a rock). In fact, it would not be an aberration—or out of character—for Easterners to focus (while meditating) tandemly upon the mannerism of the founder and upon an object contained in the universe.

In Christianity, however, there is an essential paradigm shift. For the Christian's credo, as it relates to meditative practices, simply does not comport with the modus operandi of any other religions. Rather, orthodox Christians, unlike many who have been persuaded to join Eastern-born sects, do not empty themselves of thoughts; they do not focus on inanimate objects, per se. Neither do Christians, when meditating, concentrate on the universe or upon the lives of the founders. Indeed, it is solely upon the word of God (or some aspect of Jehovah/Yahweh, who the adherents insist is quite animate), which is believed to be found exclusively in the holy Bible, on which Christians meditate. Most Christians would like to believe that all their thoughts are pure and that there is never a moment of even fleeting nefariousness. The mind, though, is in constant litigation, binarily championing the positions of both virtuous and nefarious motives. This is what the Apostle Paul had to say of the matter: "The flesh lusteth against the Spirit, and the Spirit against the flesh: and these are contrary the one to the other: so that ye cannot do the things that you would" (see Gal. 5:17). 1

John 1:8 will provide further insight into the matter. The triumvirate meditation, prayer, and fasting (when practiced biblically), however, will allow the Christian to experience a more spiritual, fulfilled, and victorious life. Meditation provides one (whether Christian, Jew, Muslim, or otherwise) with equanimity, which is necessary when facing difficult or otherwise precarious situations. Try it. Of course, Christians pray adamantly; however, for most, fasting and meditation (crucial components of Christianity) appear to be of little concern. Many adherents are under the false impression that meditation is the monopoly of Eastern religions, that is to say Buddhism, Hinduism, Taoism, etc. The scriptures, however, mention meditative practices often: twice in the New Testament (Luke 21:14, 1 Tim. 4:15), and eighteen times in the Old (some are Gen. 24:63, Joshua 1:8, Ps. 1:2, 63:6, 119:15, 97).

    Sanctimoniousness and its allies, pride, and self-righteousness, must be marginalized and carefully avoided, for they could insidiously lead one to assume that the equanimity exuded by meditation and fasting is unnecessary. However, the Apostle Paul's debacle, as delineated in Romans 7:15–25 (a must-read), may bring the pious and holier-than-thou down a notch or two. In those passages we see, arguably, the greatest, most celebrated apostle of all ages (although he named himself the least in 1 Cor.15:9) in quite a conundrum. Sin has reared its ugly head, and he (Paul) appears to have occasionally succumbed to it. Finally, he concludes that there is nothing within the repertoire of his "human nature" or flesh (that is to say, piety, dutifulness, etc.) that could serve as a formidable champion of his spiritual desire, which is to live totally for Christ. The tormented apostle concludes—Rom. 7:25—that his only escape from the prevalent crucible is through the panacea, Jesus Christ.

    Lastly, the Christian, when meditating, does not harbor a compelling need, nor is he or she obliged, to assist God in his effort to communicate with man. For "God himself" (while hanging on the cross in the form of his incarnate word, Jesus) agonizingly screeched, "It is finished" (see John 19:30). The Christian, then, while meditating, is seeking directions from a monotheistic (although triune) God that is attentive to her or his every need. Such attention and propitiation were gained at Calvary. The following scriptures may illuminate further: Matt. 7:7, Luke 11:9. Also, according to the Greek lexicon for the description of "meditate" (*skeptomai*: to affix the eye on a certain mark, or to look carefully at), it is quite possible to meditate in the midst of a seemingly disastrous situation; this is exemplified in Matt. 14:22–29. In Matthew's narrative, the Apostle Peter was not reacting under an episode of hypnosis, nor was he being driven by the secular notion of mind over matter. Rather, he was performing an act of meditation; his eyes were affixed on a certain mark. That mark was Christ.

    Millman (2000), although novelistic if only briefly skimmed, can be quite telling, for his *Way of The Peaceful Warrior* provides many glaring truths, truths that can be realized through either seated or in action meditation (as it was when Peter walked on the waters of the Sea of Galilee). Admittedly, some Christians might be offended by much of Millman's prose for his exposé—borrowing copiously from Zen Buddhism and Sufism—could be perceived as a proverbial "bridge too far." But if an open mind can be maintained throughout the bestseller and preconceptions held at bay, not only will resonance exude, but higher cognitive dimensions—through meditation—could possibly be realized.

Many students of theology—when debating or discussing Peter's actions during that boisterous situation mentioned in Matt. 14:22–31—will abruptly limit their conclusion to an absence of faith exhibited by the apostle. Upon further reflection, however, one will discover that Jesus never (as it relates to that particular episode) admonished Peter because of a lack of faith. Rather, it was the apostle's cessation of faith for which he was derided. Moreover, we notice in Matt. 14:31 that Jesus actually reminds the legendary apostle that he (Peter) has a modicum of faith. It requires faith to even contemplate (not to mention succeeding for approximately four to five meters) walking on the Sea of Galilee. His defeat, therefore, must not be attributed to an absence of faith, for the scriptures clearly explain that "God hath dealt to every man the measure of faith" (Rom. 12:3). His faltering, therefore, was precipitated by the inability to maintain his meditative posture. That is to say that at some point Peter allowed external circumstances (e.g., the turbulent waters, gale-force winds, etc.) to detach his fixation from his mark (hence the Greek *skeptomai*), Jesus Christ.

Decalogue

Zen Buddhism has a charter that's somewhat similar to the Judeo-Christian's pledge to the Ten Commandments. Those that stand out are (1) no lying (Ex. 20:16), (2) do not murder (Ex. 20:13), (3) commit no theft (Ex. 20:15), and (4) do not commit fornication (Ex. 20:14). The others (viz., no use of perfumes, no sleeping on beds that are not "actually" on the floor, etc.) are insignificant and are not commensurate with the Christian credo.

Contrasts to Orthodox Christianity

Reincarnation

Considering the fact that Buddhism predates Christianity by nearly six centuries—even though philosophically, theologically, and pragmatically indifferent—it was not designed to negate nor serve as an answer to Christianity. Subsequently, the practitioners do not consider themselves at variance or opposed to Christianity. However, as it is with most sects born on Continental Asia, when juxtaposed with Christianity, there are striking contrasts. Take, for example, one of its major tenets, reincarnation. This concept is foreign and contradictory to Christian orthodoxy. Many Christians, moreover, are not cognizant of the meaning and implications of such scriptures as "all the prophets...prophesied until John...this is Elias, which was for to come" (Mat. 11:13–14) or "he shall go before him in the spirit and power of Elias" (Luke 1:17). The preceding verses (Matt. 11:13-14, and Luke 1:17) are two of several scriptures which—on the surface—may appear to support the theory of reincarnation. When relying upon one's own understanding, the etymology of such passages remains fleeting, elusive, aloof, and may never be captured. However, we are instructed from the book of Proverbs to "lean not unto thine own understanding" (3:5). God is not the author of confusion; he has insisted, rather, that his followers study and search the scriptures so that they may avoid any miscalculations (John 5:39, 1

Cor. 14:33, 2 Tim. 2:15). The narrative of Luke 1:17 (e.g., "in the spirit and power of Elias") indicates that John the Baptist would have the same power (translated *dunamis*, or dynamite-like strength) that was revealed in Elias. John the Baptist and Elias were, therefore, separate, and distinct individuals. Also, as concerning the subject of reincarnation, the Bible concludes that "it is appointed unto men once to die, but after this the judgement" (Heb. 9:27).

Impermanence of the Soul

The Buddha is alleged to have asserted that the concept of the permanence of anything—material or otherwise—is incredulous. This allegation (the impermanence of the soul) pierces to the very ether of Protestant theology itself for it impiously impugns not only orthodox Christian beliefs, but the beliefs of most other Western-formed religions as well. The concept of the impermanence of the soul infers, of course, that eternal life is also (of necessity) a misnomer. Christians, however, both orthodox and heterodox, maintain that the Buddha's antithesis is absurdly flawed, for it interferes with the teachings of the Old and New Testament canons, the Koran, and Judaism. It is interesting to note that Siddhartha Gautama (Buddha) promulgated such a belief based solely upon his own alleged higher plane (nirvana) of thoughts, whereas most charlatans would've insisted that it was a revelation from God. Therefore, as philosophically and theologically misguided as the legendary sage appears to have been, Siddhartha Gautama is not to be labeled a charlatan. For unlike Joseph Smith Jr. and Brigham Young, or Charles T. Russell and Joseph

F. Rutherford (two of the Mormon fathers and two of the Jehovah's Witnesses founders, respectively), the Buddha never mentioned, not even once, that his actions and dogma were precipitated by God or an angel. Nonetheless, he is not absolved. For the mere fact that he never filibustered, pontificated, or presented the appearance of a charlatan doesn't lend credence to the veracity of his teachings.

Moreover, the Bible is, of course, abounding with scriptures that do, in fact, debunk this portion (impermanence of the soul) of the Buddha's ideology. Just a few exemplifications will be expounded upon here: (1) First of all, according to Gen. 2:7, and 1 Cor. 15:45, the soul of man ("soul" in Greek=*psychi*; "soul" in Hebrew=*nephesh*) is the breath of God that giveth life. And (2) as pertaining to the soul's permanence, 1 Thess. 5:23, and Matt. 10:28 are quite reassuring. The gospel according to St. Matthew lets us know that only God can—pursuant to man's sins and disobedience—destroy the soul ("destroy" in Greek=*apollumi*, to ruin the well-being of, but not extinction). Moreover, the Apostle Paul's narrative to the church at Thessalonica (1 Thess. 5:23) alerts us and mitigates any doubt that man's soul can be preserved ("preserve" in Greek= *pri'zerv*, to maintain or to retain) until Christ makes his return.

The Eight Ways to End Suffering and Acquire Everlasting Peace

Siddhartha Gautama (Buddha) is alleged to have espoused an eightfold route that must be adhered to if an individual wishes to be released from inevitable suffering. The paths to end suffering were briefly painted under the heading Basic Beliefs and Rituals but will be retouched and framed at this juncture. The eightfold path or route consisted of: (1) right motives, (2) proper speech, (3) correct understanding, (4) right actions, (5) the right profession, (6) the right effort, (7) correct thoughts, and (8) proper meditative techniques. The Buddha's espousal, of course, is inconceivable by the orthodox Christian and inextricably imbued with elitist and cultic sways. While Christianity does, of course, promote right motives, proper speech, correct understanding, and correct thoughts, the Buddha's codification is foreign—among Christian circuits—as it relates to one's relationship to God or man's eschatological expectations. Nevertheless, while demonstratively inaccurate, the eightfold path has found an enthralling courtship among Westerners. It has managed to capture the hearts and minds of a great number of unsuspecting Americans and Western Europeans. Misguided by what the charlatans have redacted from and added to the biblical dogma (and marketed and sold to them as Christianity), the unsuspecting inevitably seek other avenues by which to eliminate their conundrums. Zen Buddhism, because of its Western lure and attire, ostensibly and insidiously welcomes them; it appeals to the Westerner's ego, intellect, and sense of individualism. Westerners, as well as many others, are taught that with hard work, a high IQ, and proper interpersonal skills, they can achieve. That's true. Those attributes, viz., proper work ethic (which is heavily influenced by the ego), correct interpersonal skills, right actions, etc., should be desired in the secular domain. They lack currency, however, as it relates to finding the path to God.

Soteriological Views

Buddhists are not monotheists, polytheists, nor henotheistic; they are, invariably, pantheistic in that they contend that the whole world and all that is therein is God. During my discussions with Buddhist monks (bhikkhus) in Tokyo, Japan, it was discovered, that contrary to what Christians have been led to believe, Buddhists are not atheists, not in the usual sense of the word. Nor are they agnostics either, for they believe—and are sure—that there is a higher power. That higher power, the fundamentalists maintain, is not concerned with and is completely indifferent to the fate and behavior of mankind. This position was corroborated, cross-culturally, by the monks that I conversed with on the Korean Peninsula (Seoul). The Hare Krishnas further south in Busan (Pusan) provided similar information. I also learned from a group of hermetic ascetics in Manila, the Philippines that theirs is not a concept of avoiding hell or finding peace or salvation by a God-agent but one of self-salvation or reaching the spiritual plane of nirvana, or total enlightenment. East of the Pacific in San Francisco, the consensus—with a few insignificant variances—remained. The basic theme of Buddhism, subsequently, amounts to the theology of neo-humanism/universalism.

To the Buddhists salvation is not conceptualized within the framework that Christians would conceive and codify. For the Buddha, we are told, never appropriated the idea of a God. His philosophy—long before Desiderius Erasmus and other proverbial giants of the Renaissance—was a philosophy of humanism. He insisted that the fate of man lies within himself and his ability to, as mentioned elsewhere in this narrative, end his inevitable suffering by being released from the cycles of rebirths or reincarnations. The ending of these reincarnations, the fundamentalists insist, can only be accomplished by following the eightfold path, which was codified in this narrative under the heading Basic Beliefs and Rituals. These paths, if adhered to, are alleged to eventually lead one to nirvana or enlightenment. Once nirvana is obtained, the Buddha concluded, rebirths are no longer necessary; man is at peace because karma has been eliminated. Salvation (the end of suffering), then, is realized when the individual ceases to be reincarnated and, therefore, no longer exists in any form after death. Hence, self-actualization or enlightenment is obtained by the individual; no aid is necessary or fathomed from external sources or other powers. As incredulous as it may sound, this is what salvation means to those of the Zen persuasion.

    The Zen method of self-salvation, or nirvana, however, does not fit within the framework of Christian theology. Moreover, the writings of the Apostle John, all of Paul's epistles, the writer of Hebrews, in conjunction with all the gospels, clearly denudes the Zen ideology of its insidious facade. The Apostle John concluded, "If any man sin, we have an advocate with the Father, Jesus Christ the righteous...he is the propitiation for our sins" (see 1 John 2:1–2). The resolve of John Wycliffe is also quite interesting. Ferrell (2019), in his reference to the fourteenth-century recalcitrant English evangelist, indicated that Wycliffe, while challenging the papacy over its errors of granting indulgences and private confessions, insisted that one should live a life of *solus Christus*, or a life totally dedicated to Christ alone and dependent upon Christ's atonement. Wycliffe also warned against pursuing propitiation or salvation by means other than by faith, or *solae fide* in Jesus Christ alone.

One may possess the right motives, the right actions, the proper speech, etc.; these tenets will not, however, prevent the person from suffering. They will in no way provide a segue for, nor are they able to appropriate, salvation. The life of Job, the character with the same name as the eighteenth book of the Bible and who is also featured therein, may serve as a paradigm. For he was a man who possessed all the correct initiatives (e.g., right actions, proper speech, and right motives), yet he was absolutely acquainted with grief and suffering (see Job 1–3). Moreover, the eightfold path requires works of the individual, but at some point, according to the biblical narrative, faith has to be included into the mix. Here's how Hebrews 4:2 explains it: "The word preached did not profit them, not being mixed with faith." The Apostle Paul's pontification to the churches of Galatia (3:2) will provide further insight.

The eightfold path must've seemed—to Siddhartha Gautama—to have been the right way to salvation (or enlightenment, the preferred term of Buddhists); however, the Bible concludes, "There is a way which seemeth right unto a man, but the end thereof are the ways of death" (see Prov. 14:12). Jesus Christ needed no eightfold path; in fact, he is the one and only path to salvation and enlightenment. Jesus insisted, "I am the way, the truth, and the life: no man cometh unto the Father, but by me" (John 14:6).

To conceive of following the eightfold path, one must necessarily possess, at the very least, a modicum of narcissism. And, since it is narcissism that Zen embraces, it can be reasoned that the vainest (or conceited) individuals are easy prey for the Zen cult. So then Zen and Christianity are paradoxically similar; they both seek to embrace. The former embraces the intellect and the works that can be derived from such; the latter embraces the faith of the individual and in turn reciprocates with grace or unmerited favor. The similarity soon withers, though, for the ubiquitous and legendary sage Apostle Paul maintained, "For by grace are ye saved through faith; and that *not of yourselves*: it is the *gift* of God: *not of works,* lest any man should boast" (emphasis added; see Eph. 2:8–9).

To learn of other narratives that denude the concept of the inevitability of suffering, the reader is advised to revisit the following scriptures: Heb. 2:10, 13:12, 1 Pet. 1:11, Mark 5:26, 1 Thess. 2:2, 2 Tim. 2:12, and 1 Pet. 4:16.

Eschatological Perspectives

Zen purports that man is essentially at the helm of his own salvation or enlightenment. It promulgates that narcissism, the love of one's self, is the very first step in the attainment of *summum bonum*, or the highest or ultimate good. Eventually, however, as espoused by Buddhist practitioners and their liturgy, one must obtain nirvana, or the highest level of intellectual enlightenment. Once nirvana has been obtained, the adherents allege, man's consciousness is one with the universe, much like the oceans, trees, and vegetation are. The practitioners insist that ignorance, not the love of money (the ecclesiastical proverb that would resonate among those of the Christian faith) is the root cause of all evil. Zen Buddhism, therefore, insists that it be unencumbered with the ideals or concepts of God, fate, heaven, or hell. These are such trivial matters, the practitioners have concluded.

Concerns and Implications for the Orthodox Christian

The summary of Buddhism and all Eastern-born religions and sects that predate Christianity must be treated somewhat differently than religions that originated after the advent of Christianity. Some followers during Buddhism's infancy and adolescence had not the opportunity to hear the gospel. Nonetheless, many have judged Siddhartha Gautama quite harshly and perhaps, to some degree, rightly so. One must take into account, however, that, as it is with anyone, man—devoid of the Spirit of God, left to his own devices, and without access to information upon which to make decisions—is necessarily oblivious to the fact that he's merely ego-driven, neo-humanistic, and essentially blind.

The Buddha died at least a century before Socrates began his monologues; he took his last breath long before Aristotle came into the world. Consequently, he wasn't privy to the sources of Greek etymology/literary translations that are quite prevalent today. Of the works of Aquinas, Polycarp, Luther, Jerome, or Whitfield he had no knowledge; more importantly, though, neither Jerome's Vulgate nor other New Testament literature arrived during the Buddha's lifetime. Does that absolve him, you ask? Absolutely not! For had he the resources—which only became available after his death—perhaps he would have rejected the gospel still. Allegorically, even most Western judicial systems don't apply the same sentence to a thirteen-year-old to, let's say, a thirty-two-year-old who commits the same type of crime. Similarly, to judge the Buddha, who lived and died before the Common Era (BCE), by employing the exact same criterion as one would use to judge a bishop, pope, or, let's say, a local pastor of the Common Era (CE) would be unjustifiably fallacious.

One must wonder, however, that, had the Buddha lived during the current era with the opportunity to even dabble in Christianity, if he would've been drawn toward Christianity "to some degree." It's quite possible, since his was a philosophy founded during an outcry against an ethos which ostracized the masses and some of the proletariat from mainstream society. Of his possible affinity for Christianity (had he lived to witness the religion), we shall never know; however, considering the biography that we have of him, it is certainly worthy of conjecture.

Realistically, however, perhaps the Buddha would've rejected any tenets of Christianity. Mohandas Gandhi (Hindu) and most of the fourteen Dalai lamas (Buddhist), if we can draw any similarities between them and the Buddha, had absolute, unlimited access to copious forms of Judeo-Christian literature, yet they never wavered. Most were quite pejorative in their view of Christianity. They stood firm and resolute in their Hindu and Buddhist persuasions. Of this narrative, let this be the sum: "That servant, which knew his lord's will, and prepared not…neither did according to his will, shall be beaten with many stripes…he that knew not, and did commit things worthy of stripes, shall be beaten with few stripes" (see Luke 12:47–48).

Suggested Readings:

(1) Edelglass, Williams; Garfield, Jay L. *Buddhist Philosophy: Essential Readings*. Oxford University Press (2009) 198 Madison Avenue. New York, NY. 10016.

(2) Kornfield, Jack. 2000, 2001. *After the Ecstasy, the Laundry*. Bantam Books, 1540 Broadway, New York, NY. 10036.

(3) Osho International Foundation. 2007, 2008. *The Buddha Said...Meeting the Challenge of Life's Difficulties*. Watkins Publishing, 75–76 Wells Street, London, UK.

(4) Salzberg, Sharon. 2011, 2019. *Real Happiness, the Power of Meditation*. Workman Publishing, New York.

(5) Trungpa, Chogyam. 2005. *The Myth of Freedom: And the Way of Meditation*. Shambhala Publishers, 300 Massachusetts Ave. Boston, MA. 02115.

(6) Walpola, Rahula. 1959, 1974. *What the Buddha Taught*. Published by Open Road + Grove/Atlantic. 841 Broadway, New York, NY. 10003.

Dr. A.J. Handy, Ph.D.

Section Three

Christian Identity Groups

Founding/Brief History

Christian Identity groups or movements didn't spring up overnight, nor was the premise conceived in a vacuum. Rather, the belief exuded from and is the metamorphosis of its precursor, British-Israelism. British-Israelism came to the fore in England in or around the mid-1660s. It espouses the idea that the British people, too, (like the Jews in present-day Israel) are the progeny of Isaac's son, Jacob. They are in the direct lineage of the lost ten tribes of Israel, the adherents maintained. The faithful also purported that the Jews can, in fact, lay claim to the lineage of Jacob; that lineage, however, was a lineage of inferiority, as propagated by British-Israelism. Whereas British-Israelism made accommodations for the Jewish people as the concept continued to mature into its Anglo-Israelite stage on American shores, the Jewish people began to be shunned and excoriated. During the early to mid-1920s, men who cradled the Anglo-Israelite stage of British-Israelism's evolution (e.g., Ruben Sawyer, Ralph Roy, Charles Totten, Howard Rand, and others) began to promulgate the ideology that Jews could stake no claim to being in the lineage of Jacob. This position, of course, was radically different from that of its progenitor, British-Israelism. It is also worthy of note that Henry Ford, the prolific automobile manufacturer, and a somewhat quiet and inconspicuous sympathizer of Adolf Hitler's Third Reich, was very instrumental (from, say, the 1920s until his death in 1947) in the development of the Anglo-Israel/Identity movement. Ford, allegorically taking a back seat to his employee William J. Cameron, assisted Howard Rand, Harry Bennett, and others in copiloting the ideology. And able copilots they were; however, it appears that whenever the movement encountered any variance or hurdles, it would be Cameron who would, metaphorically, navigate it through the most atrocious of gales and turbulences. Frequent sips from the bottle, however, would engender his downward spiral; he became addicted to alcohol, defected, and never returned to his position within the movement. As instrumental as Cameron, Bennett, Sawyer, and others were in providing the catalyst for the Anglo-Israel movement, it was the next generation of men—entering into the early 1960s and beyond—who would truly animate, transform, and provide the ideology with its vital nutrients. It was men such as Gerald Smith, Ben Judah, John Lovell, and other exponents who would fashion and provide Christian Identity with its own uniqueness, severing it from its predecessors, British-Israelism and Anglo-Israelism. Lastly, Barkun (1994) explains that, as perceived by the Anglo-Israelites, the Jews are the progeny conceived by the miscegenation between Satan and the biblical Eve. Unfortunately, even today among the loyalists the consensus remains.

Of course, no serious exegesis or chronicle concerning the Christian Identity Movement can be complete without mentioning, at least briefly, Nathan Bedford Forrest (the Ku Klux Klan's first Grand Wizard). Forrest and five or six other members of his upper brass (shortly after the American Civil War, about 1866–1870) absolutely terrorized the recently emancipated. Moreover, after the demise of the Night Riders, patterollers, and

Klansmen of that era, others much more atrocious, devoid of compunction, well organized, and determined, would follow. They were formed in conjunction with the erection of statues of prominent Confederate leaders as means to intimidate and curtail the advancement of those who were the direct beneficiaries of Lincoln's Emancipation Proclamation, the former enslaved. These groups (Christian Identity) are more concerned with hate and culture than with anything else. The term "Christian," as observed in the Christian Identity's nomenclature, is therefore a gross misnomer. Theirs is a quasi-motif of Christianity, "Christians in name only." The duality that plagues them is either they've not heard the true gospel or the gospel preached unto them was not properly conceptualized (see Heb. 4:2). The participants of these groups tend to admire, look up to, and be the surrogates of Robert E. Lee, Stonewall Jackson, Nathan Bedford Forrest, David Duke, Adolph Hitler, and Hitler's most trusted generals: Joseph Berchtold, Karl Hanke, and the infamous Franz Halder. Many among the Hitler Youths and within the Neo-Nazi circuits are much more familiar with Hitler's *Mein Kampf* than the King James, New International version, or the Revised Standard Version.

Basic Beliefs and Rituals

All Christian Identity Groups, regardless of the brand, (for there are quite a plethora) maintain that White Anglo-Saxton Protestants, or WASPs, are the only peoples that can be identified—hence the term "Identity"—as the progeny of the lost ten tribes of Jacob. Also endemic to Christian Identity Groups is the mendacious insistence that as a result of Noah's son Ham's transgression against his father (Gen. 9), Black peoples of the world are cursed with Black or dark skin and that they must, consequently, always be reduced to a position of servitude. The Jews, the loyalists argue, are in no way, not even remotely, related to the House of Israel. Instead, as maintained by Identity Groups, Jews are the offspring that resulted from the intercourse between the Devil and Eve; hence, allegedly, they are the children of Satan. One must wonder, nonetheless, why Luke's prose in Acts 17:26 is such an enigma to Christian Identity Groups, for Paul pontificates, "And hath made of one blood all nations of men for to dwell on all the face of the Earth." Accordingly, because of Christ's atonement at Calvary, all peoples from every nation are related.

    The adherents also aver that the geo-economic system is controlled and underwritten by a Jewish conspiracy. Subsequently, as surmised by the occult's followers, Western governments are doing the Jews' bidding and must, therefore, not be trusted. Identity Groups loathe the US government. However, the following far right-wing inspired events are but a few exemplifications of Christian Identity's anathema of governmental agencies: (1) Timothy McVeigh's destruction in 1995 of a federal building in Oklahoma City, during which one hundred and sixty-eight were killed. (2) The Ruby Ridge confrontation of 1992, featuring White nationalists led by Randy Weaver, which militarized their compound and dared federal officials to advance. Two were reported killed. (3) The Charleston (SC) Church massacre, in which the twenty-two-year-old White supremacist Dylann Roof, after spending nearly forty minutes in bible study with predominately Black members at Mother Emanuel Church, fired seventy rounds, killing nine parishioners. That was the kind of hate that only Satan himself—and those whom he would enlist—are accustomed. (4) The mass killing of eleven at the Tree of Life Synagogue in Pittsburgh, on Oct. 27, 2018. (5) The hate-filled insurrectionists' attempted overthrow of the United States government on January 6, 2021; during this cauldron—billed as the storming of the United States Capitol building—one law enforcement officer was killed, many others were bludgeoned by the culprits. The revolutionaries numbered in the thousands. Angry mobs, roaming the halls, could be heard chanting, "Hang Mike Pence! Hang Mike pence!" A Gallows was erected on the Capitol grounds in order to satiate their thirst. Nancy Pelosi – the Speaker of The House of Representatives – was also in danger of wearing the noose. However, they both managed to elude the rioters. Lastly, among the plethora of events (developments which would require a separate digest to write about), there were (6) The unforgettable episode of White supremacists marching and carrying glowing torches (in August of 2017) through the streets of Charlottesville, Virginia. As they went along they repeatedly spewed the visceral and derogatory chant: "Jews will not replace us! You will not replace us! Jews will not replace us"!

Cross lighting or burning—the signature of many (not all) Identity Groups—is performed periodically as a display of contemporary relevance and intimidation. In a failed attempt to ameliorate some of the hatred and scare tactics trafficked and spewed by the Ku Klux Klan, the US High Court ruled in 2003 that cross burning, if designed to intimidate, is a crime. Nonetheless, the practice continues.

Parallels to Orthodox Christianity

The basic tenets of orthodox Christianity resonate with Christian Identity Groups. That is to say that the virgin birth of Christ, Christ the redeemer, the concepts of heaven and hell, water baptism, a tribulation period, and a millennium reign are not foreign concepts within the Identity circuits. The Rapture concept, however, a pivotal eschatological construct—and an event vigilantly awaited by those of Christian orthodoxy—does not comport with the apocalyptic theology harbored by those of the Christian Identity movement. We will learn what Christian Identity Groups have purported and espoused concerning the apocalyptic age in our next section, Contrasts to Orthodox Christianity.

Contrasts to Orthodox Christianity

Whereas Christian orthodoxy purports that the Battle of Armageddon will be a war between the forces of good and evil unrelated to phenotypes and ethnicities, Christian Identity groups maintain that Armageddon will evolve into a race war, a battle between God's allies and chosen people, the White race, and the axis powers, or all other ethnic peoples—Jews in particular. However, the obstacles to Christian Identity's assertions are enormous. For example, it is impossible to simply plow through the intersection of Romans 2:10 and 2:11: "glory, honor, and peace...to the Jew first...there is no respect of persons with God." John 4:22 requires caution as well, for it cannot be hurdled: we know what we worship: for salvation is of the Jews." Notice in John 4:22 that Jesus says "we." He, therefore, is aligning himself with the

Jews, the very population that Identity Groups seeks to excoriate. There is absolutely no way to navigate around 2 Corinthians 5:14: "If one died for all, then were all dead." To impiously ignore 1 John 4:20 is to engender the wrath of God: "For he that loveth not his brother whom he hath seen, how can he love God whom he hath not seen?" Moreover, it would be theological "malpractice" and absolutely unconscionable to ignore the luminous warning signs of Romans 1:16: "Salvation to every one that believeth; to the Jew first." To reiterate, the Bible—the scriptures touted by Identity Groups and orthodox Christians alike—clearly states and is quite unequivocal that "there is no respect of persons with God" (Rom. 2:11). Such egregious and impious indictments brought against the scriptures (briefly mentioned above) is one reason why those who would preach, or teach, the gospel should be, first of all (as opposed to being academically decorated), "born again." It would also be helpful for one to be well versed in New and Old Testament theology and early Church history. Academic prowess, Ivy League letters, and sheepskins are wonderful and are to be pursued; however, without the born again experience, unnecessary blunders, misinterpretations of scriptures, and cynicism shall always be one's unsolicited and inextricable companions.

As was addressed in *Comprehending the Pauline Epistles: A Study Guide (Handy*, 2019), the Apostle Paul while traveling on his missionary journeys almost invariably displayed a proclivity to court and attempt to share the gospel with the Jews first. If there were any disruption or rejection of his benevolence by the Jews, then he would turn his attention to the Gentiles. This assertion is nowhere better exemplified than in Acts

13:14–15, 44–46, a "must read." See also Act 2:5, 3:26, Rom. 10:12–13 and Gal. 3:28. Most cults that laud and extol the Bible (e.g., Mormonism, Adventism groups) exhibit some semblance of orthodoxy; within Christian Identity, however, orthodoxy is, to say the least, severely wanting, and essentially—with the exception of a few critical conduits—nondescript.

While orthodox Christians maintain that the fall of man was the result of Adam's and Eve's disobedience in the Garden of Eden, Christian Identity Groups insist, rather, that the fall of man came about due to the salacious and sexual relations between Eve and Satan. This is a momentous and, needless to say, very impugning and mendacious break from orthodoxy for it impiously flies in the face of—and is quite an affront to—the very ether of Christianity, Judaism, and Islam. The fallacious constructs harbored by the Christian Identity groups' members seek to impeach not only Christianity but most of the world's major religions.

Soteriological Views

Christian Identity Groups further maintain that White Anglo-Saxons are not only the true Identity of the biblical Adam, but that they are the progeny of all who are in the lineage of Christ. They insist that they are the lost sheep of the House of Israel. It is promulgated that many of them lost their identity due to miscegenation with other groups of peoples during their biblical post-wilderness experience. It is also asserted that they, because of their phenotype, are the only race that will be granted salvation.

Dr. A.J. Handy, Ph.D.

Eschatological Perspectives

Not unlike Charles T. Russell's false millennial prophecy that the Second Coming of Christ would take place in the year 1914, Edward Hine, a reputed and proud exponent of the Identity Movement, falsely claimed that the battle of Armageddon would unfold and play out during the years of 1995 through 1997. That didn't pan out. Following this, he extended the arrival date of the Second Coming to be in excess of some 244 years. That, of course, is yet to be confirmed. The adherents insist that the Rapture concept does not comport with biblical theology, for they maintain that a Rapture occurrence would mean the supplanting of the Tribulation and Armageddon. Rather, Identity Groups allege that those who are the primal identity of Christ (that is to say, White Anglo-Saxons) who have fulfilled all other scriptural requirements will be the ultimate victors at Armageddon. During this battle, as purported by the loyalists, God will destroy the Jews and those of mixed, tainted, and non-White Anglo-Saxon blood. Afterward, as alleged by the faithful, White Anglo-Saxons will reign with Christ in heaven for a thousand years. During that same millennia, the fundamentalists have concluded, all non-Anglo-Saxons will be left to pine away while being tormented with great tribulation. Christian Identity adherents insist, moreover, that they will return to Earth with Christ after the Tribulation.

Concerns and Implications for the Orthodox Christian

On the surface, Christian Identity Groups are not all that different from other cults that cloak themselves with many of the premises of Christianity. For all in the run of their deceits initially go to great measures to avoid showing any traces of the evil and mendacious motives that lurk within. Jesus pontificated, "Beware of false prophets, which come to you in sheep's clothing...Ye shall know them [false prophets/dogmas] by their fruits" (Matt. 7:15–16, emphasis added). These groups will invariably seek to justify their unscriptural orthopraxy (how to behave as a Christian) while remaining nestled and secure (as they believe) within the confines of Christian orthodoxy. Proper orthodoxy will always exude—albeit perhaps slowly—proper orthopraxy, or Christian conduct. The two (e.g., proper orthodoxy and proper orthopraxy) are not mutually exclusive; one cannot have proper orthodoxy and ignore proper orthopraxy. For any sects, Christian Identity Groups or otherwise, to identify themselves as Christian while at the same time maintain such a high standard deviation from scripture is nonsensical and self-deceiving. Concerning biblical Israel (which remains quite relevant), the Apostle Paul harangued, "They have a zeal of God, but not according to knowledge...they being ignorant of God's righteousness, and going about to establish their own righteousness, have not submitted themselves unto the righteousness of God" (Rom. 10:2–3). So it is with Identity Groups and others that rely more upon culture and phenotype to secure their salvation than they do the righteousness of God. Moreover, Eurocentric cults and sects are not alone in their quest to appropriate salvation from the predicate of race and ethnicity, for Afrocentric cults (e.g., Abakua, Rastafarianism, and Santeria) have employed similar schemes in order to provide fodder for their ethno-religious sways. We've touched briefly upon this in section one, Abakua. However, in sections ten and eleven we shall abandon the tranquil, placid, and shallow waters of Abakua and brave the pernicious and recalcitrant swells and undercurrents of Rastafarianism and Santeria. It is at that confluence where Rastafarianism and Santeria meet where we will attempt to delve further into and take a much closer look at two of the most prominent Afro-religious cults.

Of course, racism, xenophobia, bigotry, and other related pathological mental disorders and comorbidities do not, as we shall explore further in section eight (Mormonism), comport with the ethos and values of the Christian and other religious communities. Rather, the goal of evangelism is to move a person from darkness to light, from sin to righteousness and salvation. The predicate of all rebellions against God is sin. Therefore, those of the Christian Identity groups are not unlike anyone else who have not truly accepted Christ. Moreover, all unrighteousness is sin (1 John 5:17). Therefore, if one can bring themselves to look beneath the surface or the prima facie facade of the Identity group members, they might begin to ask themselves, "Are these members in such an inextricable quagmire that it would be fruitless to share the gospel with them?" Those who are not cognizant of the power or *dunamis* of God will, of course, write these groups off as hopeless and unreachable. But, as the born again will attest, the born again experience gives one a different prospective or outlook. How so? It allows one to look beyond the superficial or outward appearances, to see what's within the heart and soul of an individual. For the Lord admonished Samuel with "the Lord seeth not as man seeth; for man looketh on the outward appearance...the

Lord looketh on the heart" (1 Sam. 16:7). The Apostle Peter—notions not too conceptually different from that of Samuel—harbored similar misconceptions (see Acts 10:23–48, a must-read). But how say the scriptures? For the same Apostle Peter, writing from prison in or about 66 CE, insisted, "The Lord is not slack concerning his promise...but is longsuffering to us-ward, not willing that any should perish, but that all should come to repentance" (2 Pet. 3:9; see also John 3:16, 6:37, and Matt. 28:19. Salvation is for all, and it can be obtained by all. Once members of Christian Identity Groups conceptualize the Apostle Peter's narrative to the Sanhedrin, some (not all) will accept that they are on the wrong path. For true Christianity (not the misnomer "Christian" Identity to which they've become accustomed) is never fueled by hate and its undercurrents but by love and by the power of the Holy Ghost. They must become cognizant of the fact that, as Peter explained to the Sanhedrin Council, "Neither is there salvation in any other: for there is none other name under heaven *given among men*, whereby we must be saved" (Acts 4:12, emphasis added). Moreover, allowing one's self to become encapsulated by a name (e.g., Identity, Baptist, Pentecostal, Lutheran, etc.) is to— in many instances—deny the power of God. He, indeed, has the power to save anyone, no matter the denomination or stripe. And, as we have shown elsewhere in this corpus, phenotypes can certainly be discounted. Lastly, there isn't one denomination that doesn't (cynically) purport and promulgate the idea that its theology is totally correct and that there is, something (at least a modicum of flaw) indictable about all others. It follows, then, that the Christian Identity Groups' enigma, as well as many of orthodox Christian groups, is why is theology (properly taught and promulgated) so important? If the reader should manage to keep the mind slightly ajar, along with euthanizing anecdotes and preconceptions, the answer to that enigma will be serendipitously (or otherwise) revealed within these pages.

Suggested Readings:

(1) Anderson, Carol. *White Rage, the Unspoken Truth of Our Racial Divide*. Bloomsbury Publishing, 2016, 2017.

(2) Diangelo, Robin. *White Fragility: Why It's So Hard for White People to Talk About Racism*. Beacon Press, 2018.

(3) Duke, David. *A Path to Racial Understanding*. Free Speech Press, 1998.

(4) Gordon, Linda. *The Second Coming of the KKK: The Ku Klux Klan of the 1920s and the American Political Tradition*. Liveright, 2017.

(5) Katz, William L. *The Invisible Empire: The Ku Klux Klan Impact on History*. Open Hand Publishing, LLC, 1986.

(6) Speer, Albert. *Inside the Third Reich*. Orion Publishing Group, 1969.

(7) Stallworth, Ron. *Black Klansman: Race, Hate, and the Undercover Investigation of a Lifetime*. Macmillan-Macmillan Publishers, 2018.

Dr. A.J. Handy, Ph.D.

Section Four

Confucianism

Founding/Brief History

Confucianism emerged originally as more of a philosophy than a religion. After the collapse of the Chinese feudal system (a concept that began around 1122 BCE and lasted until 256 BCE), a system not too different from India's caste system, vagrancy and decadence began to permeate the land. This land was the area just south of what is known today as Beijing, China. Founded between 553 BCE and 479 BCE by Kong Fuzi (Kung Fu Tsu, or Confucius), the ethical teachings of Confucius would not be thought of as a religion until approximately 202 BCE. That was some two hundred and eighty years after the founder's death. However, it wasn't until well into the twelfth century that the neo-Confucian scholar Zhu Xi would provide Confucianism with its metaphysical animation. What Confucius allegedly taught (as well as the philosophy of the neo-Confucian Mencius) concerning divination, intellectualism, human nature, the universe, and interpersonal relations have been annotated and conveyed to us through several works. According to Roberts (2004), Confucius's followers would codify much of his teachings in what would be called *The Four Books* and within four ancillary works which were later added. *The Five Classics*, however, is believed to have been written by Confucius himself.

The Four Books (penned after Confucius's death) and *Classics* (composed by Confucius) are considered as the canon of Confucianism. *The Analects* features

Confucius's dialogues with his disciples; *The Book of Mencius* was penned by the author with the same name and includes much of his teachings; *The Doctrine of The Mean* addresses the balance between heaven and the Earth. Lastly, *The Great Learning* is a narrative concerning the paradigm of a venerable, or virtuous, person. Those are *The Four Books*. *The Five Classics* are *The Spring and Autumn Annals* (with references to Confucius's hometown), *The Book of History* (which chronicles the lives of ancient leaders of China), *The Book of Rites* (which purports to identify many of China's ancient ceremonies), *The Book of Poetry* (which, as the name suggests, is a compilation of poems not written by Confucius but chosen by him), and *The Book of Change* (which is said to be used to predict future occurrences, predictions predicated upon the outlay of the universe. In essence, it's a book describing techniques for divination).

    The concept did not originate in a vacuum, however, for Confucianism has much in common with and is deeply rooted in the dogma of its Chinese contemporary, Taoism. Their relationship to one another and to Buddhism can be observed from the name "China's Three Doctrines." For in many areas of China and other Sinitic societies (e.g., China's tributary Taiwan, the Korean peninsula, Vietnam, and Japan), the Three Doctrines are often indistinguishable, and quite often all three are featured during ceremonies. Confucianism mimics Taoism in that it, to some degree, seeks to bring the practitioners not only into harmony with one another, but into the rhythmic harmony of nature. The caveat to the relationship between Confucianism and Taoism, however, is that whereas Taoism is primarily concerned with nature and man becoming one with it, the

Confucians are more concerned with man's proper exploration and treatment of nature, which can only be accomplished when people learn and practice proper etiquette toward each other.

Basic Beliefs and Rituals

Even though Confucianism can stand (albeit much more subtly) on its own merits as a religion, it appears more so when syncretic with Taoism and/or Buddhism. For not unlike Laozi's Taoism, it seeks to bring mankind into Tao, or perfect harmony, with the forces of the universe. This Tao is also considered to be the "right way," which is predicated upon the concept of the Yin and the Yang. This principle (the Tao as a whole) purports that, just as the Yin and the Yang are opposite and opposing forces yet complementary, the Universe is consistent with the same, that is to say, the universe also consists of conflicting yet complementary powers. As such, according to Confucianism, humans must be taught how to affect and become one with that force or power. This, the sage alleged, will keep the universe in equilibrium. Contrary to the teachings of Confucius, however, Laozi argued that the Tao cannot be taught, for he insisted, rather, that it is innately within everyone and everything. That which was created as a philosophy would evolve over the centuries into a distinct religion. Because Confucianism does not fit the bill or script of what they conceive of as a religion, many Westerners, however, refuse to recognize it as such. It certainly falls within the criteria of a religion nonetheless. The criteria are: (1) an organized set of beliefs, (2) a group that adheres to that set of beliefs, (3) a view of a connection/disconnection between man and a higher power, along with its implications, (4) sacred texts/writings, and (5) periodic rituals or ceremonies. Confucius's followers eventually felt that they could enlist divination tactics to make predictions that would assuage their worries and anxieties. Confucianism embraces Buddhism in that, not unlike Siddhartha Gautama's ideas, Confucius's concepts are quite humanistic.

His was a pedagogical construct of producing superb individuals; because of that many have rushed to conclude that Confucius was an elitist. That's not so, for quite the opposite is true. In order to realize the maximum benefit of the remainder of this narrative, it will be necessary at this juncture to take a microscopic look at the term "superb." The term is etymologically Latin, *superbus*. It gives the connotation of being excellent. The sage Confucius simply believed that to properly affect society and subsequently realize Tao (harmony with the universe), humans, no matter one's stripe, social or economic status, must learn through rigorous academic curriculums and study how to behave toward one another. Confucius promulgated that as one enters the Literati group (that is to say, the well educated), he or she would know how to treat the less educated and those of less fortune because they've been properly taught and because the Literati were once in that position themselves. Therefore, the notion of elitism, as conceived in Western thought, would remain a misnomer and never become a factor in Confucian ideology.

However, Confucius (Kong Qiu/Fuzi), a government official, failed to take into account the possibility of a Machiavellian/oligarchical despot rising to power. For such was the case of the Qin dynasty, during which epoch, according to Renard (2012), China's Emperor Huang ordered nearly four hundred and sixty Confucian scholars to be buried alive. The cruelties would continue, for during Chairman Mao's (Mao Zedong) mid-twentieth century reign of terror or Cultural Revolution, the despot boasted of more egregious atrocities. He allegedly sentenced over forty-six thousand Confucian scholars to be buried alive (Rummel, 1994). These facts alone seriously debase, unseat, and throw the Confucian pedagogical model into disarray.

Taoism and Confucianism averred that the Tao is the originator of all life; it is the origin of all astronomical, terrestrial, and celestial bodies; it encompasses the wind, rain, cold, heat, light, darkness, and all things seen and unseen. It is quite apparent that, like all Sinitic and some Eastern-developed religions, Confucianism shares little symmetry with orthodox Christianity. Many of the enormous dichotomies that are very pronounced between the two sects (orthodox Christianity and Confucianism) will be addressed under the heading Contrasts to Orthodox Christianity. However, attention will be focused within the next section upon the little symmetry that the two do have in common.

Parallels to Orthodox Christianity

Like Christianity, Confucianism emphasizes man's proper relationship (e.g., kindness, frankness, courtesy, benevolence) with or toward one another. The two also promote proper interactions between civic officials and the populace. Confucianism's methodology, however, for accomplishing these goals differs markedly from that employed by Christianity. As the Yin and the Yang (briefly discussed earlier), which is often illustrated as a circle containing two congruent comma marks lying opposite of one another, each half a different color while sharing a small dot of the other's color, makes for a proper balance or equilibrium of the universe, so, too, would superb individuals (Yin) and civil authorities (Yang, which emerged from those superb individuals) maintain a similar environmental symbiosis. Confucius's, of course, was a method or pedagogy of teaching mankind the proper etiquette for coexisting with others.

While I do not purport nor intimate to be the intellectual equivalent of the venerable and learned sage Confucius, I do humbly yet audaciously take comfort in (and am assured of) my knowledge of the life and works of Confucius and that of his most prolific exponent, Mencius. That knowledge, coupled with in-depth knowledge of *The Analects* and impeccable God-given biblical acuity, gives me great confidence and assurance in my ability to expose and denude much of Confucius's erroneous philosophical and intellectual constructs. Confucianism, when juxtaposed with Christianity, divulges many salient and epistemological arguments. Perhaps the most arguable, as pertaining to ethics, is that one can never be certain of the veracity of the curriculum that he or she is being taught, for the curriculum and the syllabi are designed by man, not by God. Confucius's concept of a superb person, resulting from being properly taught, is a misnomer in and of itself. No one can become superb in the sight of God by mimicking the behavior of or being taught by another. At best, the pupil can be required to acquire skills, talents, or concepts that would identity him or her as meeting certain criteria. But a superb person can hardly be the product of a secular pedagogy, for even with continued practice and modeling, he or she will merely vicariously absorb many of the traits of the mentor. The mentor or teacher—prior to being qualified as such—however, honed his or her talents and social skills vicariously as well. So then what is being learned via any secular pedagogy is only what another individual (or individuals through books, recordings, etc.) has learned and passed on from his or her pedagogical experiences. Consider, for example, the intellectual prowess of Sir Isaac Newton, Albert Einstein, or perhaps the unsung William James Sidis. All these celebrated men (Newton for gravity, Einstein for physics, and Sidis for math and thermodynamics) registered an intelligence quotient (IQ) of well over two hundred. Einstein's IQ was between two hundred and two hundred and twenty; Sidis' towered Einstein's by seventy to eighty-five marks. And, no doubt, if the IQ of St. Augustine of Hippo (theologian and philosopher), Cicero (Roman scholar and lawyer), Virgil (Roman poet), and Aristotle (Greek philosopher) could've been measured, that data would have looked similar. These men were quintessential and remain greatly renowned for their contributions to human knowledge. They will always, of course, be lauded for their ability to assuage geo-social and political fractures. Great men they were; superb they were not, for, if one could be so persuaded to delve further into the backgrounds of these individuals, it would soon be discovered that (as we have learned under the preceding heading Basic Beliefs And Rituals) the great minds of the world are not always the most superb, magnanimous, or benevolent. Rather, more often than not, they tend to be quite malevolent. In the following paragraph we shall inquire of the scriptures concerning this matter.

In the context of Christianity, however, we are to portray the life and behavior of Jesus Christ. The Apostle Peter plainly states, "Christ...leaving us an example, that ye should follow his steps" (1 Pet. 2:21). John expands upon his colleague's assertion with "ye need not that any man teach you" (1 John 2:27). One can also infer from John 14:26 that it is the born again experience (predicated upon accepting Christ as savior) that teaches us proper values, morals, and mores and thereby makes the person superb or excellent in God's sight. The sum of the matter, however, is inextricably embedded and rooted in love (*agape*). Jesus insisted, "That ye love one another *as I have loved you*" (emphasis added, see John 13:34). It's interesting to note the phrase "as I have loved you," for it lets us know that Jesus's (hence God's) love was and is *agape*.

Of the plethora of love types (viz, *eros*, *agape*, *storge*, *philia*, *ludus*, etc.), there is one that dwarfs all others. The term is *agape* (Greek *agapi*, meaning God's love for man and the love that man is to reciprocate). Unlike the others (e.g., *eros*, *philia*, *ludus*, etc.), *agape* is an unconditional love, or one based not upon any perceived set of circumstances. This is the love that God requires not only to be shown toward him but toward others as well. The following are a few scriptures that will accentuate the *agape* concept: 1 John 3:18, 4:20, 1 Cor. 13:2–13 (in 1 Cor. 13:2–13 and others where Paul uses the term "charity," it would be within the norms of the Greek lexicon to translate the word "charity" as "love"), Gal. 5:14, Eph. 5:2, John 13:35, Col. 3:14, and 1 Pet. 2:17. There are, of course, an abundance of other scriptures from which to borrow. Albeit clearly explained and exemplified (John 3:16, Rom. 5:8) in the scriptures, the uninitiated will find it unconscionable to imagine that mankind can harbor *agape* (unconditional) love. How is it possible, they will ask, to love someone—particularly those who are unkind, malevolent, or even bellicose—by displaying the same love that Jesus portrayed? Nonetheless, revisiting John 13:34, we see that *agape* is exactly what Jesus intended.

The following scriptures are a succinct summation of how one is able to display *agape* to others: "as many…as have been baptized into Christ have put on Christ" (Gal. 3:27). As such, one has become a new creature (2 Cor. 5:17) while simultaneously acquiring the persona of Christ. It must be concluded, then, that it is not the Yin and Yang concept promulgated by Taoism and Confucianism that keeps the universe in perfect balance. Rather, God (Yahweh/Jehovah) is the architect, although incomprehensible to man, who sketched the universe, framed it, and assures its equilibrium, or perfect balance (Job 14:5, 26:7, 10, Acts 17:26, Heb. 11:3).

Solomon's Book of Proverbs vs. Confucius's Sayings (*The Analects*) A Comparison

King Solomon (King David's son) is credited with the authorship of the vast majority of the Proverbs. The attributions of other Proverbs have only been the subject of conjecture, speculation, and mere presumptions. Suffice it to say, however, that they were all penned by those who were moved and inspired by God. The Apostle Peter proclaimed in his second letter that "holy men of God spake as they were moved by the Holy Ghost" (1:21). Moreover, when reading *The Analects*, which is comprised of twenty books or sections, one finds that it presents many striking similarities to several of the Proverbs. These similarities have enticed some theologians of the Christian persuasion and otherwise to espouse that Confucius's disciples, when completing Confucius's unfinished work borrowed significantly from Solomon's Proverbs. Upon thoroughly examining both works (the Proverbs and *The Analects*), one can easily come away with the same conclusion. However, while the use of many third-person narratives within *The Analects* does suggest that the work was completed posthumously, the similarities do not necessarily lend credence to plagiarism. The reader, after critically examining and comparing both works, will be in a more conducive position to draw his or her own conclusion.

Most of the passages or verses of *The Analects*, if you will, begin with the phrase "The Master said" or "Confucius said." The sayings of Confucius address such topics as virtue, benevolence, the gentleman, and the Way or Dao/Tao. Laozi, the founder of Taoism, characterized the Dao/Tao as the forces that cause the universe or nature to behave in multiple fashions; Confucius, however, would characterize the Way as the Right Paths. We shall examine some resemblances between the Proverbs and *The Analects*. Only briefly, however, will the comparisons be entertained at this juncture. This is so that the reader will not be unduly influenced or prompted to accept the author's position or intimations, rather, that the reader will become inquisitive and emboldened to delve further into the two sources and draw his or her own conclusions. As a result of further research, the inquisitive will ultimately become more knowledgeable and cognizant of the word of God. While the author has borrowed sufficiently from *The Analects* in order to present dichotomies and comparisons, it is advised to obtain a copy. One final and extremely important note before we examine the resemblances: when comparing any ancillary and secondary works to the Bible, one must necessarily ensure that he or she has a tenacious command of and is solidly grounded in the scriptures themselves. Accordingly, when serendipity or eureka moments occur while the Bible is being juxtaposed with other sources, all such enlightenments must be validated and confirmed by biblical scripture. Moreover, if those illuminations are allowed to go without question or validation, the unsuspecting could possibly begin to, unwittingly, subscribe to concepts that are antithetical to scripture. If this happens, they are quite likely to become entangled in Satan's subterfuge and be swept away by his duplicitous undertows and swift currents. Hence, while *The Analects* and other sources can be insightful, it is imperative to search the scriptures to ensure that such insights are in accordance with them.

The comparisons between Confucius's *Analects* and Solomon's Proverbs are as follows:

(1) Book XV and verse 40 of *The Analects* (Lau, 1979, pg. 137). It advises one against seeking advice from those who are following a different path than him or her.

Compare this to Proverbs 13:20, which speaks about the benefits of accompanying the wise, as opposed to being in the company of fools.

(2) Book Vll and verse 20 of *The Analects* (Lau, 1979, pg. 88) speaks of one not having congenital cognition but seeks to acquire knowledge.

Juxtapose this with Proverbs 1:5, which explains how a wise man furthers his learning and seeks wise advice.

(3) Book I and verse 15 of *The Analects* (Lau, 1979, pg. 61) addresses the matter of the poor.

Compare this portion to Proverbs 14:20–21, 31; 29:7, 13, each of which points to the treatment or character of the poor.

(4) Book XlX and verse 1 of *The Analects* (Lau, 1979, pg. 153) is a narrative describing the gentleman who does what is right even though it's more economical to engage in wrongdoing.

Consider this narrative in relation to Proverbs 16:8, which insists that having little but being honest has great benefits.

(5) Book IX and verse 29 of *The Analects* (Lau, 1979, pg. 100) teaches that a man that has wisdom is never a double-minded man.

Compare this to Proverbs 8:11–12; 16:16, both which compare wisdom to precious jewels (i.e., silver, gold, or rubies).

(6) Book XII and verse 22 of *The Analects* (Lau, 1979, pg. 116) discusses Confucius's narrative after being confronted by Fan Ch'ih. When asked about wisdom, the sage insisted that one should know his fellow men.

Compare this to Proverbs 2:1–2, 5:1–2, in which we find the suggestion of having an attentive ear to those who are imbued with wisdom.

(7) Lastly, although the similarities continue to be quite copious, Book I and verse 14 of *The Analects* (Lau, 1979, pg. 61) presents a discourse about being guarded or cautious when speaking.

Juxtapose that discourse with Proverbs 10:19, 13:3, 15:1, 17:28, and 29:11, all of which explain the importance of knowing when to speak.

The preceding comparisons are only a modicum of instances citing Solomon's and Confucius's similar writings. The similarities, however, are enormous. They should prompt one to question the novelty and originality of Confucius's works. Nevertheless, as positioned elsewhere in this narrative, to decide whether or not Confucius's followers borrowed from the works of King Solomon will be left to the reader after painstakingly and critically examining the sources to conclude.

Contrasts to Orthodox Christianity

Among Confucius's *Five Classics*, penned by Confucius himself, is the *Classic of Changes*, or *I Ching*. This work was designed as a source of instruction in divination whereby the diviner uses eight trigrams to form sixty-four equilateral triangles (or Stars of David, which some may be more familiar with). The early disciples of Confucius and Laozi (Lao Tzu), the father of Taoism, alleged that this activity was beneficial for predicting weather patterns and life's future events. Orthodox Christianity, however, finds no currency in this nor does it invest in such a scheme. While the scriptures are unequivocally clear and replete with warnings concerning such matters (i.e., divination, soothsaying, witchcraft), we shall examine but a few.

(1) In the book of Leviticus (The English Standard Version), from verse 26 to 31 of chapter 19, Israel is warned of relying upon the shapes of the clouds or cloud patterns as a means of divination or fortune-telling. They were also forbidden from looking into the future by eliciting the assistance of necromancers or fortune-tellers.

And, yes, within that same narrative, cutting oneself or tattooing was also strictly forbidden.

(2) The book of Numbers (chapters 22, 23, and 24) addresses the scenario of Balak and Balaam, wherein Balaam the false prophet and diviner is summoned and instructed to employ his craft in an effort to curse God's people. However, we find that despite his several attempts and best practices, his tactics prove fruitless, for God has promised that no weapon formed or crafted against his people will prosper (Isaiah 54:17).

(3) Lastly, while studying the works of the Prophet Isaiah, in the nineteenth verse of chapter eight, another warning is revealed. God's people are warned against mimicking and assimilating the behaviors of the Assyrians; such behaviors included seeking direction from those who were influenced by familiar spirits (apparitions) and such as employed wizardry. There are copious scriptures, primarily contained within the Torah/Pentateuch and the history books that denounce the practice of divination. Some among the plethora are Num. 23:23, Deut. 18:9–14, 1 Sam. 28:7, and 2 Kings 17:17.

While Confucians do not acknowledge nor disavow a God and therefore have no pantheon, their pedagogy includes an undertow of heaven and Earth worship. Heaven and Earth, however, not unlike nature and creation, are not God. Rather, they are but mere manifestations of God's power, or *dunamis*. The Apostle Paul pontificated, "The invisible things…from the creation of the world are clearly seen, being understood by the things that are made, even his eternal power…" (See Rom. 1:20). The Confucian-Taoist heaven and earth philosophy is further defused by the Apostle Paul's narrative to the church at Rome, for in it he explains (from the New International Version): "They worshipped and served created things rather than the creator." The Living Bible expresses succinctly, "They prayed to the things God made, but wouldn't obey the blessed God who made these things" (Rom. 1:25). When reading Romans 1:25 from the King James version or any scripture in which Paul mentions the term "creature," it is etymologically correct to equate the word "creature" with the term "creation."

Moreover, contrary to Confucian and Taoist belief, man will never become one with nature, for such an amalgamation is not nature's desire. Moreover, in spite of the espousals of Freud (1923) and promulgations within his subsequent work (1961), man's ego has no desire—nor will it allow him—to become one with nature. For nature/creation itself groans (Greek=*stenazo*, to express desire or grief from within; grief that is caused from the labor of pushing forward from within), as does mankind in anticipation of being one with God. To obtain a better illustration of this premise, it will be necessary to explore Romans 8:19–23. Lastly, but of no less importance, according to biblical scripture, while there is a symbiotic relationship between the Earth/nature and man (See Gen. 1:26–31, 3:17–19), bringing man into union with nature as a mean of salvation was never God's plan. Rather, God's modus operandi or plan was— through the atonement or death and resurrection of Christ—to bring mankind back to himself (see 1 Cor. 15:22, 2 Cor. 5:19, 21, Eph. 1:7, Gal. 1:4, and others).

Soteriological Views

Confucians do not comport with the definition of

heaven nor hell, not in the sense of the classical Christian concept, that is. They're not Christians, of course, nor can they be characterized as atheists. Rather, the fundamentalists insist that there is a Nothingness, or Tao, that controls the universe. Although they espouse that Tao is inexplicable, the mere fact that they believe that there is some higher power (albeit incomprehensible) exculpates them of atheism. Agnostics, they absolutely are; Confucians simply do not wear the proverbial badge of atheism, however. Confucians emphasize the symbiosis among man, the heavens, and the Earth.

Eschatological Perspectives

Neither Confucius nor his immediate followers were concerned with the rewards of a heaven for the avoidance of sin. Nor did the sage consider giving credence to a hell. He and his followers were/are far too humanistic to entertain such premises. Instead, Confucius's was a concept of heaven that purported that mankind was ultimately responsible for his own fate and enlightenment. The adherents maintain that there might be a God as Christians and others allege; maybe there's a heaven in which he dwells. Perhaps there's a hell, too, a place where—as espoused by Protestants—wicked people end up. Such trivial matters, the Confucians maintain, are the headaches and opioids of Christianity and must not be entertained. Moreover, in Confucius's doctrine, the custodians of any heaven or hell—if the two actually existed—would be indifferent to man's behavior. Hence, man is not to behave in such a way as to avoid hell or acquire heaven, for heaven and hell, as Confucianism promulgates, have not been proven to actually exist.

Therefore, man is not to concern himself with such trivial, unsubstantiated cosmic extremes. For humans, the sage and his disciples averred, were to commit themselves to upholding the five virtues of life, i.e., wisdom, love, devotion to one another, propriety or proper decorum, and justice. In summary, Confucius's ego would've never allowed him to subscribe to holistic Christianity or Christianity in the main. The ego is very deceptive, for it fills one with the notion of individualism, pride, and self-centeredness. It's the alchemy behind Confucianism. Schucman and Thetford (1976) implied (within their copious pages of *A Course In Miracles*) that the ego is selfish and conceited; they also maintain that it blinds us from the clarity and reality that there is a higher power (regardless of the nomenclature) beyond one's ego. Consequently, Confucius's was not a notion of heaven as Christians would think of it. For he thought of heaven—if it indeed existed—as merely a nebulous, spiritual motion oblivious to the presence and actions of mankind. Lastly, while there are no ecclesiastical motifs, hierarchical priesthood, or ordinations, the Confucian concept of ancestor veneration, albeit esoteric, is indicative of their belief of an afterlife. Ancestor veneration, of course, does not comport with the orthodox Christian construct.

Concerns and Implications for the Orthodox Christian

Confucianism, not unlike Buddhism, Taoism, or Hinduism, has no elaborate master plan or scheme for proselytizing, nor is its literature and liturgy dogmatic, per se. Consequently, it has never posed an existential threat to the more vigorous, incessant, and principal religions (viz, Orthodox Christianity, Islam, Catholicism, Judaism) of the world. Nonetheless, it remains quite a subtle, insidious, and pernicious force, for Confucianism hinders the proselytizing efforts of Christians throughout the continent of Asia and other pockets that have assimilated its axioms. It is important, therefore, for those who would evangelize or serve as missionaries among this population to possess some basic knowledge of the teachings of Confucius and the ethos of his period. Proverbs 11:30 lets us know that the wise winneth souls. And, of course, the Apostle Paul concluded that Christians—not only his protégé Timothy—should study the scriptures in order to properly share them with others (See 2 Tim. 2:15).

    Confucianism was well established and promulgated throughout China and other Asian lands far afield many hundreds of years before the beginning of Christianity. Confucianism does not predate the world's arguably oldest religion, Judaism, however, for Christianity, in its own right (that is to say separate from Judaism), didn't come about until, arguably, between 27 CE and 32 CE but certainly no later than 35 CE. Confucianism, contrastingly, was present in Asia since from about 553 BCE to 479 BCE. Hermeneutics and biblical studies teach us that timing coupled with ethos speaks volumes to not only the beliefs of an individual, but to how the individual will view biblical and religious constructs. Colloquially speaking, most people (except where there is a spiritual, intellectual, or scientific enlightenment) tend to accept conditions as they are. They get by in life by proverbially marching to the drum of the status quo. On the other hand, others choose to voice their concerns and become champions for changing the milieu and social environment that they've inherited. Confucius and others who founded religions either prior to or long after the advent of Christianity are not without exception. From Proverbs 23:7 we learn that "as he thinketh in his heart, so is he." Had Confucius been a young man coming of age in, let's say, Rome, Germany, Greece, Turkey, or Palestine from about 7 CE to 16 CE, perhaps—being influenced by the ethos—his ego would've presented itself differently. Subsequently, he would have possibly acquired an affinity for Christianity. Given the sage's gravitas and intellect, it's profoundly inconceivable that Confucius, if active at the places and during the periods mentioned above, would not have been on par with Luther, Jerome, Huss, Wycliffe, or Calvin.

Instead of Luther's Ninety-Five Theses, perhaps Confucius's; rather than Luther appearing before the Diet of Worms in Germany, maybe it would've been Confucius; rather than Jerome or Huss succumbing to the flames, perhaps Confucius would have been the martyr. It could've been a real possibility, considering the character of the venerable sage. Of course, the opposite is also not without plausibility. For Confucius could've just as well gone the way of Voltaire, Erasmus, or René Descartes (who coined the phrase "I think, therefore I am"), philosophers and humanists who rejected God. Nonetheless, Christians must not conclude that all hope is loss for this cult, for the scriptures reminds us that God is not willing that any should perish (see 2 Pet. 3:9).

Suggested Readings:

(1) Benedict, Gerald. 2008. *The Watkins Dictionary of Religious and Secular Faiths*. Watkins Publishing, London (UK).

(2) Gardner, Daniel K. 2007. *The Four Books: The Basic Teachings of the Later Confucian Tradition*. Hackett Publishing, Incorporated.

(3) Ni, Peimin. 2016. *Confucius: The Man and the Way of Gongfu*.
Rowman & Littlefield.

(4) Rainey, Lee Dian. 2010. *Confucius And Confucianism: The Essentials*. Wiley-Blackwell Publishers.

(5) Waley, Arthur. 1996. *The Book of Songs, the Ancient Chinese Classic of Poetry*. Grove Press.

Dr. A.J. Handy, Ph.D.

Section Five

Hinduism

Founding/Brief History

Hinduism, arguably one of the two oldest religions of the world, had its infancy in the area of what is today called India, specifically in the northwestern section near the fertile Indus River valley not far from present-day Pakistan's eastern border. However, as concerning the actual founder of Hinduism, antiquity has betrayed us, for, unlike most eastern cults—let's say, Taoism, Confucianism, or Buddhism—neither antiquity nor anthologies provide a specific initiator. In Hinduism we're not presented with a Laozi (Lao Tzu) who through Taoism taught that mankind could live in perfect rhythm with the forces of nature and the changing environments. Nor are we given a Confucius who wrote and taught concerning the morals, mores, and ethical behaviors of man, how humans are to behave toward one another, and how the government should respond toward its citizenry. In the study of Hinduism, we're not introduced to an eremitical Siddhartha Gautama (The Buddha) who at the age of nineteen became disillusioned by the sublime confines of aristocracy, subsequently abandoning his wife and child, trading wealth for poverty, disappearing into the quiet of the night, assuming the persona of a mendicant ascetic, and embarking upon a nine-year odyssey until finally experiencing an epiphany. Hinduism does not release such a biography.

Radiocarbon dating, however, has enlightened us, for it has amalgamated critical data, derivatives, and relics to allow conclusions to be drawn. With Carbon-14 dating, archaeologists have been able to conclude that, prior to the Aryan occupation (which began around 2002 BCE), the Harappa people inhabited the lands along the fertile Indus Valley of India. Their cultish practices, however, are said to have been those that would not have supported Hinduism, relative to how it has been practiced over the past centuries. Hinduism is a syncretic belief in that it is an appropriation of some aspects of the Aryans' Vedic religious system, which was synthesized with their own pre-Aryan religion of Sanatana Dharma.

As has already been touched upon in the chapter addressing Buddhism, after establishing hegemony, the Aryans expanded the preexisting caste system. This was easily accomplished, for the Aryans were the only ones who could speak Sanskrit. This social construct was ostensibly designed to introduce God (Brahman) to the people. In actuality, though, it was fabricated in order to maintain the purity of the Aryan race, thereby perpetuating and ensuring themselves the highest quality of life. The Aryans considered it their "manifest destiny." As a rebellion against the Aryans' tactics and their Vedic practices, which sometimes included animal sacrifices, many natives simply adopted the lives of ascetics and retreated to the forests in search of spiritual attainment.

Whereas Buddhism and its splinter sects (i.e., Theravada, Vajrayana, and Mahayana) promote a proclivity toward meditating in more relaxed positions, Hinduism insists, however, upon its grandiose precursors (i.e., yoga poses, chants, oblations, and occasional circumambulations) to meditation.

Dr. A.J. Handy, Ph.D.

Basic Beliefs and Rituals

Contrary to Western thought, Hindus are not atheists; rather, Hinduism incorporates polytheism, monotheism, and henotheism. It's polytheistic in that the faithful believe there are many gods; it's monotheistic in that, although there are many gods, a person can choose to follow only one; it's henotheistic in that although the believer only worships, let's say, one god or several others, he or she will tolerate other gods. Most Hindus tend to be monotheistic, however. Nevertheless, in order to obtain a proper perspective of and appreciation for Hinduism, it will be necessary to rid the palate of its cravings for fallacies and myths—the tastes of which it has perhaps become accustomed—and refresh it with a taste of accurate, substantiated, and well-documented facts.

Because there is a plethora of gods from which to choose, the practices of one sect or cult will be, in most respects, foreign to a neighboring Hindu order. The practitioners are, therefore, not invariably monolithic. The same can, of course, be said of Zoroastrianism or Jainism, for they have various incognito splinter groups as well. Some Hindu practices, which of course are recognized by those of a particular order, are completely imperceptible to other practicing Hindus. This is because many of the smaller branches and factions have amputated several of the orthodox tenets. Regardless of the sect or individual persuasion, the orthodox (if the term orthodox can be attached) Hindu prefers to worship their god(s) or goddess(s) through a tangible object of some sort. Brahman is said to be the supreme god, the god that allows one to experience spiritual and divine reality.

Among Brahman's pantheon, there is that which many have termed the Hindu Trinity (the Trimurti). This misnomer has mistakenly been compared to
the Trinity, which resonates with Christian thought.

The trinity is said to consist of: (1) the god Brahma; (2) the god Vishnu; and (3) the god Shiva. To obtain a better understanding of these three, it is important to grasp the concept of the socioeconomic structure, or caste system, of India, the system "popularized" by the Aryans. It will lend much to the understanding of the caste system if one can imagine Maslow's (1954) theory of man's hierarchy of needs. Although sketching a much different construct (for Maslow purports that man's basic and more important survival needs must be met before his social and less important self-actualization needs can be realized), Maslow's illustration is somewhat analogous to India's caste system. At the apex of the triangle were the Brahmins (Aryans) who insisted that they were to be considered priests/intellectuals. They were, therefore, considered to be in a class of their own. Below them were the militia or battle-ready caste, third were the agrarian/agricultural-merchant caste, and moving further toward the bottom of the spectrum were the peasants whose lot it was to serve those at the top of the pyramid, the Brahmins. Fifth and finally at the very bottom were (and still are) those who are colloquially known as the outcastes or untouchables. As the name suggests, they are treated with abject disrespect; they need not be reminded that certain mundane tasks are theirs to be completed. They are, of course, not allowed to participate in certain forums. The blend of the peasant caste and the outcaste are often indistinguishable, however. To some degree the caste system still exists today. It is prevalent in regions where Hinduism, Buddhism, or their derivatives are the dominant religions.

We see then that the Aryans' Vedic system was but a ruse; however, it gained momentum and cascaded throughout the centuries. At this juncture it is important to continue our examination of the three: Brahma, Vishnu, and Shiva. Brahma was alleged to be the god who primarily attended to the needs of the priestly class (the Brahmins). Vishnu is said to be the god who keeps the universe in order, providing the universe with illumination and equilibrium. Vishnu is associated with several (perhaps as many as eleven) avatars as well. In contrast to Vishnu, Shiva, the third in the triumvirate, is the god who destroys. This concept is readily accepted among Hindus, for it gives credence to their concept of reincarnation, that all things (i.e., life-forms, structures, etc.) must change their appearance.

Cults and sects that harbor the precepts of reincarnation almost invariably tend to give credence to some form of divination as well. Hindus are not exempted, for they imperiously and unapologetically wear the proverbial badge of divination. Acts of premonition and signs of augury are expected and widely practiced among the ranks. Hindus are believed to often rely heavily upon the uncharacteristic behaviors of animal species (i.e., unusual patterns of birds and cows, etc.), as well as astrological phenomena to predict future occurrences. Of the four Vedas, the *Atharvaveda* addresses the subject of divination more copiously.

The holy texts/canon of Hinduism are known as the Vedas (Books of Knowledge). Fundamentalist Hindus insist that the Vedas are *apauruseya*, (that is to say, not of human nor divine origin). This belief coincides with that of Knipe (1991), who alleged that the writings should be viewed as one unit; they are eternal and were not given to the world through any human or deity. However, many have insisted that when reading the Vedas, they seem to imply that they are, indeed, of human origination. In fact, many theologians have credited the authorship of the Vedas to the Vedic (Aryan) sage Veda Vyasa (often referred to as Krishna Dvaipayana), with the date of penning between 1500–1000 BCE. The four Vedas and much of the Hindu ancillary texts are as follows: *Rigveda* (the oldest), *Samaveda*, Yajurveda, and *Atharvaveda*. An ancillary work, the *Bhagavad Gita* (known as the fifth Veda), was later added. The Brahmanas, Samhita, Aranyakas, and the Upanishads are the four sections or divisions of any given Veda. At this point we will briefly examine the four Vedas.

(1) *Rigveda*

The *Rigveda* is believed by some to be the world's oldest religious writing that remains in practice. It's comprised mostly of mythological Aryan-Hindu hymns. There are ten sections or books within the *Rigveda*; within those ten books there are some one hundred and twenty-eight hymns or songs of praise.

(2) *Samaveda*

This book contains carols and mantras that are borrowed quite extensively from its predecessor, the *Rigveda*. Of the *Samaveda*'s 1,538 plus verses, approximately 1,474 of them are seen within the *Rigveda*. Two of the over two hundred *Upanishads* (the "Chandogya" and "Kena"), which were written as an antithesis or opposition to the Vedic (Aryan) ethos, are included in the *Samaveda*.

(3) *Yajurveda*

The *Yajurveda* consists primarily of mantras or incantations uttered by a priest during many ceremonial rituals. For example, if a worshipper is offering a sacrifice or propitiating God (done usually before a contained fire), the priest will offer the incantations and mantras. Not unlike the *Samaveda*, it, too, takes from the older *Rigveda*.

(4) *Atharvaveda*

This later-arriving text is considered by many as the repository of knowledge for daily existence. It's primarily a compilation of songs of worship or hymns, all of which are comprised within its twenty sections or books. Approximately 80 percent of the text employs poems. Like the *Samaveda* and *Yajurveda*, the *Atharvaveda* integrates with sections of the *Rigveda*.

Parallels to Orthodox Christianity

Like most predominantly eastern religions, Hinduism is not easily swallowed by the Western palate; it bears little resemblance to Christianity. There are some subtle similarities, however; Christianity is divided into certain denominations (e.g., Methodist, Baptist, Episcopal, Lutheran, etc.), and so, too, is Hinduism. Some of the Hindu divisions are Krishnas, Vaishnavites, and Shaivites. Like Christianity, Hinduism has its trinity: Brahma, Vishnu, and Shiva. The Hindu triad or triumvirate, of course, does not remotely resemble the Protestants' codification of the Trinity with the Father,

Son, and the Holy Ghost. Christianity has its holy literature, the one and only source, the Bible. Hinduism has its holy literature, several sources including the *Bhagavad Gita*, the Vedas, and the Puranas.

The Vedic-Hindu Scripture and the Bible
Similarities of Scriptures

Upon objectively scrutinizing and juxtaposing Vedic literature and the Bible, one will notice that there are some quite salient similarities in tone and expression between much of the two canons. Nevertheless, at this juncture comparisons will be limited to narratives found in the Bible and portions of the *Bhagavad Gita*. Before attempting to extrapolate, however, it will be helpful to give a synopsis of the *Bhagavad Gita*.

The *Bhagavad Gita* ("The Song of God") is basically a dialogue among Sri Krishna, Arjuna, blind King Dhritarashtra, and Sanjaya. Most of the conversation (90 percent or more), however, is between Sri Krishna and Arjuna. In the narrative Arjuna is saddened that his relatives, teachers, and friends have allied themselves and come out to do battle against him. He pities them. Distraught, he refuses to engage for he loves them. Sri Krishna, however, tries to encourage Arjuna. The classic goes on to express the importance of being united with Brahman, which, according to Vedic-Hindu mythology is the supreme God or force which inhabits all living things. This God-force, not to be confused with Brahma (the creator God), is alleged to be the giver of all life, the knower of all yet unknown by all. After much dialogue or question-and-answer sessions, Arjuna comes to the realization that Sri Krishna is correct in all his teachings.

Even though the *Bhagavad Gita* doesn't culminate with any Justinian, Napoleonic, or Tet Offensive type battlefield tactics, Arjuna becomes very emboldened and promises to engage. We shall now attempt to delineate some of the similarities shared by biblical scriptures and the Vedic Hindu narratives:

(1-A) In the *Bhagavad Gita* (chapter 2), as he addresses Arjuna, Sri Krishna alleges that man's inner spirit (*atman*) is without a beginning; it was never born. It is unchanging, without death, and will not cease (Isherwood and Prabhavananda, 1995).

Compare Sri Krishna's dialogue with Arjuna pertaining to the atman (The Hindu term for inner spirit) in (1-A), to the book of Hebrews' description of Melchizedek in (1-B):

(1-B) Hebrews 7:3: The writer explains that Melchizedek is "without father...mother, without descent, having neither beginning of days, nor end of life" (Scofield, 2015).

(2-A) In the *Bhagavad Gita* (chapter 2), as Sri Krishna continues his dialogue with Arjuna, he insists that grieving for Arjuna's relatives should not be a consideration. Sri Krishna continues by asserting that death is inevitable; he reiterates by explaining what happens between the birth and the death of an individual (Isherwood and Prabhavananda, 1995).

Juxtapose Sri Krishna's position concerning life and death in (2-A) with Job's debacle in (2-B):

(2-B) Job 4:1–7, 6:1–2, 7:1–2, 14:1–3, 5, 7–10, 12, 14. In these narratives Job is severely distraught and subsequently lamenting the death of all his children. Like Arjuna in the *Bhagavad Gita*, this quagmire sends him into a proverbial tailspin of grief; to venture out of the doldrums, he is offered advice from his friends. In the end, however, it is only God himself who can offer genuine comfort (Scofield, 2015).

(3-A) In chapter three of the *Bhagavad Gita*, the narrative opens with Arjuna's complaints to Sri Krishna. He's confused, for it appears that he is receiving contradictory advice from Sri Krishna. Sri Krishna responds by informing Arjuna that in the genesis or beginning of time, God created men for specific purposes and duties (Isherwood and Prabhavananda, 1995).

Compare (3-A), Sri Krishna's pontification to (3-B), in which Moses talks about the creation of mankind.

(3-B) Genesis 1:26–30, in which God creates man to be the stewards of all that he'd previously created. Man is also instructed to be fruitful, multiply, and to replenish or continue adding to the Earth (Scofield, 2015).

(4-A) In chapter three of the *Bhagavad Gita*, Sri Krishna informs Arjuna of the importance of clinging to his (Sri Krishna's) dogma and sayings. He informs Arjuna that the person who loathes his instructions will be lost or adrift. This is extremely similar to Jesus's sayings (Isherwood and Prabhavananda, 1995).

Juxtapose (4-A), the wisdom of Sri Krishna with (4-B), the words of Jesus:

(4-B) Matthew 7:24, in which Jesus says, "Whosoever heareth these sayings of mine, and doeth them, I will liken him unto a wise man" (Scofield, 2015).

(5-A) In the latter section of chapter nine of the *Bhagavad Gita*, Sri Krishna explains the fate of the person who loves him; he insisted that if a person loves him, he or she will never expire or perish (Isherwood and Prabhavananda, 1995).

Analyze (5-A), the assertion of Sri Krishna, and the prose of the Apostle John in 5-B:

(5-B) John 3:15: "Whosoever believeth in him should not perish."

John 3:16: "Whosoever believeth in him should not perish, but have everlasting life."

John 10:28: "They shall never perish" (Scofield, 2015).

Contrasts to Orthodox Christianity

In Christianity, as well as in Judaism, it is believed that there is one God who is the creator of all things seen and unseen (see Col. 1:16 and Deut. 6:4). As has been explained elsewhere in this text, this perception is untenable among Hindus, Confucians, and Buddhists. The Christians' holy text, the Bible, purports that man dies only once (see Heb. 9:27); in contrast, the Hindu's holy texts, i.e., the Vedas, the *Bhagavad Gita*, etc., promote the concept of reincarnation and multiple lifespans. In Christianity, while there are pastors, teachers, evangelists, etc., the faithful believe that God—not a guru—is their ultimate teacher (see 1 John 2:27). In Hinduism, however, this is not so. Whereas in Hinduism Brahma is said to be primarily the god of the upper caste (the Brahmins), Christianity teaches that God is not a respecter of persons (see Acts. 10:34, Rom. 2:11–16). Moreover, the Bible explains that, as it would be in the case of the "intellectuals" or Brahmins, God has hidden certain things from the wise and prudent and revealed them unto babes (see Matt. 11:25). Wisdom and knowledge, therefore, are not the monopolies of any particular socioeconomic or political group. They can be obtained, however, through the favor of God: "the Lord giveth wisdom: out of his mouth cometh knowledge and understanding" (Prov. 2:6). See also James 1:5, Prov. 1:7, 8:5–17. Furthermore, as it pertains to a nation's caste system, which ultimately affects every aspect of a person's life including where, when, and sometimes how someone worships, Christianity is quite clear concerning the matter. The Apostle Paul pontificated, "There is neither Jew nor Greek…neither bond nor free…neither male nor female: for ye are all one in Christ Jesus" (Gal. 3:28). Lastly, and of equal importance to those dichotomies mentioned previously, is a discourse concerning Hinduism's purported Three Avenues to Salvation. The three are: (1) the Avenue of Knowledge, (2) the Avenue of Works, and (3) the Avenue of Devotion. While the triumvirate are foreign to orthodox Christian thought, only one of the criterion—the one over which many Christians continue to be torn—will be examined at this juncture: the Way of Works.

      The beauty of Christianity and what makes it stand alone is, of course, first and foremost the death, burial, and resurrection of Jesus Christ. Second to the resurrection is the fact that grace, which was appropriated via the resurrection, is freely given. Jesus told not only the few disciples who had the courage to remain close to him during his final hours, but all who looked upon him at Calvary, "it is finished" (John 19:30). To some it is absolutely unconscionable to suggest that salvation could be obtained without some works or periodic pathological rituals on their part. Hindus, however, are not alone in this quagmire, for the concept of combining works with grace extends far into the fabric of Protestantism. This is particularly true in the West (i.e., America, Canada,

United Kingdom, France, etc.) among those who are truly born again. They search the scriptures regularly, they attend weekly bible studies, and their presence can be taken for granted on Sunday mornings. However, the implications and inferences of the atonement of Christ continues to elude them. It was well articulated concerning those who the Apostle Paul predicted would fall prey to apostasy in the last days: "Ever learning, and never able to come to the knowledge of the truth" (2 Tim. 3:7). The same can be said of Christians who would affiliate works with grace. Considering the varied theologies amid Hinduism, it is of little surprise that Hindus would harbor such a concept. They do not get a pass, however.

    The Christian, on the other hand, is without excuse, for unlike the Hindus, the Bible is his or her primary source. Rhetorically, why then do some Christians insist upon blending grace with works—even though they have read and studied several scriptures that speak to the contrary? Perhaps it is because faith is not included. For the writer of Hebrews makes his or her homily very plain: "Unto us was the gospel preached, as well as unto them: but the word preached did not profit them, *not being mixed with faith*" (emphasis added Heb. 4:2). They've read and heard sermons regarding Ephesians 2:8–9, which explains, "For by grace are ye saved through faith; and that not of yourselves: it is the gift of God: Not of works." Moreover, God has no strict terms that must be met for his endearment. Nor can he be persuaded by one's performances (that is to say, extended prayers, tithing, etc.). His love is unconditional! Whether sinner or saint, pauper or tycoon, sage or illiterate, God's love remains the same. It's irrevocable and everlasting

(See Jer. 31:3 and Rom. 5:8).

Western ethics and ethos, however, teaches colloquially that "nothing is free." That concept tends to follow Christians into the spiritual domain. However, the "nothing is free" narrative is only true via the economic models (that is to say Keynesian, Classical, Neo-Malthusian, etc.) or in the secular domains. Grace, nonetheless, is absolutely free! Exploring further we find: "the blessedness of the man, unto whom God imputeth righteousness without works," (Rom. 4:6). Finally, we must consider: "There is a remnant according to the election of grace. And if by grace, then is it *no more of works*" (Rom. 11:5–6). Of course juxtaposing Christianity with any Eastern-born religion will reveal many stark contrasts. So great are the dichotomies that they would have to be described in a separate compendium.

Soteriological Views

In Hinduism, the equivalent of the Christian term "salvation" is *moksha* (not to be confused with the Buddhist term nirvana). *Moksha* is achieved when the soul (*atman*) becomes one with Brahman. When the *atman* and Brahman have become one and the same—and are, therefore, indistinguishable—the individual has experienced divine enlightenment. At this point—and only then—the individual perceives that all life-forms share the same divine energy. It is believed that *moksha*, or spiritual insight, can be triggered by various chants, mantras, and yoga/meditative practices. Through them, the person is set free from individuality. As was mentioned in the section concerning Buddhism, karma, reincarnation, yoga, and samsara all play a role in one's quest for spiritual enlightenment. Many are of the opinion that yoga is a religion; yoga and its many contortions are not a religion separate from Hinduism. Rather, it's only one aspect and arguably the most pivotal tenet of the religion. Without yoga there can be no Hinduism, for the religion is inextricably entrenched in, identified, and animated by yoga practices. Succinctly, yoga is to Hinduism as prayer is to Christianity (that is to say that, without yoga, Hinduism—in its classical form—would be nonexistent).

Eschatological Perspectives

As in Buddhism, the Hindus have no hell to fear and no heaven to look forward to, at least not in the Christian context, that is. Although, according to Isherwood and Prabhavananda (1995), in their translation of the *Bhagavad Gita* (arguably the most revered work in the Hindu canon), as revealed in chapters two, nine, and eighteen in particular—of their work—we notice that Hindus do, in fact, acknowledge a heaven. Arya (2003, pg. 62–63), in agreement with Isherwood and Prabhavananda, further explains that the Hindus' concept of heaven is to be as one, or in union, with Brahman. Hinduism alleges that all bad karma can be atoned for by (as in Buddhism) samsara, or continuous cycles of reincarnations. Those reincarnations, however, are said not to transpire immediately after the death of the organism (whether man, frog, butterfly, etc.). Rather, it is purported that the organism goes back to Brahman from which it originated until such time as it is recycled back into the universe's life force. Hence, theirs is an eschatological perspective of being one with the universe by attaining the highest level of spirituality, or *moksha*. *Moksha* as we've learned, is Hinduism's equivalent of nirvana, a Buddhist concept. It is interesting to note, though, that neither Hinduism nor Buddhism definitively answer the question of what happens to a person's lifeless body. Christianity, however, does offer an antidote. Look for this to be discussed further under the heading Concerns and Implications.

Concerns and Implications for the Orthodox Christian

At this time, Hinduism does not trigger any alarms, for, because of its rigidity and esoteric and grandiose motifs, it has not had widespread appeal to American or Western European audiences (unlike Buddhism or Confucianism). Transcendental Meditation (TM), a splinter of Hinduism, has, however, found its way into the Western mainstream. It was popularized and championed by Paul McCartney, John Lennon, Ringo Starr, and George Harrison (the legendary Beatles group) during the mid-to-late twentieth century (Arya, 2003). Many believe that John Lennon was somewhat influenced by Hinduism/Buddhism when he debuted his 1971 piece "Imagine," for much of the lyrics, many Protestants maintain, are accusatory and somewhat of an indictment of orthodox Christianity.

As was said elsewhere in this text, neither Hinduism nor Buddhism adequately explain the fate of the individual upon death or during the afterlife (as far as the opponents of reincarnation are concerned). The Bible is replete, however, with scriptures concerning the enigma of the spiritless body. Those passages assiduously denude the concept of reincarnation and other erroneous eschatological viewpoints. The Apostle Paul in particular and the anonymous writer of the book of Hebrews addressed the topic brilliantly. A few examples will be examined: Phil. 3:20–21 states, "Our conversation is in heaven...the Savior, the Lord Jesus...shall change our vile body, that it may be fashioned like unto his glorious body." Here, the apostle clearly explains that one's congenital body, which he refers to as "vile" ("vile" is etymologically Latin, *vilis*, meaning "worthless" or "of low value") will not enter into heaven. Instead, it will be fashioned to be "like" Christ's glorious body prior to its entrance into heaven (*endoxo*s=Greek for "glorious" or "illustrious"). Paul's pontification to the church at Philippi soundly comports with his narrative concerning the same when addressing the church at Corinth. For he explained, "Also is the resurrection of the dead...It is raised in incorruption...it is sown in dishonour; it is raised in glory...it is raised in power...it is raised a spiritual body" (1 Cor. 15:42–44). The following scriptures will provide further assistance: John 5:28–29, 11:25–26, 12:25–26, 14:2–3, 1 Thes. 4:13–18, and Heb. 9:27. There is a plethora of other scriptures—all of which cannot be delineated within this section—that provides further insight into the enigma of habeas corpus after death.

Suggested Readings:

(1) Ayra, Virender Kumar. 2003. *The Book of The Vedas: Timeless Wisdom From Indian Tradition.* B. E. S. Publishing. Hauppauge, NY.

(2) Chatterji, Jagadish. 1992. *The Wisdom of the Vedas (Revised edition).* Quest books, IL.

(3) Prabhupada, Bhaktivedanta Swami (A.C). 1968, 1972. *Bhagavad- Gita, as It Is.* Bhaktivedanta Book Trust, 3764 Watseka Avenue, Los Angeles, California, 90034.

(4) Sharma, Ram Sharan. 1999. *Advent of the Aryans in India.*
Manohar Publishers.

(5) Trautmann, Thomas R. 2004. *Aryans and British India.* Yoda Press. New Delhi, India.

Section Six

Islam

Founding/Brief History

The founding of Islam (Islam means "total submission") was precipitated by the polytheistic ethos of pre-Islamic Arabia that disturbed Muhammad ibn Abdullah in the year 610 CE. Legend has it that in that same year Muhammad, now nearly forty-five years old, sought respite on Mt. Hira near Mecca, Saudi Arabia, when suddenly the angel Gabriel miraculously appeared unto him. Esposito (1988) explained that it was actually a cave on Mt. Hira into which Muhammad sought solace. The angel is alleged to have announced that Muhammad was God's messenger and prophet. This episode is believed to have been Muhammad's first revelation from God. Following this, even though Muhammad continued to frequent the mountain, it would be another two years before he would receive another revelation. However, in the interim Muhammad is rumored to have become distraught, capitulated to confusion, and once again felt as though he'd been abandoned (for he was twice an orphan). Legend has it, however, that God's voice would once again reverberate; we're told that it would reassure Muhammad that he wasn't forgotten. Oral history puts it that God would speak to Muhammad in a way that Muslims have termed "The Sura of the Morning." The Sura of the Morning is said to have been a synopsis encapsulated in seven short verses of how God had not only enriched Muhammad's life, but how he would continue to do so. Many believe Muhammad was instructed to recite what would essentially become the ninety-sixth chapter of the Quran, a narrative of how God had created man out of a small clot of blood, how God is gracious to man and teaches him, how man was created and developed, and how man, despite all of God's goodness, continues to rebel against him. It ends by commanding Islam, or total submission to God, exemplified by prostration before God. This recitation is said to have been the infancy of the Quran. Some, moreover, purport that the verses of the Quran were revealed to Muhammad by God periodically over a period of around twenty-two to twenty-three years from 610 CE until his death on June 8, 632 CE.

Muhammad's father died prior to the founder's birth; his mother died when Muhammad was six or seven years of age. He sought comfort and guidance. Oral tradition purports to explain that, ironically, it was an Arab Christian, a relative of Muhammad's first wife, Khadija bint Khuwaylid, to whom Muhammad would turn to for consolation and reassurance (although it wasn't unusual during that epoch for Jews, Christians, Zoroastrians, Muslims, and those that practiced Judaism to live in harmony). Waraqa ibn Qusayy, it is alleged, counseled Muhammad, and insisted that it was God that was speaking to Muhammad and that Muhammad was indeed a prophet. His warning to the former orphan, however, was that he, not unlike the Hebrew seers of old, would be rejected, scorned, and impugned.

Most Islamic scholars date the founding of Islam to be factually in 622 CE, for it wasn't until Muhammad left Mecca in 622 CE and arrived in Medina about 320 kilometers to the north that the Islamic faith would come to fruition. Moreover, it was there in Medina that

Muhammad would establish his first caliphate, or community. This community did, in fact, include those religions mentioned previously in this section; i.e., Jews, Muslims, Christians, Zoroastrians, etc. This unlikely confederacy would soon be dismantled, however. Nonetheless, before his death in 632, the founder lived to see the entire Arabian Peninsula subjugated by Islamic (Sharia) authority.

Basic Beliefs and Rituals

Fundamental to the Islamic faith is the belief that Allah is the one and only God, and even though there have been many prophets (i.e., Jesus, Moses, etc.), Muhammad is and forever will be God's only messenger.

All Muslims are called to prayer five times each day by the muezzin who stands in the minaret of a mosque.

The "Five Pillars," or acts that all Muslims are obliged to perform, are also among the fundamental and identifying facets of Islam. They will, of course, be addressed under the section of soteriological views.

Parallels to Orthodox Christianity

(1) Unlike the tribal society of pre-Islamic Arabia that championed a polytheistic ethos, Muhammad promulgated a monotheistic culture (like Christianity).

(2) Also, not unlike Christianity, Muhammad was adamantly opposed to usury, the breach of contracts, and the manipulation of contracts between parties, especially when one party of the contract was far less affluent than the other.

(3) Muhammad was particularly concerned about the care of the poor, the parentless (for he, himself was twice orphaned), the widows, the aged, and those occupying the lower rung of society.

(4) Islam also promotes the concepts of a day of judgement and the resurrection of the body. These convictions, however, are not without much dissonance, for they do not completely resonate with the Judeo-Christian leanings. The basic dichotomy between the Christians' concept of the resurrection and the premise of the same promulgated by Islam is that Christians believe that the resurrected bodies at the coming of Christ will be changed (1 Cor. 15:51–52). The adherents (Christians) also maintain the premise that being allowed to take part in the resurrection will be predicated upon one having died while maintaining a belief in Christ (1 Thess. 4:16). But this thesis is foreign, peppered with polemics, and vehemently rejected in Islam. Moreover, in Islam the changed body and dying in Christ (in hopes that he will be one's propitiation) are proverbial foreign currencies that can only lead to the devaluation of their own. However, the venerable Apostle Paul during his appeal to the bellicose Claudius Felix mentions in Acts 24:15 that "there shall be a resurrection…both of the just and unjust." The Apostle John was also quite resolute concerning man's propitiation (through Jesus Christ), for he insisted, "He is the propitiation for our sins…for the sins of the whole world" (1 John 2:2). Muslims have conjectured along those lines, however, that during a similar resurrection all eternal fates will be determined.

(5) Islam also advances the concepts of heaven, hell, and the afterlife.

(6) Traditionally, the Shia sect of Islam, which

comprises approximately 15 percent of the world's Muslim population, subscribes to the Mu'tazilaian concept of a free will or man's right to choose good or evil. Christianity is also an exponent of this view.

(7) Despite polemics to the contrary, Islam, as espoused by Muhammad, did not (like Christianity) condone killings and military aggression outside of the war zone, nor did Muhammad insist that Christians, Jews, Zoroastrians, or others convert to Islam. Moreover, these (killings, forced conversions, and aggressions) are post-Muhammadian persuasions. Armstrong (2000) argued that Muhammad insisted that Muslims should respect the religious rights of others.

(8) Not unlike Christianity, classical Islam (under Muhammad's leadership and according to the Quran) promotes the empowerment and enfranchisement of women, for not all women during the reign of Muhammad were required to be veiled, nor were they relegated to a separate section of the household. Paradoxically, these practices were adopted by Muslims from the Byzantium (present-day Istanbul) Christians two to four generations after the demise of Muhammad.

(9) Like the Bible, the Quran reveals the following:

(1) The book of Genesis is not inaccurate in its description of the creation of mankind.

(2) A distinction can be clearly made between God's creation and God the creator.

(3) Satan was forced to plummet from heaven, and his objective is to deceive mankind and sever any ties that mankind may have with God.

Contrasts to Orthodox Christianity

In Islam, the Christian concept of the separation of religion from the state is inconceivable, for the religion of Islam and the caliphate/community are inextricable, symbiotic, and must necessarily harmonize. Islam, adherents insist, should always be guided by the caliph and his interpretation of Sharia law or the Sunna and Hadith of the prophet. In situations where Sharia law is vague, reliance is made upon the Sunna and Hadith of the prophet, i.e., how Muhammad would've most likely decided the outcome of similar cases. Moreover, Islamic law, the Sharia, represents a theocracy throughout the United Arab Emirates (UAE), as well as most other predominately Arab/Muslim nations. Philosophically, therefore, Sharia law and the social milieu of the orthodox Muslim are one and the same. Furthermore, Sharia law is supplemented by what is known as the Grievance Courts. The Grievance Courts oversee the prosecution of nefarious and criminal aspects; the ancillary Sharia courts are responsible for hearing domestic and family disputes. The Grievance Courts and the Sharia courts, however, exist under the auspices and at the pleasure of the caliph, hence recognizing the legitimacy and enhancing the credibility of the theocracy, Islam.

Also, unlike Christianity, Islam has what is known as a muhtasib, a position or duty similar to that of a constable designed to enforce day-to-day Islamic observances, i.e., the absence of alcohol consumption, the prohibition of gambling, the calls to prayer, the abstinence from certain foods, etc.

According to the principles of Islam, all sins are forgivable except polytheism (even if one has abandoned the practice). In Christianity, however, although denominations argue and debate over the narrative of Matt. 12:31 ("All manner of sin...shall be forgiven unto men: but the blasphemy against the Holy Ghost shall not be forgiven"), most orthodox denominations conclude that all of man's sins are forgivable by faith in the atonement and resurrection of Jesus Christ (See 2 Pet. 3:9, Rom. 8:35–39, John 19:28–30).

Traditionally, the Sunni sect of Islam, which as of this date comprises about 85 percent of the world's Muslim population, subscribes to the Al-Ash'ariaian theology of predestination. Many Bible students will recall that John Calvin (given name Jehan Cauvin) promulgated a similar unorthodox concept. For further information concerning Calvin's theology, some of which is quite untenable, acquire a copy of *Concerning the Eternal Predestination of God* by Calvin (1997). Some of the works of St. Augustine and John Wycliffe—although heavy reading and requiring much diligence to make it through them—will leave one with a great appreciation of the topic. Predestination (of the Calvinist persuasion), of course, is not a tenet of Christian orthodoxy (See Rom. 5:1–2, 10:8–13, Eph. 2:8–9). Therefore—that is to say, based upon the plethora of antithetical scriptures—Calvin, borrowing primarily from Eph. 1:4–5, and Rom. 8:28–30, capriciously inferred in error, for the scriptures upon which he predicated his thesis are not in reference to any particular "individuals," but rather they are pertaining to all of subsequent ages or epochs who would accept Christ and live through him by faith. Notice the prose in Eph. 1:5: "Having predestinated us unto the adoption of children by Jesus Christ." When Eph. 1:5 is placed alongside Gal. 4:4–5 and 1 Cor. 2:7, the portrait continues to be painted: "When the fullness of time was come, God sent forth his son...to redeem them that were under the law, that we might receive the adoption of sons" (Gal. 4:4–5). 1 Corinthians 2:7 (NASB) completes the picture with "we speak God's wisdom in a mystery, the hidden wisdom which God predestined before the ages to our glory." Colloquially, those scriptures are saying that at a certain time only known by God, God would "hand mankind over to Jesus Christ, to be adopted by him." This would relieve man of the "non-accomplishable" requirements of the law (see also Rom. 8:15, 9:26, Gal. 3:26).

Islam, because of its concept of salvation (see Soteriological Views), does not promote the premise of the Trinity. Also, unlike Christianity, polygamy is traditionally a fundamental aspect of the Islamic ethos, for it is permitted by the Quran for a man to have four wives simultaneously if his financial status is such that he is able to provide for all equitably. Muhammad is reported to have had a family consisting of as many as twenty wives. He is also alleged to have married a six-year-old (Nichols et al. 2006). However, as Muslims venture into Western theaters (i.e., the U.K., Canada, the U.S., etc.) and begin to assimilate, such practices are invariably abandoned.

Unlike Christianity, Islam doesn't seem to put a very high premium on egalitarianism in marriage even while it maintains, as Christianity does, that marriage is the proverbial atrium of a wholesome society. Traditionally, the husband is at liberty to divorce his wife or wives "at will." All that is required to terminate the marriage is to summarily state to the wife "I divorce you" three times in succession.

Esposito (1998) implied that the unfair treatment

of women as espoused by the ethos of Islam can be further exemplified by the requirement of women to gain the permission of their husbands in order to simply venture outside the home. Further research reveals that failure to obtain such permission could result in the wife's home confinement. This internment could last as long as the husband desires or until the spouse has learned obedience.

Islam also promotes a form of idolatry, for during their pilgrimage (Hajj) to Mecca, the faithful can be seen briefly kissing the black stone that is lodged in the wall of the Kabah.

Animal sacrifices are also performed in Mecca during the annual pilgrimage. In Christianity, of course, Christians maintain that animal sacrifices and other obligations adhered to under the old covenant were "done away with" by the sacrifice of the body of Christ once and for all (see 2 Cor. 3: 7, Heb. 10:1–10, Gal. 3: 19).

The following section (Blasphemous verses) will codify some of the more poignant dichotomies between Islam and orthodox Christianity.

Blasphemous Verses

The Quran's Blasphemous Verses and the Bible's Antithesis

(1) The Quran: Ch. 4, verses 171–172 vs. the Bible: John 1:1–2, Mat. 3:16–17, Mat. 16: 13–17, 1 John 5:7, Luke 24:39, 42–44.

One will find in those verses (171–172), of the Quran, that Jesus's deity is disputed, for he is made out to be no more than a spirit messenger created by God. The Trinity is vehemently repudiated. The people of the Book

(Christians and Jews) are warned not to elevate Christ as deity. The gospels, however, help Christ's case (that he is in fact God) by presenting us with exculpatory evidence. For the Apostle John articulated, "the word was God" (John 1:1). As for the Trinity, Matt. 3:16 shows us the triumvirate Godhead. Other scriptures, listed above, are also quite telling. They will help to reveal the actual truth concerning Jesus's deity and person.

(2) The Quran: Ch. 5, verse 75 vs. the Bible: John 1:1–2.

In this verse of the Quran, we observe much of the blasphemy (Section 1, above) that was spewed in Ch. 4, vs. 171–172, the continuance of the impugning of Christ's deity. However, the first few verses of St. John denude or lay bare the charges and indictments brought against Christ.

(3) The Quran: Ch. 19, verse 30 vs. the Bible: John 10:30, 14:9, Acts 2:36.

In this passage the Quran alleges that Jesus proclaimed that he was merely a servant of God and a prophet. That's quite contradictory to Jesus's pontification in John 10:30; "I and my father are one," Jesus proclaimed. Acts 2:36 corroborates Jesus assertion, for Peter enunciated during his first sermon "God hath made that same Jesus, whom ye have crucified, both lord and Christ."

(4) The Quran: Ch. 3, verse 59 vs. the Bible: Heb. 7:1–3, 17, John 8:58, Rev. 22:13, 1 Cor. 8:6, 1 John 5:20.

This verse, (59) located in the Muslims' holy book, falsely accuses Jesus of being created by God from the dust, as was Adam. Chapter seven of the book of Hebrews, however, (in its comparison of Christ to Melchizedek) exonerates Christ. So too does John 8:58, 1

Cor. 8:6, and other scriptures listed above.

(5) The Quran: Ch. 5, verses 116–120 vs. the Bible: John 10:30, 14:7–9, Acts 2:36.

This narrative, found in the Quran, has the tone, and reads much like that of chapter 19, verse 30 (referenced in section 3 above). It purports that Jesus rejected any claims of deity. John 10, 14, and Acts 2, of course, refute those egregious accusations.

(6) The Quran: Ch. 4, verses 157–58 vs. the Bible: 1 Cor. 2:1–2, Gal. 3:1, John 19:16, 18, 30, Matt. 27:22, 1 Cor. 15: 3–8.

These verses in the Quran, proclaim that Jesus was not crucified; rather, God disguised another and (as is commonly held among Muslims) allowed him to be crucified in lieu of Jesus. During the episode of the crucifixion, God is said to have taken Christ back to heaven amid the confusion and chaos in Jerusalem. When we read 1 Cor. 2:1, however, we learn that the Apostle Paul is confident that Christ was, in fact, crucified. Gal. 3:1, John 19:16, 18, 30, and a plethora of other scriptures reveal the same.

(7) The Quran: Ch. 3, verse 84 vs. the Bible: Heb. 1:9, 13, 3:3, 7:1–7.

The Quran espouses the belief that there shouldn't be any distinction made between Moses, Jesus, and any of the prophets. The book of Hebrews, nonetheless (chapters 1, 3, and 7, in particular), illuminates the fallacies of such a notion. (Khattab 2016, Scofield, 2015).

Soteriological Views

In Islam, contrary to the Christian concept, salvation does not connote redemption; rather salvation is codified in the Five Pillars, which will be explained elsewhere in this narrative. There is no intercessor or propitiator to appease God on behalf of man's sin; moreover, among Muslim liturgy the names Jehovah, El Shaddai, or Yahweh are not common and are therefore not recognized in the broader scheme of Muslims' daily activities. As it applies to God (i.e., Jesus, Jehovah, Yahweh, etc.) only the name Allah is recognized, hence, an atonement or propitiation is unnecessary. Furthermore, there is no spirit that leads man from sin into righteousness and alerts him when he has strayed. Rather, man, although accountable to Allah, must determine his/her own actions (that is to say, will he/she adhere to the Five Pillars, choosing good, or will he/she reject them, subsequently choosing evil?) for it is alleged that he will be held accountable for all inappropriate actions, actions that are recorded along with the favorable ones in the Book of Deeds.

The Islamic conceptualization of salvation involves availing one's self of and becoming a part of the creation of a society that is just and wholesome. The following, the adherents insist, are the Five Pillars, which are fundamental to Islam's soteriological beliefs:

(1) The Shahadah
Reciting the Muslim profession of faith. The profession is recited with the mantra, "Allah is the one and only God, and Muhammad is his messenger."

(2) The Salat
Praying (preceded by ceremonial washing of the feet, mouth, and hands) five times each day, at daybreak, noon, midafternoon, at sunset, and during the evening. The worshippers (in a prostrate position if possible), facing

Mecca, recite the mantra, "Allah Akbar (God is great)! Muhammad is Allah's messenger! Prosperity is in Allah!

(3) Zakat

Contributing a portion of one's income/assets to assist the poor, orphans, and others. Muslims maintain that the Zakat will also facilitate the promulgation (and assimilation when in non-Islamic theaters) of Islamic practices and dogma.

(4) Sawn

This fast during the ninth month of the Islamic calendar, or Ramadan, from sunrise to sunset commemorates God's favor bestowed upon his people as well as what most Muslims refer to as the Night of Power, wherein Muhammad is alleged to have received the first of his instructions (the Quran) from God.

(5) Hajj

After Ramadan, provisions are made for the obligatory—at least once in a lifetime—pilgrimage to Mecca, Islam's most revered site. Ablutions or cleansing are required prior to the journey. After the cleansing, men are arrayed with white attire; the women usually don white dresses. When just outside the city of Mecca, members of the group will begin to announce their arrival with the mantra, "I am here, Allah! Allah, I have arrived!" Upon entering Mecca they proceed to the Kabah, the center of focus, which is circumambulated seven times (following the revolution of the sun around the Earth and planets). The Kabah is particularly significant among Muslims, rivaling the tomb of Muhammad, for many believe that in pre-Islamic, polytheistic Arabia, the idols of false gods were housed there. Muhammad is alleged to have toppled those idols during his raid on Mecca and dedicated the Kabah to a god that he determined to be Allah. Prior to the end of the pilgrimage at Mecca, several animal sacrifices are made in honor of Abraham's faithfulness to God.

Eschatological Perspective

Appealing to the nexus between primordial man and his unregenerated, salacious character, Islam purports that men, during the afterlife, in what is termed The Garden of Paradise, will be surrounded by not only their spouses (plural) but also with many young females that they, perhaps, never even knew while on Earth. Islam's tenor, as promulgated by its two most revered texts (the Quran and Hadith), is as though heaven will mirror the patriarchal milieu that exists within Muslim, Christian, and other religious societies today. Such conjecture is highly unlikely, if one is to believe biblical scripture (see Gal. 3:28, Philip. 3:21, 1 Cor. 15:51–52).

Islam teaches from the Hadith (Islam's second most revered text) that there will be a resurrection of the righteous and the unrighteous; this will be followed by a period of tribulation, during which time the antichrist (Masih ad-Dajjal) will deceive. It is also espoused that during the tribulation period, the Earth will, of course, be plagued with chaos; Jesus (Isa) will finally appear to quell the confusion caused by the antichrist and allow for a period of peace. There will be an Armageddon (*fitna*, Al-Malhama Al-Kubra), followed by the annihilation of all life forms. Finally, as purported by the Hadith, there will be a day of reckoning/judgement, during which time the righteous will be allowed to enter paradise (Jannah); all others—apostates and infidels—must be relegated to the consuming fire of hell (Jahannam).

Concerns and Implications for the Orthodox Christian

Islam purports to explain that man is not in need of redemption, an intercessor, or an atonement. The orthodox Christian, however, is well aware that, when left to rely upon his own devices, man—even though he will reject some sins based upon philosophical or moral reasons—will invariably choose sin over righteousness. Moreover, contrary to the soteriological dogma espoused by Islam, man (lacking the born again experience) simply does not have the credentials necessary to guide him spiritually. Hence, he/she is much out of place if attempting to preach or teach the gospel (without the born again experience). Such a person is profoundly and very noticeably "ill-equipped," their academic achievements, accolades, or theological prowess notwithstanding. One of the most telling biblical exemplifications of this can be found in Acts 18:24–28: "A…Jew named Apollos…mighty in the scriptures, came to Ephesus…he spake and taught…the things of the Lord, knowing only the baptism of John…when Aquila and Priscilla had heard, they took him unto them, and expounded unto him the way of God more perfectly…he…helped them much…he mightily convinced the Jews…that Jesus was Christ." Luke's narrative in Acts 1:8 is also quite enlightening.

Orthodox Muslims argue that it was Abraham's son Ishmael (not Isaac) who God commanded to be sacrificed by the patriarch; however, this concept is one of many designs to impiously excoriate Judeo-Christianity. The idea, promulgated by Islamic clerics, that the offering up of Isaac was not the predicate and consummation of Abraham's faith would, of course, decimate Christianity as we know it. For if it could be proven that Ishmael was the intended sacrifice, then Christianity would have to be discarded. Why so? Ishmael's (the son of the bondwoman, Gen. 21:10–12, Gal. 4:22–31) lineage could not show the deity nor lead to the coming of Christ; to supplant Isaac with Ishmael would essentially render Christianity a misnomer. After examining the forty-two generations and each and every progenitor leading to Christ, I've painstakingly sought to determine if Ishmael could be positioned within the direct lineage of Christ. However, I found no avenue by which it could be accomplished. Ishmael simply cannot be accommodated within the confluence.

Moreover, to accept Islam's premise that Abraham offered up the wrong son would be to refute the fact that the patriarch was, in fact, the harbinger of Jesus Christ. Contrary to the polemics leveled against the feats of Abraham, his consummation of faith (the offering up of Isaac) would reach across the ages and profoundly affect the salvation of man. For it (that is to say, Abraham's offering up of his son Isaac) is the nexus between the old covenant, which was based upon works, and the new, which is according to faith. The fact that Abraham believed God allows mankind to approach God (via the Abrahamic Covenant and the subsequent atonement of Jesus) and obtain salvation through faith, *sola fide*, or through faith alone. The following scriptures will provide further illumination of the premise: Gen. 22:2–12, Rom. 4:1–9, 13, 16, Gal. 3:9, Jam. 2:23.

The religion of Islam is absolutely replete with monumental discrepancies, and there are serious questions which Muslims must ask themselves, the most fundamental and urgent of which is this: are they willing to entrust their eternal destiny to the dictates of a man who—according to reputable sources, including Hazleton (2013)—grappled with suicidal ideations? For Muhammad thought to cast himself down upon the jagged protrusions of Mt. Hira after allegedly hearing from God prior to hurrying home to bury his sorrow in Khadijah's lap. Twelve years his senior, she would console him until he, sobbingly, drifted soundly asleep.

Other questions that the serious practicing Muslims (and clerics) must consider are these: what, if anything, did Muhammad experience on Mt. Hira that evening in 610? Did the Qurayhian discover some types of hallucinogens along the Silk Road that could have just possibly altered his mental status? Could those months-long camel drives from Mecca north to Damascus or south to Yemen and other lands far afield, encumbered by dry, parched desert and treacherous steeps, have caused the premature atrophy of portions of his cranial network? Did the twice-orphaned Hashemite, born without an inheritance, fall prey to depression that may have caused sound reasoning to betray him? As a child, he occupied the lowest of the lowest of class statuses. All of the questions listed above, including if it is possible that Muhammad heard only human voices from distant lands while upon Mt. Hira in 610, are questions that Muslims, surely, at one time or another, have asked themselves.

Nonetheless, a rush to judgement here, one way or the other, must not be made; instead, rational thoughts must be allowed to prevail. It must be at least entertained, however, that perhaps any voices that the founder perceived on Mt. Hira were only imagined. The voices could've arisen from indiscriminate echoes resounding from contiguous camps or from the echoes of unseen camel drives. For the majestic sands of Saudi Arabia are quite vast and reverberate. During the epoch of pre-Islamic Saudi Arabia, it was not uncommon for shouts or sounds to echo for miles during the still of the twilight. The alleged experiences simply cannot be corroborated. There have been many who have argued a case for their inexplicable encounters with the unknown or the metaphysical; however, all but those who have espoused Christianity are yet to be substantiated. For example, one might argue colloquially that just as Muslims cannot be sure whether Muhammad actually heard God's voice on Mt. Hira, how can the Christians be sure that, let's say, John the Baptist actually heard God's voice in the wilderness of Judaea, the voice that Christians allege led John to Jesus? The relationship and ministry between Jesus and John the Baptist have been validated and were predicted long before the birth of the cousins (Luke 1:13, 30–36). See also; Mal. 3:1, Isa. 40:3, Matt. 11:13 (The Living Bible), and Jn. 1:33.

Furthermore, and this is one of the most unsettling issues as it relates to Islam, if Muhammad could mistakenly recite utterances from Satan, then it would not be unreasonable to assume that some, if not all, of his revelations, were simply imaginations or illusions. For it is well documented that in his rush to reconcile differences between himself and the elite of pre-Islamic Mecca, he recited that Lat, Uzza, and Manat (tribal totems and allegedly the three daughters of al-Lah, the head deity of pre-Islamic Mecca) were somehow made to become three enormous winged creatures that could also (like Muhammad is alleged to have done) intercede for the people.

Although Rushdie (1988) concluded that his novel, *Satanic Verses*, was a work of fiction, many in the Islamic world took offence and conceived that the volume was an indictment of Muhammad himself. Subsequently, the Rushdie Affair spawned, a *fatwa* or license to kill Salman Rushdie because of his controversial narratives. To this day the *fatwa*, issued by the theocratic Ayatollah R. Khomeini in 1989, has not been officially rescinded. In conclusion, it is important to avoid equating Islam to the radical quasi sects, sects such as ISIS (Islamic State of Iraq and Syria), al-Qaeda, Hamas, Hizballah (Hezbollah), etc. It's quite a misnomer to refer to them as "radical Islamists" for they're not Muhammadian (true Muslims)! These groups seek to polarize, hijack, and rebrand Muhammad's religion, the religion of peace. Going to war to protect the sovereignty of one's homeland is more than reasonable; however, beheadings, rapes, and placing opposition members in cages (even during war) and drowning them in the ocean simply does not comport with the values of Islam. Those are radical, unconscionable paradigm shifts; those tactics would have never been among Muhammad's modus operandi! Muhammad would be ashamed! He would adamantly disavow such atrocities! While there are many true Muhammadians across the globe, including areas where Islam is the theocracy, it would be a difficult task to find greater representatives of Muhammad's modus operandi than the majority of those Muslims of Dearborn, MI, New York, NY, Liverpool, and Manchester England (two UK. cities which often compete with Leeds for recognition as

England's third largest city), or those currently suppressed by China's—under the iron fisted Xi Jinping—regime. Islam, not unlike Christianity and many other theologies, is really a religion of peace; however, after the 9/11 incident (Sept. 11, 2001), most Westerners, particularly in the United States, closed their minds to such a possibility. Therefore, they began to proverbially paint the entire portrait of Islam with a very broad brush and view Muslims and Arabs with unwarranted suspicion, not considering the fact that some Arabs are Christians. The disfigured portrait that has been painted of Islam is not marketable to those who, although rejecting Islam, have studied the religion. They are able to differentiate between the Muhammadian motif and that of mere imposters or those who "masquerade" as Muslims. As one cannot truly understand Christianity without becoming cognizant of the life and deity of Christ, so, too, is it with Islam. One cannot begin to appreciate Islam without becoming somewhat aware of the life and history of Muhammad. Following this narrative under Suggested Readings, the reader will find eight impeccable sources that will provide more insight into the life and intentions of Muhammad.

Dr. A.J. Handy, Ph.D.

Suggested Readings:

(1) Ali, Kecia. 2104. *The Lives of Muhammad.* Harvard University Press. Cambridge Massachusetts, London, England.

(2) Alkhateeb, Firas. 2017. *Lost Islamic History, Reclaiming Muslim Civilization from the Past.* Hurst & Company Ltd. 41 Great Russell Street, London, WC1B3PL.

(3) Esposito, John L. 1999. *The Oxford History of Islam.* Oxford University Press. 198 Madison Avenue, New York, New York. 10016.

(4) Fakhry, Majid. 1970, 1983, 2014. *A History of Islamic Philosophy* (Third edition). Columbia University Press, New York.

(5) Haykal, Muhammad Husein. 2008. *The Life of Muhammad.* Islamic Book Trust, 607 Mutiara Majestic Jalan Othman, 46000 Petaling Jaya, Selangor, Malaysia.

(6) Levtzion, Nehemia, and Pouwels, Randall. 2000. *The History of Islam in Africa.* Ohio University Press. Athens, Ohio.

(7) Ramadan, Tariq. 2007. *In the Footsteps of the Prophet, Lessons from the Life of Muhammad.* Oxford University Press, 198 Madison Avenue, New York, NY. 10016.

(8) Syed, Muzaffar Husain; Akhtar, Syed Saud; Usmani, Babuddin. 2011. *A Concise History of Islam.* Vij Books India Pvt. Ltd. Ansari Road, Darya Ganj, New Delhi, India.

Section Seven

Jehovah's Witnesses/Watchtower Bible and Tract Society

(Joseph F. Rutherford, 1869–1942)
(Charles T. Russell, 1852–1916)

Founding/Brief History

Floundering at the fringes and attempting to weave its way into a more salient position within the fabric of Christianity is the cult Jehovah's Witnesses. After dabbling in Presbyterianism, congregationalism, and skepticism or doubting the veracity of the religions of his day, Charles T. Russell set his sights on Adventism/millennialism, the belief that the second coming of Christ is imminent or on the horizon. Russell promulgated that Christ's second coming would happen in the year 1914 (Hall, 2003). Jesus, of course, did not accommodate his wishes. Mr. Russell also founded the Watch Tower Bible and Tract Society in 1884. His was not, however, a millennial concept founded in a vacuum, for pioneers such as Ellen White and William Miller had earlier hatched similar perceptions. Russell was very impious, not only toward the idea of the Trinity, but also toward the orthodox belief that Jesus Christ is divine or actually God. He insisted, as do the adherents to the Watch Tower Bible and Tract Society of today (JW's), that Jesus was "created" by God and therefore not a deity.

    After Charles T. Russell's death in 1916, Joseph F. Rutherford assumed de facto leadership of the Watch Tower Bible and Tract Society until the following year in which de jure authority was awarded him. For the next several years until his death in 1942, Rutherford would continue advancing Russell's vision for the Watch Tower Bible and Tract Society. This was accomplished by embarking upon an unprecedented religious literature marketing campaign. The most prolific of which was perhaps the publication and distribution of the Golden Age/Awake pamphlets.

To portray himself as a prophet and to elevate himself above his predecessor—Russell, who erroneously prophesied that Christ would return to Earth in 1914—Rutherford, known to many as Judge Rutherford, in his work titled *Millions Now Living Will Never Die*, predicted that Christ would descend in 1925, and the world as it was known would be no more. These unfulfilled promises caused a rift and disillusion among the ranks. Many began to reexamine the trajectory of Russell's and Rutherford's doctrine. Thousands abandoned the founders' opiates. To assuage disturbances and rekindle illusions, Rutherford colored the society by renaming it Jehovah's Witnesses in 1931. Although prima facie Rutherford's and Russell's theology appears distinguishable, upon further reflection, however, it becomes obvious that they are one and the same.

Basic Beliefs and Rituals

The Jehovah's Witnesses (JW's) reference Isaiah 43:10 as the fundamental basis of their theology; it's fairly clear, however, from a contextual approach, that within that narrative, God is appealing to the houses of Israel and Jacob for reconciliation. He pleads with them to reminisce and reflect back over the feats witnessed by them and their progenitors that he'd accomplished for them. Further along in that chapter (43) from verse 22 onward, God shows his *agape* or unmerited love, for even though his people have all but forgotten him, he insists that he will not remember their sins. The JW's cult also promulgates their belief that the war of Armageddon will happen before the death of the last of those they've determined to be of the anointed class.

To further exude their influence and indict Christianity, the Watchtower Bible and Tract Society/Jehovah's Witnesses assert and continue to maintain that their own New World Translation (NWT) Bible should be considered the only infallible and inerrant word of God. The NWT was fabricated by the Society over a period of eleven years (from about 1950 to 1961) under the reign of Nathan Knorr. The Witnesses also purport that salvation will only be granted to two groups of people: (1) The anointed class of 144,000 (who were persuaded to join the fold prior to 1935) that they allege is referenced in Rev. 14:3–4, and (2) the earthly class, or Little Flock; these are said to be those who have modeled their lives according to the suffering of Jesus Christ so that they may mimic him.

If the JW's are to maintain that salvation is only forthcoming to those of the two previously mentioned groups (the earthly class and anointed class), they must determine what to do with the Apostle Paul's narrative in 2 Tim. 4:8. The Witnesses' theory simply doesn't comport—nor can it be amalgamated—with Paul's prose. There is absolutely no resonance; indeed, the dissonance couldn't be any more demonstrative. For the "aged" apostle (he would've been between sixty-two and sixty-six years of age when addressing his last letter to

Timothy) unequivocally, resolutely, and emphatically explains that salvation is for all those who await and long for Christ's appearing. The JW's will also have to reckon with or determine how to explain away 2 Pet. 3:9. In the apostle's prison letter, he categorically maintains his resolve that Christ is "not willing that any should perish." Nichols et al. (2006) revealed that in 1961, at a global communion service, there were 13,284 of the 144,000 anointed class who were served the Eucharist. As of Nichols et al. (2006) authorship, there were only about ten thousand of the anointed class still alive. The math is elementary. Hence, it appears that according to the Witnesses' calculations, because the youngest of the remaining ten thousand are now (as of the date of this penning) somewhere around eighty-four or eighty-five years old, the world should prepare for the battle of Armageddon to be unveiled in, let's say, fifteen or so years from now. It's absolutely unconscionable that only very little was learned or doubted from Russell's unfavorable court litigations and from prior failed prophecies (of both Russell and Rutherford) of Christ's "imminent" return. Rather, millions continue to, proverbially, swallow Russell's opiates; hence, in their constant stupor and sedation they remain oblivious to an urgent need for a meaningful paradigm shift.

Parallels to Orthodox Christianity

This cult, not unlike Christian orthodoxy, espouses the belief that the Bible is the final authority for all of life's circumstances; the JW's insist, however, as explained elsewhere in this corpus, that their own translation (NWT) is the only true source of biblical doctrine.

They believe that Jesus was born of the Virgin Mary; however, the caveat is that he was only a "spirit" or a personification. Hence, they reject Christ's hypostatic union or Christ as God and man.

The Witnesses also, in agreement with orthodoxy, believe in the resurrection of Christ. Again, however, there is a caveat, for they maintain that Christ's was not a physical but merely spiritual body.

The cult aligns itself with the requirement of water baptism and the concept of heaven and the Devil. They do not subscribe to the concept of an eternal hell, though. Instead, their belief is that, along with the disobedient, Satan will be annihilated. Christian orthodoxy has it, however, that Satan will undergo an everlasting torment (see Rev. 20:10). As concerning the disobedient, the following scriptures are worthy of note: Ps. 9:17, Ezek. 31:16–17, Matt. 10:28, Acts 2:27, 2 Pet. 2:4, Rev. 1:18, 20:13–15.

Along with orthodox Protestant Christians, the Jehovah's Witnesses maintain that, during the Eucharist, the bread and wine only symbolize the blood and body of Jesus. Both groups (that is to say, JW's and the adherents to orthodox Christianity) have rejected the papacy's position of transubstantiation or the premise that the bread is the actual body and the wine is the genuine blood of Christ.

The Witnesses also maintain, as do orthodox Christians, that meats with traces of blood remaining, should not be consumed by humans (see Lev. 17:10–14, 1 Sam. 14:32–35).

Dispensationalism is also promulgated by the Jehovah's Witnesses. It is commonly accepted among Christians that dispensationalism (the gradual sequences leading to Christ's return to Earth) is codified by the following areas of progression: innocence, conscience, human governments, promise, law, grace, the kingdom/millennium.

Contrasts to Orthodox Christianity And The Gospel According to Charles T. Russell

Like several other Unitarian groups, the Jehovah's Witnesses (the cult spawned by the gospel according to Russell) do not subscribe to the concept of a triune Godhead. This hetcrodoxy is exemplified by the fact that the sect promulgates that Jesus Christ is not divine and that he was only a created being. The Jehovah's Witnesses do not stop there. They, of course, hand down a similar indictment against the person of the Holy Ghost, supposing that he was only a source of kinetic energy that God enlisted from time to time to accomplish his purposes. To lend credence to this theory while subsequently notarizing the theology according to Russell, they've inserted the phrase "God's active force" (The New World Translation) in order to supplant the phrase "the Spirit of God" in Gen. 1:2. They are extremely impious, although their impiousness in no way dwarfs their ingenuity. For to initially impugn the Holy Spirit in the very first one or two verses of the Bible will lead the unsuspecting to accept the fallacious etymology throughout the entire corpus of scripture. That's remarkably clever. Proper etymology speaks volumes and is not to be taken lightly, for without it, one cannot begin to properly comprehend or realize the correct epistemological construct of the scriptures. Even a word or phrase taken out of context or supplanted here and there (in the text) is enough to perniciously lead one to unwittingly adopt an erroneous belief.

At this juncture, it will be necessary to explain (by contrasting the NWT and the King James version) how Gen. 1:2 should be interpreted. For that narrative is only one of many examples of how, through inaccurate definition of terms (espoused by the JW's), the unsuspecting could quite possibly be lead astray. Gen. 1:2 reads, "And darkness was upon the face of the deep. And the Spirit of God moved upon the face of the waters." Now, the phrase "Spirit of God" used here in the King James has the connotation of the Spirit being connected to or with God; the same is not so in the New World Translation. Here is what the Jehovah's Witnesses wish you to believe: "There was darkness upon the surface of [the] watery deep; and God's active force was moving to and fro over the surface of the waters" (NWT). The phrase "God's active force," as used here, implies the energy of wind or geophysical activity. However, let it be known and emphatically proclaimed that the Spirit of God has emotions; he has a personality; he speaks, he can be saddened; he teaches; he guides, etc. Consider the following:

(1) "The Holy Ghost said, 'Separate me Barnabas and Saul'" (Acts 13:2).

(2) " And grieve not the holy Spirit of God" (Eph. 4:30).

(3) "Then the Spirit said unto Philip, 'Go near'" (Acts 8:29).

(4) "The mind of the Spirit, because he maketh intercession for the saints" (Rom. 8:27).

(5) "Now the Spirit speaketh expressly" (1 Tim. 4:1).

(6) "The Holy Ghost…shall teach you all things, and bring all things to your remembrance" (John 14:26).

(7) "When he, the Spirit of truth, is come, he will guide you into all truth" (John 16:13).

From what has been previously explained about, contrasted, and juxtaposed with orthodox Protestantism, it is clear that the gospel as espoused by Charles T. Russell simply does not comport with that recorded by Matthew, Mark, Luke, or John. Moreover, unlike orthodox Christianity's concept of salvation by grace through faith alone, or *sola fide*, the Jehovah's Witnesses maintain that works/labor intensity (i.e., field service/evangelism) must be incorporated. The field service that is required is formulated into three tiers: (1) publisher, those who evangelize at least an hour each month and submit a field service report to that effect; (2) irregulars, those who spend some time evangelizing but fail to spend the required minimum of one hour each month proselytizing; subsequently, a report is not necessary; and (3) the inactive, those who fail to spend any time evangelizing for up to six consecutive months.

There are numerous other striking dichotomies that distinguish Christian orthodoxy from the Jehovah's Witnesses doctrine; the differences are so enormous and profound that it would make for a separate volume to even attempt to give an accurate description of them all. One, however, that will ruffle the proverbial feathers of the born again Christian is that because the Jehovah's Witnesses, following Russell's idea of the gospel, fail to acknowledge Jesus and the Holy Spirit as deity (hence the Unitarian concept), they therefore maintain the belief and widely proclaim that only those who worship in the name of Jehovah can be referred to as the true worshippers.

Granted, the faithful of every denomination regard their idea of Christology, salvation, and eschatology as inerrant; there is something amiss (albeit, perhaps minuscule) concerning the three (Christology, salvation, eschatology), they maintain, within all other sects. Those denominations, however, differing from Jehovah's Witnesses, Mormons, Seventh-Day Adventists, and Oneness Pentecostals, do not invariably conclude that accommodations cannot be made for other sects.

They (JW's) do not observe holidays (i.e., Christmas, Easter, birthdays). However, as concerning whether to recognize holidays or festivals, the Bible is not at all ambiguous. Rather, quite the contrary, for God demanded the observance of certain venues. Consider the following: (1) the Passover/Feast of Unleavened Bread—Ex. 12:15–39, 43, Lev. 23:5–6, Num. 9:2–14; (2) First Fruits/Feast of Harvest: Ex. 23:19, 34:22, 26, Lev. 2:12; (3) Feast of Tabernacles/Ingathering (aka Sukkot)—Ex. 23:14–16. The Apostle Paul, during his pontification to the church at Colossae, deliberately and without equivocation, quiets any controversy concerning one's recognition of holy days or any days held as memorials. The apostle explained in Col. 2:16, "Let no man…judge you in meat…drink, or in respect of a holy day…or of the Sabbath days." The apostle employs similar tones and rhetoric when issuing instructions concerning the observances of certain days to other Gentiles (those of Rome) as well. See Rom. 14:5–12. It's quite telling.

This cult does not pay homage to any flag (that is to say, their country's national flag, the flag of an alma mater, etc.) and adamantly refuses to participate in any war efforts or military tactics. Surely the founders must've considered how easily refuted this premise would be. One need not be familiar with Josephus's *The Wars of The Jew*s (Pfeiffer, 1974)—the narrative that describes the Jews' failed efforts to hold Masada against the notorious Roman general Lucius Silva in CE 73 and the Jews' efforts to prevent the destruction of Jerusalem three years earlier—to know that God sanctioned Israel's/Judah's military campaigns as long as God was first consulted concerning the maneuvers. One need only turn to the history books (Joshua through Esther); they are absolutely abounding with events describing Israel's and Judah's military exploits, conquests, and quite often unsuccessful campaigns.

Moreover, God even quite often instigated Israel's/Judah's attacks on their enemies; there are copious examples of such measures scattered throughout the scriptures. These maneuvers are, arguably, nowhere best exemplified (in scripture) other than in the narratives explaining the battle of Jericho (Jos. 6) and the account of King Saul's disobedience (1 Sam. 15). These pro-military venues are not only found within descriptive Christian sources (i.e., King James versions, New International version, Good News Bible, English Standard Version), but they are all right there in the Jehovah's Witnesses own pernicious New World Translation.

This heterodox group also refuses to receive certain vaccines or inoculations; the cult also emphatically rejects any blood transfusions, whether as a donor or recipient. These rejections have resulted in the senseless, untimely, and otherwise preventable deaths of thousands of Americans, children in particular. Moreover, due to the fact that Jehovah's Witnesses are monolithic in their practices, these untimely deaths are not only endemic to North America, but they are quite ubiquitous.

Fortunately, medical science has proven over and over again that the processes of undergoing blood transfusions and that of consuming blood, as in digestion, are medically and physiologically unrelated. Moses's narrative in Lev. 17:10–14 is obviously addressing the consumption of blood (from meats or any other source) through the digestive system. The transfusion of blood, however, is such that blood is allowed to pass intravenously through other portals. The following verses from the Torah emphatically forbid the consumption of blood: Gen. 9:4, Lev. 3:17, 7:26–27, 19:26, Deut. 12:16, 23–25. Moreover, the abstinence of blood consumption was not only an Old Testament warning, for Luke's prose (Acts 15:20) is quite corroborative.

The Witnesses insist that the Eucharist should only be served to the 144,000 anointed class; however, others may attend the service. This stance, of course, runs counter to orthodox Christianity, for nowhere in New Testament scripture can it be found—except as it pertains to those who are apostate (1 Cor. 11:27–28)—that Communion (the Eucharist) should be withheld from someone who has accepted Jesus Christ as Lord and Savior. Moreover, as it relates to the 144,000, the Apostle Peter makes it plain that God is not a respecter of persons. During his homily in Cornelius's house, the evangelist proclaimed, "Of a truth I perceive that God is no respecter of persons...But...he that feareth him, and worketh righteousness, is accepted with him" (Acts 10:34–35).

JW's resolutely reject the premise of the inerrancy of orthodox Christian scripture, hence the formulation of the esoteric New World Translation Bible. The truly born again understand, however, that "all scripture is given by inspiration of God" (2 Tim. 3:16).

The aged Apostle Paul was, of course, referring to the scriptures as "originally ordained by God, and accurately translated." The scriptures need not be rewritten or tweaked so that they conform to the values and ethos of modern societies. Nor should the scriptures be realigned, relabeled, and disguised in hopes that its guise can be employed to promote a new religious thought. That is exactly what the JW's have done in their fabrication of the New World Translation Bible. More will be addressed concerning this in the latter portion of this narrative. Suffice it to say at this point, however, that modern societies will have to align with the word of God and not the other way around. Otherwise, modern societies, elevating themselves above the word of God, will inevitably "capitulate to illusions." Colloquially, they're fooling themselves. Lastly, this cult assiduously espouses that all governments, capitalist or otherwise, are inherently corrupt and can only lead to economic entrapment. This economic entrapment or slavery, the faithful insist, is a harbinger of God's wrath upon those who put their trust in establishments rather than in God.

Soteriological Views

The Jehovah's Witnesses maintain that salvation is dependent, to some degree, upon labor intensity (i.e., house-to-house preaching/outreach). They are also of the opinion that the soul of any individual is not eternal. Rather, their belief is that the soul dies upon the death of the individual. This group also espouses the Calvinist idea that God predetermines the salvation of certain individuals. JW's insist, as orthodox Christianity proclaims, that Jesus did atone for man's sin. However, the Witnesses' concept is very divergent, for they maintain that Jesus atoned for man's sins only in the form of a perfect human and not as deity.

Eschatological Perspectives

The Jehovah's Witnesses purport that those born after the year 1914 cannot be considered as members of the anointed class of 144,000. This is based on Russell's belief that God's kingdom was established on Earth at the advent of Jesus in 1914. Subsequently, only the anointed class—and a few others, they insist—will enjoy the bliss of God's kingdom. Those who traffic in sin along with Satan will not suffer in an eternal hell but will be summarily annihilated. The 1914 Advent theory mentioned earlier was actually born of Russellism (the notion that only a chosen few should receive the Eucharist, etc.). The theory was widely espoused by Charles T. Russell, Judge Rutherford's predecessor. From his literature, Rutherford would have us believe that he abandoned the 1914 Advent theory in 1931 when he renamed the group Jehovah's Witnesses. Those of us whom have painstakingly dissected and scrutinized Russell's and Rutherford's theologies, however, have almost consensually concluded that the trajectories remain the same.

Concerns and Implications for the Orthodox Christian

The Jehovah's Witnesses have architected arguably the most insidious masterpiece of deception that anyone could have ever imagined. They have copied, pasted, and strung together an amazingly elaborate scheme, the idiosyncrasies of which will be debated throughout the ages. It is without controversy, moreover, that Russell, Rutherford, and their underwriters have managed to pull off the most elaborate religious scheme in the entire history of mankind. Their blueprint, albeit eccentric, is elaborate and quite frankly second to none (as concerning cults). The annals of history do not reveal the fabrication of a Western cult like it or more embedded with existential implications than that bequeathed by Russell. Search the annals, inquire at the archives, browse the repositories—a cult with more existential qualities will not be found. Rather, it will be revealed that the only Western-devised cult that even comes close (that is, to say a distant second) as it relates to shrewdness, insidiousness, perfidiousness, or cleverness would be Smith and Young's Mormonism/Latter-Day Saints. The Witnesses (JW's) have certainly mastered the art of copying and pasting, for by employing such technique, they have managed to piece together quite a deleterious, and mendacious montage.

    Since their inception, the dogmas of the Watch Tower Bible and Tract Society and that of the Jehovah's Witnesses have been embroiled in much quagmire, for their ideologies are replete with theological malpractices. Those philosophies bequeathed by Russell and Rutherford must be seriously reconsidered. Nevertheless, as a result of their aggressive outreach efforts—which requires all adult members to evangelize—their ranks continue to bourgeon. While far from being the largest religious group in North America or worldwide, they are one of the fastest growing religious bodies in North America. There are just over a million followers in the U.S. alone; a little over 155,000 are located in Canada; nearly 137,000 reside within the confines of the United Kingdom (JW's Country and Territory Report, 2018). The report also revealed that Jehovah's Witnesses are located throughout the African continent in Nigeria (nearly 390,000), the Democratic Republic of Congo (with about 230,000), and Zambia (where nearly 205,000 are faithful), assembling a large majority. Globally, there are approximately 8.5 million practicing Jehovah's Witnesses.

    It is conceivable that, had Russell availed himself of the Azusa Street Holy Ghost Revival in the city of Los Angeles during the early twentieth century, the Watch Tower Bible and Tract Society would've possibly never come into existence. This is a bold statement; nonetheless, it is a realistic one, for if he'd attended that great revival along with William J. Seymour and others, he would've experienced for himself the persons of the Holy Ghost and Christ. Admittedly, however, there were some Unitarian groups that arose from that movement. Nonetheless, although many charismatic sects spawned from the Azusa Street Revival, including some which would identify with Unitarianism, very few came away with Russell's theological perceptions, perceptions that are an affront to God's display of his presence at Azusa Street during the period of April 9, 1906, until roughly nine or so years later. The Witnesses, nonetheless, refuse to acknowledge that the issues concerning whether Jesus Christ and the Holy Ghost are deities were settled centuries ago. The Council of Nicaea, convened in 325 CE, settled the question of Jesus's deity. Pronouncing Jesus as deity was, however, quite unsettling and remains so with the Witnesses today, for the opponent of this ruling, Arius and at least one of his followers (believed to be Eusebius) were excommunicated and ultimately banished into exile.

Although the Council of Nicaea cleared up the controversy of Jesus's deity, it did not fully answer the question of whether the Holy Spirit was also, like Jesus, divine. This issue would not be brought up for discussion until 381 CE by Emperor Theodosius the First. Nearly forty-four years after the death of Emperor Constantine, who convened the first meeting, the bishops would meet in Constantinople (now Istanbul, Turkey) to settle the dispute once and for all. The Nicaea-Constantinople Creed, as it would be known, acknowledged that not only is Jesus deity, but the Holy Spirit is as well.

The Jehovah's Witnesses have doubted much about Catholicism, some rightfully so; much of the doubt, however, is unfounded. Of course, and not unlike all other religious groups throughout the ages, the Catholics have made their fair share of mistakes. However, the bishops at Nicaea and Constantinople were absolutely "biblically and theologically sound." Colloquially, we could say, "the Catholics got it right." Although the Unitarianism doctrine is not only theologically but philosophically skewed, none is more so than that to which Russell and Rutherford have endorsed and attached their addendums—Jehovah's Witnesses.

Satanic Transliterations

During the latter half of the twentieth century, author Salman Rushdie introduced a novel, *The Satanic Verses*, to the world, a narrative that many among Islamic circuits perceived to have been, in part, an insult to Islamism. Rushdie (1988) insisted, however, at the very outset of his narrative that his was a work of fiction only. Nonetheless, a *fatwa* was issued by Ruhollah Khomeini soon thereafter, but it was later unofficially lifted in 1998 by Mohammad Khatami, Iran's president at that time. Unlike Rushdie's novel, however, the Jehovah's Witnesses' Bible—The New World Translation (NWT)—does not purport to be a mere work of fiction. Contrarily, it was brazenly constructed as a tool to debase and impeach the Old and New Testament canons. The New World Translation Bible, the Witnesses' self-published montage born and cradled under the reign of N. H. Knorr (the cult's third president), is egregiously and deliberately flawed. Look for several of those deceptions to be addressed further along in this investigation. The NWT's impious disregard for sacred scripture has caused many oblivious and otherwise orthodox neophytes to go astray, for many of its transliterations are unapologetically brimming with inherent satanic connotations. Its congenital defects, coupled with inconsistent and convoluted expressions, are unparalleled. Language has been cleverly altered, the etymology of which do not resonate with Christian theology. Moreover, despite literature and research published by renowned scholars of Greek etymology (e.g., Spiros Zodhiates: *The Epistles of John*; Gustav Adolf Deissmann: *Light From the Ancient East*; Hugh Lloyd-Jones: *Greek In a Cold Climate*; Gregory Vlastos: *Socratic Studies*; K. Aland and B. Aland: *The Text of The New Testament*) that have completely debunked much of the Jehovah's Witnesses' etymological flaws, most of the faithful adhering to the JW's indoctrination and confirmation bias continue to close ranks behind Russell and Rutherford. This behavior is reminiscent of the prose employed by the Apostle Paul while addressing the Corinthian Church wherein he pontificated, "If our gospel be hid, it is hid to them that are lost...the god of this world hath blinded the minds of them which believe not, lest the light of the glorious gospel of Christ, who is the image of God, should shine unto them" (2 Cor. 4:3–4). It would, of course, necessitate a separate volume to reveal all the alterations found within the NWT. Therefore, we shall limit our critique by exposing only a few of those inaccuracies that impugn either the person/deity of Christ or the person/deity of the Holy Ghost. In the following examples the author has attempted to contrast the narratives of the Witnesses' New World Translation Bible with that of the orthodox Classic King James Study Bible. The King James Version was chosen because of its popularity, for it is the most studied among orthodox Protestant laity of all Bibles in the United States of America. Some 55 percent of all US non-clergy Protestants are said to prefer some brand of the King James Bible. Worldwide, it is by far the most desired translation among orthodox Protestant laypersons. Religious scholars, however, (religious affiliations, geography, and native origins notwithstanding) tend to choose The Revised Standard Version. Nevertheless, the following two sections represents exegeses of a few, albeit critically important, paradigms of satanic transliterations that permeate the New World Translation Bible.

Exegesis One:
Guises Designed to Impugn the Person/Deity of Christ

The New World Translation
    (1-A) John 1:1: In the beginning was the Word, and the Word was with God, and the Word was a god.

The Classic King James Study Bible's Antithesis
(1-B) John 1:1; In the beginning was the Word, and the Word was with God, and the Word was God.

Notice that the NWT says, "The Word was a god." The letter "a" gives rise to uncertainty, and the lower case "g" (in the word God) is designed to intimate that Jesus is not worthy to be equal with God, let alone be thought of as God. The King James, rather, lets us know that "the word" is used in reference to Jesus Christ, and that he is God. It also concludes that Jesus (the Word) was always in existence. Subsequently, he was not created as the Witnesses would have you believe.

The New World Translation
(2-A) John 1:14: "full of divine favor and truth."

The Classic King James Study Bible's Antithesis
(2-B) John 1:14: "full of grace and truth."

Notice that the NWT has removed the word "grace" (*chari*, to pardon, or favor that is unmerited) and inserted instead the words "divine favor," which in the original Greek lexicon is expressed by the word *theikos*, meaning "godlike." This is meant to be erroneously interpreted that only a Unitarian god is capable of bestowing grace or a pardon. However, in Jesus's case, the Witnesses insist, he was only full of divine favor, not grace. The King James, on the other hand, significantly differs, for if he is "full of grace," he must, therefore, be God. Moreover, the prose of Philippians 2:6 is quite explicit: "thought it not robbery to be equal with God."

The New World Translation

(3-A) John 1:23: "Make the way of Jehovah straight."

The Classic King James Study Bible's Antithesis
(3-B) John 1:23: "Make straight the way of the Lord."
 While the name "Jehovah" is certainly one of the names of God, in the NWT's narrative, however, it is intended to be misleading. The word "Lord" has been supplanted with the title "Jehovah," intending to divert attention away from Jesus as Lord and Christ. The Apostle Paul and Luke, however, have revealed that Jesus is both Lord and Christ (see Philippians 2:11 and Acts 2:36).

The New World Translation
 (4-A) 1 John 4:3: "But every inspired statement that does not acknowledge Jesus does not
  originate with God."

The Classic King James Study Bible's Antithesis
(4-B) 1 John 4:3: "Every spirit that confesseth not that Jesus Christ is come in the flesh is not of
  God."
 The Jehovah's Witnesses are very savvy in their deceits, for they have conveniently supplanted the phrase "that Jesus Christ is come in the flesh" with the insertion of their own: "that does not acknowledge Jesus." This cult understands that if their mendacity or deception is to come to fruition, that narrative (1 John 4:3)—perhaps more than any others which they have employed—must necessarily be reconstructed, for it actually reveals, as do the plethora of others, that Jesus literally came and revealed himself in the flesh as human and as God, hence the term "hypostatic union." This scripture, as revealed in

the orthodox narrative, impeaches the very ether of the Witnesses' doctrine that Jesus did not come in the flesh and that he was only a created spirit or angel. This scripture not only allows the Witnesses to see themselves as hypocritical (for they find it profoundly unconscionable that Jesus was revealed in the flesh), it also offers an opportunity for repentance, for when encapsulated, that's the very essence of the New Testament—to "offer an opportunity for repentance." Nevertheless, according to 1 John 4:3, the Witnesses are "not of God." Moreover, it concludes that, as the Apostle Paul and Luke insist, Jesus is both Lord and Christ (Acts 2:36, Philippians 2:11). The Unitarian concept promulgated by Charles T. Russell has been an exponent of the Jehovah's Witnesses from the inception of the Watch Tower Bible and Tract Society. The JW's theory continued to be nourished, cradled, and brought to adolescence by Rutherford, and Knorr; however, it was Franz, Henschel, and Adams which would be tasked to bring it into and see it through adulthood. Since Unitarianism is at the very ether of the Witnesses' construct, it will almost certainly be kept afloat by future pilots of the cult.

The New World Translation
(5-A) John 14:9–10: "How is it you say, 'Show us the Father'? Do you not believe that I am in union with the Father and the Father is in union with me? I do not speak of my own originality, but the Father who remains in union with me is doing his works."

The Classic King James Study Bible's Antithesis
(5-B) John 14:9–10: "And how sayest thou then, Shew us

the Father? Believest thou not that I am in the Father, and the Father in me? I speak not of myself: but the Father that dwelleth in me, he doeth the works."

One will notice the redundancy of the phrase "in union with." The term for "union" in the Greek lexicon is *enosi*, which has the connotation of combining or joining together. The Witnesses, therefore, promote the idea that Jesus and God were joined together or in union, as it relates to being in constant agreement only. To divert the reader's attention away from the deity of Christ, the Witnesses have inserted, "I do not speak of my own originality." This presupposes that Jesus had a beginning or was somehow formed or created.

The King James, however, employing the phrase "I am in the Father, and the Father in me" presents us with the idea that God and Jesus are actually one entity with no inherent or fundamental differences. The orthodox Christian novice will argue, however, that God and Jesus, because they often conversed with one another during Jesus's time on Earth, exhibited their own personalities. That's not a totally accurate inference, nor is it completely inaccurate; it's one that can only be painstakingly explained. The following explanation is quite plausible. One will notice that, almost invariably, dialogues between God and Jesus (during Jesus's three and a half years of earthly ministry) were in the presence of others. For example: (1) Matt. 3:16–17: Jesus's baptism, (2) Matt. 17:1–5: The Mount of Transfiguration, (3) Matt. 26:36–43: Jesus in the Garden of Gethsemane, (4) Matt. 27:46: The Crucifixion, (5) John 12:27–29: Jesus enters Jerusalem for Passover, (6) John 16:32–17:1–5: Jesus's prayer of intercession, (7) and lastly John 11:38–42, where we find Jesus at the grave of his friend

Lazarus. The keen eye will notice in John 11:42 that Jesus uttered, "I knew that thou hearest me always: but because of the people which stand by I said it, that they may believe that thou hast sent me." It could reasonably be concluded then that God simply wanted his people to acknowledge and experience his love for them through "himself," his incarnate word, Jesus Christ. Jesus further proclaimed, "I and my Father are one" (John 10:30). Jesus, therefore, had no origin but was in the beginning with God (John 1:1–2, Heb. 7:3). These verses observed separately or in conjunction with other scriptures must lead even the congenital skeptic to conclude that Jesus is God.

Exegesis Two:
Guises Designed to Impugn the Deity/Person of the Holy Ghost

The New World Translation
(1-A) John 14:17: "The spirit of the truth, which the world cannot receive, because it neither sees it nor knows it. You know it because it remains with you."

The Classic King James Study Bible's Antithesis
(1-B) John 14:17: "The Spirit of truth; whom the world cannot receive, because it seeth him not, neither knoweth him: but ye know him; for he dwelleth with you."

One will readily notice that the New World Translation (NWT) refers to the Holy Spirit as "it." This is, of course, by design, for the term is conversationally used in reference to an inanimate object or something less than human. Of course, this is exactly the false equivalency that the Witnesses would love their readers to infer, for theirs would be a conclusion that the Holy Spirit is profoundly inanimate and therefore not God. The King James Version, however, identifies him with the personal pronoun "he," indicating and drawing attention to his personage.

The New World Translation
(2-A) Acts 13:2: "The holy spirit said, 'Set aside for me Barnabas and Saul.'"

The Classic King James Study Bible's Antithesis
(2-B) Acts 13:2: "The Holy Ghost said, 'Separate me Barnabas and, Saul.'"

Notice that the name Holy Spirit—as used at this juncture and almost invariably throughout the NWT—is not capitalized; that is meant to give the impression that the Holy Spirit is only an "active force" with no mind or personality that God activates from time to time to carry out certain purposes. However, the alert reader has already discovered from previous narratives within this corpus that the active force theory has been debunked. The Holy Spirit, not unlike God and Jesus, is always active. Simply put, the Jehovah's Witnesses have in their transliteration given the Holy Spirit only "potential" energy.

The King James Bible, however, depicts the Holy Spirit as a person speaking and giving instructions with no unreasonable pretentions.

The New World Translation
(3-A) John 15:26: "The spirit of the truth…that one will bear witness of me."

The Classic King James Study Bible's antithesis
(3-B) John 15:26: "The Spirit of truth...he shall testify of me."

Here, again, the Witnesses, by supplanting the word "he" and inserting instead "that one," refuse to give credence to the personage and deity of the Holy Spirit. Such an impious polemic as this and those addressed in the contrasts listed above are absolutely blasphemous. They are the very alchemies of theological malpractices. For how say the scriptures? (See Deut. 4:2, 12:32, Rev. 22:18–19).

The King James, refreshingly, is very specific, for it reveals the Spirit's person. The word "he" gives him status and authority equal to that of the Father and the Son.

One will do well to not dismiss these challenges as simply hyperbolic, concluding that the ploys found in the NWT are insignificant and simply religious minutiae. Those variations are profoundly important, for they will help determine the conceptualization that the reader grasps from the scriptures. Still, some orthodox Christians will naively conclude that the NWT is simply written in a more easily understood way than, say, the King James or the New International version. Nevertheless, the novice must remain cautious that he or she is not betrayed by the NWT's prima facie appearance of legitimacy. These machinations can have profound etymological/linguistic effects. One must also remain cognizant of the fact that an untruth is just as easily understood in some instances as the truth is, for to understand a prevarication only to perceive it as truth is an existential threat to one's Christian orthodoxy.

Epistemologically, therefore, if one is not aware of the veracity of the knowledge that he or she has obtained and that truth is juxtaposed or weighed against the plausibility of false equivalencies, then the "path of least resistance" will ultimately be chosen. That trajectory will invariably be that with which one is most familiar or which seems logical. However, as the avid reader will attest, the New Testament is replete with illogical events (viz., immaculate conception, Lazarus emerging from his grave, the resurrection of Christ, etc.) that—if not for the born again experience—are completely unconscionable. Nonetheless, those who have experienced very rapid spiritual maturation are those who, as concerning the comprehension of scriptures, have removed their cognitive prowess from the equation. Rather, they've learned early in their spiritual journey to avoid leaning upon their own understanding (Prov. 3:5). Moreover, as was promulgated by the proverbial giants of the Enlightenment era, logic is not always truth, nor illogic always false. That is why the scriptures must be studied, not simply read, as reflected in the Apostle Paul's instructions to Timothy in which the Apostle advises, "Study to shew thyself approved unto God…rightly dividing the *word of truth*" (see 2 Tim. 2:15, emphasis added). Moreover, the word of God, as even the most skeptical of atheists will perceive if they would avail themselves, is spiritual (John 4:24, Heb. 4:12–13). Succinctly put, Biblical content, despite arguments to the contrary, will never be understood in the same manner as, let's say, the narratives of your favorite novel, psychology, or sociology text. Moreover, as stated elsewhere in this work, one's academic and theological prowess or his or her lettered status, while employed for the comprehension of other sources (that is to say norm-referenced tests, criterion-referenced exams, textbooks, etc.), should never be relied upon to facilitate the comprehension of Biblical scriptures. However, the mere professors of Christianity will continue to struggle with this premise. It's quite an enigma to them. For while deliberately dabbling in sin they enjoy receiving accolades for their inorganic and fabricated sermons, their publication of scholarly papers, and having additional letters attached to their names. They feel inept without such lauding, works, and accomplishments. Many, of course, try desperately hard to ward off their salacious thoughts and premeditated motives, but the human willpower is simply not up to the task. Sin is very deceitful (see Heb. 3: 13, Rom. 7: 15-25). Once, and if the cynics, and naysayers acquire the born again experience though, they soon realize how spiritually inept they once were. For only through the direction of the Holy Ghost (one's lack of any formal education, or high education status notwithstanding) can spiritual awareness be gained (see John 16:7-15).

It is appropriate at this juncture to address some of the concerns that the JW's must address if they are to emerge from their many quagmires. Among the several questions that the Witnesses must ask themselves is are they so naive as to entrust their eternal destiny to the theories of Russell who—as noted by Ankerberg, Weldon, and Burroughs (2008)—insisted that one would be better off not reading the Bible alone but instead attending to his books, literature, and narratives in conjunction with the Bible? It would be fruitless, Russell alleged, to attempt to comprehend God's plan of redemption without a thorough knowledge of his narratives contained in his seven-volume book series titled *Studies in the Scriptures*.

It was as though Russell dared his constituents to disobey or even question his neo-Machiavellian tactics. The same can be said of Rutherford and all those who would later pilot the cult (e.g., Knorr, Franz, Henschel, Adams) and now, since the realignment, the board of directors. Can a modicum of scriptural conceptualization be found in such a premise (that is to say, elevating Russell's narratives above that of the scriptures), or does such an espousal appear to be advanced by those whom have succumbed to narcissistic ideations? The latter, of course. An examination of Charles T. Russell's personality will reveal that his was a personality that exactly mirrors the description of narcissistic personality disorder outlined in the American Psychiatric Association's (1994) Diagnostic and Statistical Manual Of Mental Disorders (DSM-IV, pg. 629). He certainly harbored proclivities for grandiosity and had a constant need for accolades or having his ego stroked. To insist that his followers repudiate and hate naysayers signals that he was certainly devoid of empathy. In contrast, however, consider the example of the Apostle Peter, for he encouraged his recipients to embrace not only his own instructions but the directives that they'd received from the Apostle Paul as well (see 2 Pet. 3:15–16). The apostles were not vain, nor were they self-absorbed (as were the founders of the JW's cult); they had one thing in mind: to preach the gospel with emphasis accentuating the death, burial, and resurrection of Christ.

Another lingering, unanswered, and embarrassing conundrum that this sect has wrestled with since early in the nineteenth century is, are they willing to cling to the notion orchestrated by the founding fathers that—as explained by Ankerberg et al. (2008)—hatred, not love, should be shown toward those who refuse to subscribe to the Watch Tower/Witnesses doctrine? Also, will the cult continue to follow the concepts promulgated by a man who lied about something as insignificant and mundane as the potency of his wheat? Rhetorically, do these concepts remotely resonate with the tenets of the Old or New Testament? For what say the scriptures of these things? (see Ex. 23:1, Psalms 101:7, Prov. 12:22, 14:5, 19:9, Matt. 5:43–48, Luke 6:27–36, John 8:44, and Rev. 22:1–19). Given such a superfluity of discrepancies, malpractices, and unsubstantiated content demarcated in the JW's blueprint, the faithful must admit that the veracity of their dogma should at least be looked into. Most will, nonetheless, assiduously continue along the founder's trajectory, prescribing and administering Russell-Rutherford placebos. Moreover, despite decades of confirmation biases, defection of many of their congregants and top-level officials, and the restructuring of their power base, the current pilots of this cult, the board of directors, vehemently ignore the need for any significant paradigm shifts or trajectory changes. Lastly, much of the satanic overtones and esoteric undercurrents harbored by this cult have been exposed and painstakingly denuded within this corpus. However, as it pertains to this insidious and pernicious (albeit much resilient) cult, there remains much to be suspicious of.

Suggested Readings:

(1) Dencher, Ted. 1966. *Why I Left Jehovah's Witnesses*. Lakeland.

(2) Lingle, Wilber. 2009. *What the Watchtower Society Doesn't Want You to Know: A Glimpse Behind the Walls of the Kingdom Hall*. CLC (Christian Literature Crusade) Publications.

(3) Reed, David A. *Behind the Watchtower Curtain: The Secret Society of Jehovah's Witnesses*. Crown Publications, Incorporated. 1989.

(4) Reed, David A. *Jehovah-Talk, the Mind Control Language of Jehovah's Witnesses*. Baker Books, 1997.

(5) Schnell, William J. *Thirty Years a Watchtower Slave*. Baker Books, 2001.

(6) Scorah, Amber. *Leaving The Witnesses: Exiting a Religion and Finding a Life*. Penguin Publishing Group. 2019.

(7) Wilson, Diane. *Awakening of a Jehovah's Witness: Escape from the Watchtower Society*. Prometheus Books. 2002.

Section Eight

Mormonism

The COJCO-Latter-Day Saints and the Reorganized COJCO-LDS/Community of Christ

Founding/Brief History

Poised along the periphery of Christianity along with the Jehovah's Witnesses cult is Mormonism/the Church of Jesus Christ of Latter-Day Saints (LDS). While Joseph Smith Jr. was certainly the leading man in the founding of the Mormon Church, attention must also be given to Oliver Cowdery, who was, in essence, cofounder with Smith. Thus far, however, he's been unsung, relegated to a mere footnote in Mormonism. Cowdery's contributions, without which the Book of Mormon would have never came to fruition, will be addressed in detail further along in this investigation.

Joseph Smith Jr., born in 1805 in Sharon, Vermont, was initially attracted to Methodist and Presbyterian theology. However, restless, and disillusioned, he would become increasingly disenchanted and confused concerning the direction of his spiritual journey. Profoundly distraught, he would turn to the Bible for guidance. After reading the book penned by the Lord's brother, he decided to take God up on his promise made in James 1:5 (in the King James version). The young Joseph Smith Jr. was, indeed, in search of divine wisdom and guidance. Those divine features that he sought from his former dabbling (that is to say, in Presbyterianism and Methodism) continued to elude him. At the age of fifteen in 1820, as Smith discusses in his account of *The Pearl of Great Price* (Smith, 1951), after venturing into a wooded area endeavoring to find direction from God, he began to ask God for the wisdom and guidance that he'd read of in the scriptures. Smith alleged in his prose that during his period of solitude, he was overcome by a power of diabolic proportions. He insisted that the power was so great that his tongue became uncooperative, temporarily robbing him of speech. Comparing the power that overcame him to diabolic proportions could've been the result of extreme darkness that Smith alleged surrounded him. Smith says he was contemplating surrender to this power of darkness when a bright light came upon him. The spirit of doom was supplanted. Smith noted in his manuscript that this light brought with it two inexplicable personages above him. One, referring to Smith by name, commanded that the other acknowledge Joseph Smith Jr. as God's beloved son. Smith also maintains in his writings that during this episode, he asked one of the images which sect of religion was correct and which should he join. The personage, Smith proclaimed, asserted that he should not align nor associate with any of them for they were all corrupt.

Revelations Precipitating the Development of the Book of Mormon and Cowdery as Cofounder

After pondering the meaning of his first vision, Smith decided to pledge allegiance and show obedience to God. To honor his vow, he would have to refrain from congregating with any of the religious groups of his day. Roughly three years after experiencing his first vision (September of 1823), the disillusioned Smith would decide to call on the Lord while lying awake in bed. Smith alleged that, as in his first vision, once again a bright light came upon him; the similarities, however, between the former and the latter encounter would differ in that during the second, one named Moroni, a brilliant personage, is said to have appeared unto him. Moroni is said to have revealed to Smith the location of a book that was written on plates of gold. The plates, the personage is purported to have revealed, not only contained what Smith had longed for (e.g., the true gospel), but they would also incorporate an inscription describing the lineage and plight of the indigenous peoples of America. The revelator supposedly informed Smith that he would find two tools necessary for translation, the Urim and Thummin. It would be quite some time and several visions later, however, before Smith would be told how to find and retrieve the devices.

Finally, after he fell to the ground due to unmitigated exhaustion, another vision is reported to have arrived, directing the zealot to the location of the articles. While trying to unearth the instruments, Smith was prevented by Moroni and advised to wait until four years had elapsed before retrieving the materials. Anxiously, however, Smith returned to that exact location each year for four years to receive updates and clarifications from Moroni. Finally, after the expiration of four years (September 22, 1827), the eager Smith was awarded guardianship of the plates until they were to be needed. At a later date, Smith would begin to employ the Urim and Thummin in his pursuit to translate the writings from the golden plates. This would by no means be a unilateral task; the translations would not have been accomplished without the aid of one Oliver Cowdery, for it was he who would tirelessly assist Smith. Cowdery and Smith spent two days painstakingly interpreting and translating at the Smith's residence. As Smith interpreted from the plates, Cowdery penned the same into the English vernacular. As a result of this work accomplished on May 15, 1829, the Book of Mormon would have its infancy.

However, it would be nearly one year later before the Mormon religion (that is to say, the Church of Jesus Christ Of Latter-Day Saints) would find its way onto the market. Cowdery's work was absolutely invaluable in the formulation of this cult. Moreover, many Mormons, affiliations notwithstanding (for there are several splinters), believe that John the Baptist appeared unto Cowdery and Smith as they were together praying. The occultists also maintain that during the appearance of John, John the Baptist put his hands on "the two and ordained them both." The idea of elevating Oliver Cowdery to the plane of Joseph Smith will, no doubt, irritate the palate (subsequently becoming difficult to swallow) of many Mormon historians, particularly those who are Mormon fundamentalists; they will, no doubt, assert that it, at the very least, borders on sacrilege. Nonetheless, he must not remain a mere footnote, unsung. Moreover, if the faithful sincerely believe that there is veracity in all that Cowdery is alleged to have accomplished, then surely it would not be unreasonable to assign him his rightful status in Mormonism—that of cofounder. Cowdery didn't just arbitrarily arrive at Smith's home with some serendipitous discovery, nor was he summoned. Rather, he aggressively sought out Smith and agreed to work in tandem. Cowdery's talents proved to be instrumental in the founding and ratification of the cult. Without Cowdery's invaluable contributions, this heterodoxy would have never materialized.

Basic Beliefs and Rituals

Mormons (LDS) believe that the Aaronic priesthood was restored at the time that John the Baptist allegedly laid his hands on Joseph Smith Jr. and Oliver Cowdery. The Aaronic priesthood is considered to be the lower order of the priesthoods; they are empowered with, among other duties, bestowing routine, daily tasks upon the clergy and laity. The directional or procedural concerns of the church and doctrinal matters are, however, the responsibilities of the higher Melchizedek priesthood (presidential ranks). Only males twelve years and older are allowed to be initiated into the inferior Aaronic priesthood. However, one must be an adult male to be considered for membership into the higher Melchizedek order. This anti-egalitarian/patriarchal ethos has not been without serious negative genealogical effects, though. Despite the systemic racial climate that was allowed to prevail after Joseph Smith Jr.'s death, Smith, an antislavery man, must be applauded because of the fact that during the height of the North American slavery institution, he did indeed allow Blacks to ascend to the priesthoods. Nor was his a congregation of racial separatists, for one Elijah Abel and a few other men of African descent worshipped with Smith. However, after Smith's death and during the early reign of the cult's second leader, Brigham Young (1852), egalitarianism, tolerance of racial differences and miscegenation began their acute, downward spiral. During Young's watch, males of African ancestry seeking initiation into either of the priesthoods were blatantly discouraged and frowned upon. Brigham Young and other ethnocentric underwriters sincerely believed Blacks to be inherently and congenitally inferior. Subsequently, because of the alleged primordial discrepancies of that phenotype (that is to say, those of African ancestry), the Latter-Day Saints didn't aggressively evangelize among those of the African diaspora until fairly late into the twentieth century. It was the summer of 1978, to be specific. Moreover, it was during the winter of 1978 in which the group's leader, President Spencer W. Kimball, asserted that God had instructed him to dispense with the concept of prohibiting Blacks from entering the priesthoods (hence the doctrine of continual revelations). The proclamation resonated well in media (i.e., newspapers, pamphlets, etc.); long-held prejudices, however, are not easily relinquished. They die hard, if at all.

Nonetheless, it's inconceivable that such a pathological mentality was allowed to systemically continue for more than 125 years (from 1852 to 1978). Surely there must have been some sociologists, paleontologists, anthropologists, and others among the Mormon ranks with enough bravado or gravitas to present an opposing view. Moreover, one must ask if Kimball's proclamation—if we are to believe that it was not divinely inspired—was presented in good faith, or was it simply an overture allegorically analogous to Beethoven's Fifth being supplanted by the strings of a ukulele? Succinctly put, will the harbinger deliver as expected, or will a much inferior compromise avail itself? Time will tell.

The LDS also asserts that both the Bible (the Mormons' King James version, 1981 edition) and the Book of Mormon are the infallible word of God. One, they maintain, should not be esteemed above the other.

Traditional orthodox Christian scripture, the cult contends, is the alchemy of Satanism. The Mormons refer to their other self-published literature as well. Arguably the most amplified and exponential of their auxiliary sources is the *Doctrine and Covenants*, which the adherents purport explain—among other things—why continued revelations from God are necessary. *The Pearl of Great Price* (in which Smith describes his first vision), *Gospel Doctrine* (which contains many of Smith's discourses), and the Mormons' Articles of Faith can also be found among the LDS's literary repertoire.

Continuing Revelations: Orthodoxy vs. Heterodoxy

No serious exegesis of Mormon literature would be complete without addressing the LDS's concept of continuing revelations. Actually, the basic premise is not confined to, nor is it the monopoly of, Mormonism; it certainly shouldn't be conceived of as an approach foreign to Christian orthodoxy. However, there is a caveat in that Christians do not insist that revelations from God necessitate addenda, or sources which are required to be periodically attached to or referenced along with the Bible. Insubordination and hostilities within the movement have engendered many fissures. For a great number of Mormons, mostly those leaning toward heterodoxy, have disavowed the continuing revelations concept and other aspects of Mormonism. Nonetheless, God promised that he would speak to his people in various ways. The following are but a few of the narratives in which continuing revelations—as perceived by orthodox Christians—are exemplified: Acts 2:17, 9:11–12, 10:11–22, 13:2, 16:6, 9–10, 20:23, 21:10–11,

Matt. 2:13, 27:19, John 14:26, 15:26, 16:8, 12–13, Joel 2:28, and 1 Cor. 14:24–25. Although "all scripture is given by inspiration of God" (2 Tim. 3:16), perhaps the most demonstrative of the scriptures listed above are these two—(1) Joel 2:28: "your sons and your daughters shall prophesy, your old men shall dream dreams, your young men shall see visions," and (2) John 16:12–13: "I have yet many things to say unto you, but ye cannot bear them now…the Spirit of truth…will guide you into all truth…and he will shew you things to come." Nevertheless, *The Doctrine and Covenants* explains why continuing revelations are necessary, the fundamentalist Mormons proclaim. The LDS have also concluded that the ancillary work may have to be updated periodically as God reveals supplemental information. This perspective will be further reiterated under the heading Concerns and Implications for the Orthodox Christian.

Parallels to Orthodox Christianity: Church Ordinances

Not unlike orthodox Christians, the LDS are staunch advocates of many of the ordinances of the church (i.e., water baptism, the spiritual gifts bestowed upon the church, the ministries conferred on the church, the Trinity). However, contrary to classical Protestantism, the Mormons' idea of the Trinity is pantheistic, for they maintain that the Father, Son, and the Holy Ghost are all gods with distinct personalities and therefore not one God with three representations. The latter concept (a monotheistic god with three representations), the Mormons argue, is mistakenly held among orthodox Christians. The LDS/Mormons also serve the Lord's

Supper or Eucharist; water is served, however, in lieu of wine or juice. In agreement with orthodox Christianity, the LDS constantly urges and reminds its members that government officials, law enforcement personnel, magistrates, and civil authorities must be obeyed.

The Virgin Birth

The Mormons—all brands—also believe, as mainline Christians do, that Jesus Christ was born of the virgin Mary and that he is the redeemer, the author, and finisher of one's faith.

Contrasts to Orthodox Christianity and the Gospel According to Joseph Smith Jr.

Plural Marriage

The long-held practice of polygamy, which was only denounced in order to facilitate acceptance of what is now the American state of Utah into the Union, is, of course, one of extreme heterodoxy. Although events of plural marriages can be discovered approximately forty times during the epoch of the Old Covenant, the concept is not supported by the New Testament canon in the least. Moreover, the New Testament does not speak in the plural context when referring to a "biblically acceptable" consummated marriage. The Apostle Paul, when pontificating to the church at Corinth (1 Cor. 7:2), settled the argument succinctly: "Let every man have his own wife [not wives], and let every woman have her own husband [not husbands]" (emphasis added). Nevertheless, the Mormons have decided to ignore such scripture and have concluded that polygamy was sanctioned by God. They have paid little attention to the precepts of the new covenant, which, as mentioned previously, does not sanction, or legitimize such actions. The LDS, up to the latter half of the nineteenth century, turned a blind eye to polygamy and rejected the Edmunds Act of 1882, the legislation that declared plural marriages to be a felony. The Morrill Anti-Bigamy Act of 1862 (the predecessor of the Edmunds Act), which forbade the practice of polygamy within the territories of America, was, of course, slandered. The cult would not soon relinquish the long-held erroneous concept. Much of the laity and some among the clergy of the Salt Lake City and Independence, Missouri, cults who have been forced to abandon the concept are very sympathetic to the dissenters and factions that still practice clandestinely. Nonetheless, eventually, the church was forced to denunciate the custom in order to gain acceptance into the Union. Many of the old-timers in opposition splintered, settling elsewhere outside of Salt Lake City, Utah, and Independence, Missouri. Far afield, they would reinstitute their fundamentalist practices and salacious (sexual) fascinations. Two such groups are the Fundamentalist Church of Jesus Christ Of Latter-Day Saints (founded by Warren S. Jeffs, who was, prior to his death, serving a life sentence plus additional years for sexual misconduct involving children) and the Apostolic United Brethren. Although ostensibly derided by the principals of the more prominent Mormon sects of Salt Lake City, Utah, and Independence, Missouri, these two cults, along with several other factions, continue the legacy of plural marriages to this day.

The New Jerusalem

The Latter-Day Saints (LDS) assert that the New Jerusalem that will be established by God will be located on the North American continent (Independence, Missouri, to be exact). The LDS argue this to be true based upon Joseph Smith's revelations as outlined in *The Book of Mormon* (See 3 Nephi 20:22, Ether 13:2–10). They also cite the Bible (Jer. 31:1–15) to support their convictions. During a critical examination of those verses, the following was discovered in 3 Nephi 20:22: "This people will be established in this land...and it shall be a New Jerusalem." This scripture is contextually misplaced and egregiously malignant, for to incite and instill confusion, the Mormons have placed 3 Nephi 20:22 just prior to what would be known in the King James Bible as Deut. 18:18–19. They have revised and renamed the King James version of Deut. 18:18–19 as 3 Nephi 20:23 (Smith Jr., 2013). The LDS have, of course, amalgamated those scriptures as a means of promulgating their idea of the New Jerusalem being located in America's Midwest. Not only do they wish the reader to conceive that the New Jerusalem will be established in North America, but also that the prophet that God "has raised up" is Joseph Smith Jr. In actuality, Deuteronomy 18:15–19 is in reference to the coming of the Messiah, Jesus Christ. In all fairness to the LDS, however, the Mormons are not suggesting that Smith is the Messiah but that those scriptures are in reference to Smith as the prophet "like unto Moses." Nonetheless, this does not absolve them of disingenuously misleading the masses. Even so, Luke's narrative in Acts 3:22–26, coupled with Deut. 18:15–19, has pulled away and denuded the Mormons' insidious guise, revealing it as fraudulent and subsequently impeaching their proposition. Those narratives (Acts 3:22–26, and Deut. 18:15–19) are harbingers of the coming of the Messiah/prophet Jesus Christ.

Not only that, but the Mormons' New Jerusalem perspective lacks credibility in other areas as well; its many fissures and proverbial fault lines make it quite difficult for the scholar to perceive of it as having any integrity. Here's why: first of all, there aren't any scriptures in the entire Bible (excluding the flood mentioned in Gen. 7) that purport that any of the activities found in the scriptures happened or were predicted to occur anywhere near what would become known as the North American continent. Moreover, eschatologically, of the two times that the term New Jerusalem is mentioned in the book of Revelations (3:12, 21:2), there is nothing explicit nor remotely implied in John's prose that can be inferred that the New Jerusalem would be located or headquartered on the North American continent. Lastly, according to Rev. 21:1, the harbinger of the New Jerusalem will be a new Earth, thus the continents as we know them will no longer exist.

The Priesthoods

The LDS's premise of the Aaronic and Melchizedek priesthoods was briefly discussed previously in this investigation; however, it is virtually impossible to draw an accurate picture of Mormonism without further reiterating the concept of the priesthoods for they are the nexus by which all other tenets of the cult are synthesized. It is also necessary at this juncture to differentiate the two (Aaronic and Melchizedek) from the priesthood of Christ.

The Aaronic and Melchizedek priesthoods were, of old, designed and implemented for God's purposes. They are now, however, incongruent with and have been made redundant by the current epoch with the dispensation of grace. For in the period of the New Covenant, the true believer is his or her own priest through the "atonement of Jesus Christ." This is referred to by Christian theologians as the priesthood of the believer. Moreover, unlike those under the priesthoods of old, the true believer, under the auspices of the atonement (that is to say, because of the death, burial, and resurrection of Christ), has "direct access" to God by faith. Therefore, the repentant or those seeking salvation are not obliged to pursue grace through indulgences or confessions before a priest here on Earth. Jesus put it plainly as he hung on an old, rugged cross, drenched in blood, over 2,500 years ago: "Jesus knowing that all things were now accomplished…he said, it is finished" (John 19:28–30). All former priesthoods (Levitical or otherwise), Jesus was asserting, were dissolved at his death. The priesthood of the believer would take effect (Heb. 7:23–28). The twenty-sixth verse of that narrative (Heb. 7:23–28) is particularly telling for it reveals, "For such an high priest became us." Hence, the priesthood of the believer. Under the Old Covenant, only the high priest was allowed behind the "second curtain" into the holy of holies, for there he frequented annually to offer up sacrifices for the sins of the people and for himself as well. Now, however, under the dispensation of grace and because the veil of the temple was torn from top to bottom (and has been removed), Christians (and those seeking to become such) can petition God for themselves without the aid or intervention of an earthly priest. Hence, the penitent is at liberty—by faith in Jesus Christ's atonement and resurrection—to enter into the true holy of holies (not into that which was but a shadow of what was to come, Heb. 8:2, 4–5, 10:1) through repentance and faith. There, in the presence of God (although even as a sinner he or she was always in God's presence, albeit obliviously, Rom. 10:8–10), the neophyte can commune with God without requiring an earthly priest to do his or her bidding (see Matt. 27:51, Heb. 10:19–22, 1 Tim. 2:5, 1 John 2:1–2).

When comparing the Aaronic priesthood and the priesthood of Melchizedek to the faith of Abraham, the following is what the Bible explains: Gen. 15:6 coupled with Rom. 4:3 implies that it is by faith that we are saved. As such, the law, which was inaugurated four hundred and thirty years later (that is to say, after Abraham demonstrated his faith), could never undo or supplant what Abraham symbolically did (offering up his son) through faith (Gal. 3:17). The law, as observed by those of the antiquity, was "not of faith" (Gal. 3:12). Faith during the period of law did not provide a nexus between God and man, nor did it comport with the epoch of law. In summation, as explicated in Heb. 7:8, all priesthoods prior to the resurrection of Jesus (which were not predicated on faith but upon works) were supplanted by the everlasting priesthood of Jesus Christ (Heb. 7:23–28, 8:2, 4–6). It is not only an affront to God but also egregiously sacrilegious for the LDS—and the papacy as well—to install "mortal men" into the priesthood, elevating them, in essence, to the same plane as Christ himself.

Baptism for the Dead

The baptism for the dead (proxy baptism) is a concept popularized by the founders. It remains a practice of the Mormons of Salt Lake City, Utah. However, many other sects have denounced the concept. The fundamentalists (i.e., those who adhere strictly to Smith's/Young's ideas), however, assert that the procedure is necessary for the absolution and exoneration of those who died prior to the founding of the Church of Jesus Christ of Latter-Day Saints (1830), God's only recognized church. This baptism, the LDS proclaim, will give the deceased a glimmer of hope. To have this ritual performed on behalf of the deceased, the intermediary must be baptized in an LDS/Mormon temple in the presence of several witnesses. The Apostle Paul addressed this topic in his first recorded letter to the church at Corinth. He pontificated, "What shall they do which are baptized for the dead…why are they then baptized for the dead?" (1 Cor. 15:29).

Much can be surmised and concluded from that scripture; however, that Paul is championing proxy baptism is among that which would be unreasonable to conclude. In other letters, Paul makes it plain—though many orthodox Christians will disagree—that water baptism is not required for salvation (Rom. 3:28, 4:2–3, 5:1–2, 6:3–4, and Eph. 2:8–9). Rom. 6:3–4 is an enigma to and has been improperly conceived by some. MacArthur (2010) concluded that those scriptures (Rom. 6:3–4) are not referring to water baptism. Moreover, if we are to believe the preceding scriptures mentioned within this paragraph, one must conclude that MacArthur is exactly correct. Those scriptures listed above, when synthesized, reveal that only faith (or *sola fide*) is required for salvation. Water baptism, therefore, is not essential. Also, it would not be unconscionable to conclude that those scriptures (Rom. 6:3–4) are in reference to accepting Christ as Savior and, hence, corollary receiving the Holy Spirit. As pertaining to the Apostle Paul's discourse in 1 Cor. 15:29, it becomes clear, when viewed contextually, that the apostle is addressing those who were bordering on apostasy. Several were conspiring to renounce the concept of the resurrection, without which none can be saved. To ameliorate, the missionary accentuates the importance of the resurrection of Christ while simultaneously framing his narrative within the confines of faith.

The Adam-God Doctrine

Brigham Young, Smith's successor, asserted that God was a man before becoming God. He also maintained that Adam is actually God. He insisted that, subsequently, all LDS/Mormon males can acquire godhood. This ideal, however, has been rejected by the majority of present-day Mormons.

Soteriological Views

The Mormons' soteriological perspectives and the nexus between the individual and salvation is codified in section 3 and 4 of their Articles of Faith. Belief in the atonement of Jesus is required as well as strict obedience to the word of God. Faith in Christ, of course, is essential as well as repentance and water baptism. The LDS/Mormons, not unlike the Oneness/United Pentecostals, also maintain that one must acquire the gift of the Holy Ghost as a requisite for salvation. To obtain the gift of the Holy Ghost, they argue, one must undergo the laying on of hands by the presbyter.

Purgatory

This controversial, systemic abstraction resonates and rings loudly among Mormons, papal circuits, and Catholic loyalists; it does not, however, comport with Christian orthodoxy. The concepts of purgatory and indulgences were the cause of Martin Luther's split from his once beloved Romanism. The precept of purgatory was also disavowed by John Huss, Jerome of Prague, John Wycliffe, and other reformists/pre-reformists. The notion will be discussed further in the succeeding narrative titled Eschatological Perspectives.

Eschatological Perspective

The Latter-Day Saints ubiquitously maintain that the day of judgement will be preceded by the establishing of God's lost ten tribes. It is in North America, the adherents insist (the state of Missouri), that they will finally be gathered. As Christ begins his millennial reign, those that are his will meet him in the First Resurrection and accompany him to Earth. The disobedient who have not experienced death will be engulfed by consuming fire. The souls of the unrepentant dead must be allowed purgatorial rites for there in purgatory is where they may have an opportunity to atone by languishing for their sins. Those who are in purgatory and others will have a second chance to receive salvation during the Second Resurrection after the end of the one thousand-year period. Most orthodox Christians subscribe to the notion that those people who are not taken up to heaven in the rapture will have a second chance to obtain salvation. Now, even though the term rapture is not located in the Bible, it is explicated in 1 Thess. 4:15–17 as being caught up. The Greek lexicon has it as *harpazo*, or to snatch and remove from one place to another. However, the orthodox Christian's construct of an impending opportunity (that is to say, after the rapture) to obtain salvation does not exactly comport with that of Mormonism. Rather, purgatory is the Mormons' antithesis to the Christian's idea of salvation following the rapture. Purgatorial rites are a foreign concept in the realm of orthodox Protestantism. Nonetheless, the Mormons as well as the Catholics insist that the apocryphal book of Maccabees (2 Maccabees 12:45–46 in particular) displays solid evidence of a place (although not mentioned by name) called purgatory. 2 Macc. 12:45–46 reads as follows: "But if he did this with a view to the splendid reward that awaits those who had gone to rest in godliness, it was a holy and pious thought. Thus, he made atonement for the dead that they might be freed from this sin" (Catholic Biblical Association of America, 1970). Based upon the narrative of 2 Macc. 12:45–46, many liberal Protestants, in an attempt to keep their unconscious biases in check, have erred in their insistence that orthodox Christians should not summarily assume those scriptures to be hyperbolic. They bring up the point that the anti-papacy Martin Luther eliminated certain books from the Bible during the turbulent fifteenth century because they favored purgatorial rites, transubstantiation, and other tenets of Catholicism. That is, of course, well documented. Maccabees was one such book. First and

Second Maccabees were one book during that time. The broadly based or liberal Protestants also assert that fundamental Christians should ask themselves the following two questions: (1) Was Luther justified in his redactions? (2) If evangelicals can accept as fact the mind-boggling concept of the virgin birth of Christ, then why would the precept of purgatory be so unconscionable?

The following explication is an attempt to resolve the enigmas discovered above; Luther was absolutely correct to exclude the apocryphal book of Maccabees from the Protestant canon for it would be grossly negligent and a theological misstep to ignore the plethora of exculpatory scripture indicating the absence of a purgatory that acquits the firebrand. The following exemplifies such exculpatory evidence: Rom. 3:23–24: "All have sinned, and come short of the glory of God; Being justified freely by his grace through the redemption that is in Christ Jesus"; Rom. 3:28: "We conclude that a man is justified by faith"; Rom. 8:1: "There is…no condemnation to them which are in Christ Jesus"; Titus 2:14: "Who gave himself for us, that he might redeem us from all iniquity, and purify unto himself a peculiar people"; 1 John 1:7: "The blood of Jesus Christ…cleanseth us from all sin"; 1 John 1:9: "He is faithful and just to forgive us our sins, and to cleanse us from all unrighteousness"; and 1 John 2:2: "He is the propitiation for our sins." Other substantiations that exonerate the Protestant Martin Luther (a former papal loyalist) concerning the issue of purgatory are presented in 1 John 4:17, Heb. 1:3, 9:27, 10:14, 1 Cor. 6:11, Rom. 5:9, John 5:24, Phil. 1:20–23, and 1 Thess. 4:13. Of all the arguments presented here (and arguably within the entire New Testament) as pertaining to purgatorial rites, perhaps the most revealing are these two: (1) "When he had by himself purged our sins" (Heb. 1:3) and (2) "It is appointed unto men once to die, but after this the judgement" (Heb. 9:27).

The Latter-Day Saints' ideal of salvation simply does not comport with that espoused within the New Testament for theirs is an untenable hierarchical motif.

This paragraph will delineate how their concept is codified. At the very pinnacle of the pyramid, they've formulated the Celestial Stage or kingdom. This position, they articulate, is reserved for the faithful who have unwaveringly adhered to the Articles of Faith. Further down the slope, they maintain, is the Terrestrial Stage or kingdom. Those assigned to this planetary experience will be those who were "subpar" in their obedience to Christ but, after experiencing purgatory, have truly repented and accepted Christ as savior. The lowest and most populated on the continuum, the LDS allege, is the Telestial Stage. This planet will consist of the unrepentant and those who ignored the Articles of Faith. Those in this kingdom, the Mormons believe, after experiencing purgatory and Satan's reign of terror, will also have an opportunity to repent and receive salvation.

Concerns and Implications for the Orthodox Christian

The Latter-Day Saints (LDS/Mormons) have quilted quite an amazingly duplicitous montage; however, its patchworks are blatantly incongruent with and do not easily mesh with the fabric of orthodox Protestantism. Their texts, *The Book of Mormon* and supplemental literature, are replete with betrayals and theological malpractices. Such negligence insinuates that they, like the Jehovah's Witnesses, have proverbially "made a deal with the Devil." Nonetheless, all but the novice will find that the seams of the LDS's proverbial quilt, when juxtaposed with Christian orthodoxy, are soon unraveled. As noted previously in this work, there is little parallelism between this cult and orthodox Christianity. The dichotomies—most of which have already been addressed—are resoundingly enormous. Hence, the following are questions, circumstances, and anomalies that Mormons must ask themselves, investigate, and consider ameliorating before blindly following the founders' trajectory and contorting the truth:

(1) If Smith's narratives were truly divinely inspired, would they really have to be revised periodically, as proposed by their concept of continuing revelations? When compared with biblical scripture, that premise harbored by Mormons is simply baseless. It does not derive from nor is it intimated within the original. The following are but a few scriptures that will attest to the erroneousness of the theology concerning continuing revelations: (A) Psalms 33:11: "The counsel of the Lord standeth for ever, the thoughts of his heart to all generations"; (B) Psalms 119:89: "For ever, O Lord, thy word is settled in heaven"; (C) Psalms 119:160: "Thy word is true from the beginning: and every one of thy righteous judgements endureth for ever"; and (D) Isaiah 40:8: "the flower fadeth, but the word of our God shall stand for ever." As stated elsewhere, these are only a modicum of the copious amounts of scriptures that denude the Mormons' perception of continued revelations. For additional enlightenment, it is advised to delve further and of course prayerfully into the scriptures,

for Jesus insisted that one should "Search the scriptures; for in them ye think ye have eternal life: and they are they which testify of me" (John 5:39).

(2) Might it be of concern to Mormons to know that it is well documented that there are some two hundred or more acts of plagiarism found among Mormon literature of the King James Bible?

(3) Would it change their minds somewhat about the character of Joseph Smith Jr. if they knew that Smith claimed that the inscriptions on the plates, which he alleged to have unearthed, were of Egyptian hieroglyphics but were proven to be fraudulent? According to the works of Martin (2003), the characters were presented to the learned and noted Professor Charles Anthon at Columbia University for authenticity. The professor pronounced them to be a hoax, and the events precipitating his (Smith's) review of the letters, he concluded, were all a scheme.

(4) To what extent would it trouble the laity—of course the Mormon scholars are aware of this—to know that Smith used peep stones to locate treasure, the practice that borders on occultism (see Lev. 19:31, 20:6, 27, Deut. 18:10–13, 29:29, Rev. 18:23)? This was well documented by Smith's neighbors and by those who knew him best.

(5) Would it be of any concern to the laity of the Latter-Day Saints to learn that much of the narrative in the book of Mormon is eerily similar to the works of one Minister Solomon Spaulding? Many quite noted theologians from both sides of the aisle (that is to say, Mormons and non-Mormons) have contended that Spaulding's works were plagiarized by the fathers of Mormonism.

(6) Should the events of Smith's contested visions

be subjected to further examination? In one narrative, he writes that the personage that he saw in his first vision was Nephi; in another, he alleged it could have been Moroni. Initially, he intimated that it was only one personage; later he concluded that there were two. Are the Latter-Day Saints willing to allow their salvation to be predicated upon the nexus of an uncertain vision of Joseph Smith Jr., a nexus cosigned by Brigham Young? The students and followers of Mormonism must understand that this is exactly what they have done.

(7) Many, of course, will think Smith a true prophet and martyr, but was he really, or was God punishing him and his brother, Hyram, because of false prophecies during the storming of the prison where they were being held for instigating the burning of a newspaper building in Carthage, Illinois, where they both lost their lives? In order to grasp this connection, it will be necessary to review Deut. 18:20–22. Within those verses we discover that God is explaining to his people the eventual fate of a false prophet. He proclaims, "But the prophet, which shall…speak a word in my name, which I have not commanded him to speak…that prophet shall die." Although it cannot be concluded as such, perhaps this was the case with Joseph and his brother, Hyram. Other scriptures—although, perhaps, not as poignant as those mentioned in the eighteenth chapter of Deuteronomy—that may also illuminate this nexus are Deut. 13:5, Ezek. 13:3, 6–10, 17, Rev. 22:18–20. Mind you, many among the mob that shattered the prison and the lives of Joseph Smith Jr. and his brother, Hyram, were fellow Mormons. It's hard to imagine that a prophet would be complicit in the burning down of a newspaper building or that a prophet would be arrested for treason.

The charges of arson and treason brought against Joseph Smith during the summer of 1844 are well known and debated among the serious students of Mormonism. A chronicle of Smith's life will leave even the staunchest loyalist disappointed, disillusioned, and prone to defection.

(8) We now turn attention to Smith's successor of whom much has already been said, Brigham Young. It is worth mentioning that in 1857 several Mormons, accompanied by some indigenous peoples, massacred over 135 Arkansas travelers as the Southerners passed through Utah. The migrants were trekking down to the Golden State. Although Young has not been proven to have been complicit, many historians have intimated that he—after becoming aware of the incident—ordered his followers to remain tight-lipped. Eventually, however, Young was forced to single out John D. Lee as a scapegoat.

All cannot be annotated here concerning the fallacies, innuendos, and discrepancies of Joseph Smith Jr. and Brigham Young, for only a separate digest specifically chronicling their lives could contain such a superfluity of such information. Suffice it to say, however, that they were certainly men of very checkered pasts. There are many other topics, along with those mentioned above, that the Mormons must certainly address if they are to find their way out of Joseph Smith's nineteenth-century quagmire. Will they continue to cohere to the gospel according to Joseph Smith Jr., or will they eventually begin, as the author of the book of Hebrews proclaims, "Looking unto Jesus the author and finisher of our faith, who…is set down at the right hand…of God" (see Heb. 12:2)?

Are the LDS willing to entrust their eternal destiny to a sect which once, from January of 1852 up until the summer of 1978 (some 126 years)—refused to obey Christ's Great Commission by ignoring those of African progeny (vis-á-vis Matthew 28:19–20)? Unlike the Jehovah's Witnesses, the Latter-Day Saints, even though they've fabricated their own brand, do refer occasionally to the authorized King James version (as long as it's not incorrectly interpreted, they maintain). Joseph Smith Jr., however, penned what he purported to be the inspired version of the King James Bible. In 1867, his text was posthumously published two decades after his death. Nonetheless Jesus's directives in Matthew 28:19 are unequivocally clear: "Go ye therefore, and teach all nations." Those scriptures, regardless of translations, cannot easily be dismissed or explained away. The early missionaries were determined to fulfill the mandate that Christ enunciated, for—except for the Apostle Peter, who nearly succumbed to his xenophobic illness and preconceived notions (Acts 10:9–16)—they refused to allow one's phenotype to thwart the word of God (notice Acts 8:4 and trace Paul's missionary journeys from Acts 13–27). For further information concerning where the apostles journeyed, their odysseys, and the precarious situations in which many often found themselves, all in obedience to Christ, explore *Down through the Centuries, Little Known Facts from Church History* (Ferrell, 2019), and *Comprehending the Pauline Epistles, a Study Guide* (Handy, 2019). Both are extremely enlightening. However, Handy's exegesis of Paul's missionary journeys is superbly delineated.

In sum, to accommodate a more cosmopolitan, twenty-first-century American/global view, the LDS's position on miscegenation, women's rights, and ethnocentrism must be more aggressively ameliorated. Some changes, however, have exuded. They have evolved too slowly, though, and they're much too minuscule. The author has been quite critical in this narrative (albeit completely objective) concerning the Christology, theology, and liturgy of the Mormon fathers. However, it was for the benefit of and love for the adherents that this investigation was begun. Lastly, while much has been exposed about the epoch, life, and works of Joseph Smith Jr. and Brigham Young (much of which the faithful will find unpalatable), it is also with a commiserate heart that the author ends this commentary. With that, the author concludes the investigation of the veracity of Mormonism.

Suggested Readings:

(1) Brodie, Fawn M. 1971, 1979. *No Man Knows My History, the Life of Joseph Smith the Mormon Prophet*. Second edition. Alfred A. Knopf. New York.

(2) Bushman, Richard L. 1984. *Joseph Smith and the Beginnings of Mormonism*. University of Illinois Press.

(3) Ferrell, Vance. 2019. *Down through the Centuries, Little Known Facts from Church History*. Harvestime Books, P.O. Box 300, Altamont, Tn.

(4) Handy, Adam J. 2019. *Comprehending the Pauline Epistles, a Study Guide*. Lighthouse Christian Publishing.

Dr. A.J. Handy, Ph.D.

Section Nine

Oneness Pentecostals (UPCI and Others)

Founding/Brief History

Pentecostals in general (i.e., Assemblies of God, Church of God in Christ, etc.) are Christologically Trinitarian. However, there are many splinter groups, among which are the more prolific United Pentecostal Church International (UPCI) that adhere to the soteriology of Unitarianism, or the oneness ideology of salvation. To them, the line of demarcation between the person of Christ and God is extremely blurred. Even though the UPCI is an American-born cult established in the mid-twentieth century, in order to put its Christology into proper perspective, it is important to note that Unitarianism—its linchpin and elixir—was ubiquitous and collaborating with other ecclesiastical issues in Western and Central Europe long before the establishment of the United Pentecostal Church International (UPCI). It was one Michael Servetus, a renowned Spanish medical doctor, who is believed to have been the first to popularize the idea of Unitarianism around 1547–1550. Such an espousal would lead to his martyrdom, however. John Calvin, a former Catholic born into French aristocracy and persuaded to adopt Protestantism, paradoxically (for his was the erroneous theology of predestination and election, which essentially criminalized God) allied himself with the pontiff, a Catholic, of course, to excoriate and drive Servetus to imprisonment and subsequently to the stake. That all occurred during the mid-sixteenth century. Of all the misguided theological concepts engendered during the epoch of the Protestant Reformation, none were more unscriptural than those of Calvin.

From the Protestant Reformation Movement, the Unitarian concept was adopted by some in England as a rebuttal to the Elizabethan-Anglican movement or Anglicanism. W. E. Channing, a Puritan, introduced his version of Unitarianism to North America around the first quarter of the nineteenth century. However, Jonathan Edwards, George Whitefield, and others were already volleying and exchanging polemics and indictments against Unitarianism and Arminianism in the New England corridor with Charles Chauncy. Chauncy was a staunch opponent of revivalism during the Great Awakening period of 1735–1745 (Wright, 1955). He and his constituents insisted that what they had observed of the Great Awakening was simply emotionalism and theological ignorance. Chauncy and many other lettered elitists of the Great Awakening epoch maintained that men of little education should resign themselves to the position of laity, for they, Chauncy continued, were unqualified to ascend the pulpit. In one of his latest works, Wright (1975, 1989, pg. xiii) reveals that Chauncy denounced the Great Awakening as "a corruption of religion." Nonetheless, several of the pro-revivalist ministers (i.e., James Davenport, Jonathan Edwards, et al.) alleged that it was the scholarly ministers who were unfit. Davenport asserted that many of the lettered were worldly and not truly born again. Such social discord and polemics would advance the premises of Arminianism and Unitarianism. Arminianism and Unitarianism are meticulously woven within the fabric of the Oneness/United Pentecostal theology, the former to a lesser degree, however.

The origin of the United Pentecostal Church International (UPCI) and other Oneness/Unitarian cults in North America goes back as far as 1916, when it was in association with the Assemblies of God, a Trinitarian group. Religious predispositions, however, would cause those ministers who harbored the Oneness concept of Christology to sever ties with and repudiate the Assemblies of God. The Oneness, or Jesus's name only, ministers were determined to unite under the Unitarian tradition. Not long after their dissociation with the Assemblies, say, two months or so (Jan. 1917), the Oneness ministers were summoned to the hamlet of Eureka Springs, Arkansas, to devise a plan that might allow them to remain confederate. During that meeting, they would found the General Assembly of the Apostolic Assemblies. However, phenotypical, and other concerns engendered wedges deeply within the sect. Those wedges would spawn several splinters (i.e., the Apostolic Churches of Jesus Christ, the Pentecostal Ministerial Alliance, the Pentecostal Assemblies of the World, etc.). However, during the ensuing three decades or so, with most fissures mended, many loyalists now dead, and social and other divisions eulogized, an alliance was formed between the sects. They agreed to assemble and unite under one banner, the United Pentecostal Church International (UPCI). The name remains unto this day.

Basic Beliefs and Rituals

Other than the belief in Unitarianism (absence of a Trinity, hence the term Oneness), the soteriological view of the necessity of speaking with tongues as a requirement for salvation and the belief that one can forfeit her or his salvation, this cult shares similar beliefs with orthodox Pentecostals. Subsequently, because this group superficially, or on its face, presents the appearance of being Trinitarian Pentecostals (e.g., Assemblies of God, Church of God in Christ, Church of God, Full Gospel Baptist, or even the nondenominational Calvary Chapel), many newcomers to the gospel have unassumingly fallen prey to the United Pentecostal's (UPCI/Oneness) ostensible motives. It is not hard to perceive why so many have been deceived by this cult, for to the uninitiated, they portray themselves with a form of godliness. The Apostle Paul warns of such in 2 Tim. 3:5. Moreover, I discovered throughout my copious years of investigation that an abundance of the loyalists (even those who had been associated with the cult for over ten years or more) cannot adequately explain the dichotomies between the Trinitarian and Oneness theologies. Subsequently, they remain oblivious to the pernicious and deleterious undercurrents that lie beneath the surface of the Oneness Christology. That's a very slippery slope.

For, not unlike orthodox Pentecostal groups, United Pentecostals speak with tongues, lay hands on the sick when appropriate, and insist that they allow the nine spiritual gifts (1 Cor. 12:8–10) to operate within the church. Nevertheless, because of their deviation from the orthodox model, much of their liturgy must remain suspect. Upon close inspection, the liturgy and doctrine are found to be based in the quagmire of counterfeit theology. Jesus's explanation is very fitting for the Oneness cults: "teaching for doctrines the commandments of men" (Matt. 15:9). As can be observed in the scriptures where God performed miracles, in many instances, the

Devil readily presented a counterfeit. This can be best exemplified in Ex. 7:10–12, 20–22, 8:6–7. The Devil's advocates, in many instances, stand ready to present a duplicitous "form of godliness." Consequently, lacking a fundamental theological background, they (e.g., those who have sought refuge among the Oneness cult as a result of disillusionment engendered by those who formally masqueraded among them as preachers) are at the mercy and in the throes of Satan. They dare not revolt. Rather, they are constantly reminded—albeit ever so subtly—that to reject the Unitarian/Oneness methods would mean a forfeiture of their salvation. That's reprehensibly false; it's theological malpractice. It emanates from the very seat of Satan.

Moreover, the Unitarian's interpretation of scripture—Acts 2:38 and Matt. 28:19 in particular—is wanting. Their interpretation does not comport with holistic New Testament directives, nor with Martin Luther's pontification. While vociferously addressing the Inquisition at the Diet of Worms, his was a position consistent with biblical scripture of *solae scriptura*, or letting the Bible alone be the source of correct doctrine (Ferrell, 2019. pg. 102–103). I shall attempt to assiduously delineate and denude the United Pentecostal's appendages of Jesus's name only baptism, the forfeiture of one's salvation, and speaking with tongues as a requisite for salvation under the heading of Contrasts to Orthodox Christianity.

Other than the ability to quote their favorite scripture, that is to say, Acts 2:38 and Joel 2:28, the rank and file, as opposed to the laity of many within orthodox sects, are essentially unskilled in the scriptures. It is as though the Apostle Paul, when addressing the church in

Rome, also had the United Pentecostal Church in mind when he pontificated, "For they being ignorant of God's righteousness, and going about to establish their own righteousness, have not submitted themselves unto the righteousness of God" (10:3). Moreover, their dress codes are the strictest, and Satan's subterfuge leaves them little room for compromise. Of course, that is one of the hallmarks of the occult: to ensure that everyone "toes the line," conforms, and thinks twice before rebelling.

Parallels to Orthodox Christianity

As has been previously stated in this narrative, the Oneness/UPCI's beliefs are, in many ways, similar to those of most Protestant sects. Water baptism, the Eucharist (without transubstantiation), the hypostatic union, salvation obtained through the atonement of Christ, the resurrection, heaven and hell as eternal places, the rapture, and an Armageddon are some of the more pivotal aspects which the UPCI/Oneness Churches share with orthodox Christianity. There are others, but those are the most significant criteria. However, as to be expected of any heterodox or splinter group, there are some caveats. These dichotomies are not only what make them so unique but are also the nexus that has caused them much scorn and repudiation. Three of the more defining symptoms of Oneness Pentecostalism are (1) Jesus's name only baptism, (2) a belief that salvation can be forfeited, and (3) speaking with tongues as a requisite for salvation. These caveats will, of course, be treated within the section that follows. Nonetheless, to appreciate and properly understand the explanations, it is paramount that the reader refer to the scriptures noted within the narratives.

Contrasts to Orthodox Christianity

(1) Jesus's name (only) baptism, a requisite for salvation: By far, the most defining characteristic or hallmark of the Oneness Pentecostal cult is its Jesus's name baptism. It is their signature. As concerning the proper method of baptism and all other church ordinances and doctrines, the Christian is obliged to the obedience of the scriptures alone (*solae scriptura*). There shouldn't be any redactions, cover-ups, or appendages. Jesus was quite unequivocal when he commissioned and mandated the apostles to go about "baptizing them in the name of the Father, and of the Son, and of the Holy Ghost, teaching them to observe all things whatsoever I have commanded you" (Mat. 28:19–20). The UPCI and other members of Oneness cults will have to reexamine their love for God for Matthew 28:19–20 is clearly a mandate. Jesus insisted that "If you love me, keep my commandments" (John 14:15). Jesus continued, "If a man love me, he will keep my words" (John 14:23). The scriptures should never be indicted or called into question by those who readily purport to promulgate it. Nonetheless, by denying the inerrancy of scripture, that is exactly what the Oneness groups and others (i.e., Latter-Day Saints, Jehovah's Witnesses, and Adventist groups) have done. A plausible case simply cannot be made for a Jesus's name only formula of baptism. It's certainly not espoused anywhere in the scriptures as being a requirement for salvation. When the jailkeeper at Philippi asked the missionaries, "What must I do to be saved?" the reply was, "Believe on the Lord Jesus Christ" (Acts 16:31). Paul's prose in Rom.

4:16 is quite convincing also: "It is of faith, that it might be by grace; to the end *the promise might be sure to all the seed*" (emphasis added).

(2) Forfeiture of salvation:
There are some who argue that one's salvation is not eternal. This Arminian concept (promulgated by Jacobus Arminius during the early seventeenth century) is an erroneous premise bequeathed to and absorbed by a variety of heterodox Pentecostals, UPCI included. However, Heb. 5:9 and a plethora of other scriptures cannot be simply ignored. The writer of Hebrews explains, as concerning Jesus, "He became the author of eternal salvation unto all them that obey him." Moreover, Jesus insisted, "I give unto them eternal life...they shall never perish, neither shall any man pluck them out of my hand" (John 10:28). In corroboration, the Apostle Paul enunciated in one of his letters from prison that "after that ye believed, ye were sealed with that holy Spirit of promise" (Eph. 1:13). See also Rom. 8:31–39, 5:1–2, John 3:15–16, 6:40, 10:10, and 1 John 5:13.

(3) Speaking with tongues, a requirement for salvation:
This concept is not ratified by scripture, nor is it intimated, implied, or otherwise documented in the canons. The premise that is ratified by scripture, however, is the fruit of the Spirit, love in particular. For the Apostle Paul pontificated the following: "The fruit of the Spirit is love, joy, peace, longsuffering, gentleness, goodness, faith, meekness, temperance" (Gal. 5:22–23). The word "charity" is mentioned no less than nine times (in one chapter of scripture, no less) in 1 Cor. 13. At the outset, the Apostle Paul enunciates that charity (love/*agape*)—

one of the fruits of the Spirit—is of paramount significance as it relates to salvation. The same cannot be found in scripture concerning speaking with tongues, however. Rather, during his homily, the Apostle Paul articulated, "Though I speak with the tongues of men and of angels, and have not charity, I am become as sounding brass, or a tinkling cymbal (1 Cor. 13:1). Actually, approximately midway through that same thirteenth chapter, it's noted that tongues will cease. Surely then, as it pertains to salvation, tongues cannot be compulsory. The Christian mantra should be *sola gratia* and *sola fide*, that is to say, let grace and faith alone be the determining factors of one's salvation.

Soteriological Views

Repentance, acceptance of Christ as savior, full emersion baptism in Jesus's name only, and speaking in tongues as a requirement for salvation are all pivotal tenets of the Oneness'/UPCI's salvation perspective.

Eschatological Perspectives

With the exception of the caveats mentioned elsewhere in this text (i.e., Jesus's name only baptism, tongues as a requirement for salvation, forfeiture of one's salvation, etc.) the end-time prospective of Oneness Pentecostals is not unlike that of orthodox Christians. The rapture, an Armageddon, the second coming of Christ, the resurrection of the dead, the judgement of mankind, etc. are all eschatological aspects which are espoused by both the Oneness sects and orthodox Christians.

Concerns and Implications for the Orthodox Christian

Unlike some of the other cults addressed in this inquiry (i.e., Jehovah's Witnesses, Rastafarians, Abakua), the Oneness sect is not one that can simply be ignored; it's well funded, extremely ubiquitous, and quite determined. Patterson and Rybarczyk (2007, pg. 123–4) revealed that as of 2007, there were approximately twenty-four million Oneness or Jesus's name Pentecostals worldwide. That's quite a swell from the days of its infancy, and a cessation does not appear to be forthcoming.

    The Oneness/UPCI (Unitarian) doctrine is a blotch on the canvas of Protestantism for it conspires with its allies Mormonism, Adventism, and Jehovah's Witnesses to deliver an insult to the face of Christianity, a scar. Moreover, deeply embedded within the fabric of the United Pentecostal/Oneness movement are microscopic strands of the British-Anglo-Israelism triumvirate, a Eurocentric construct of which we learned in section three of this text (Christian Identity Groups). Those fibers often come together, however, and can be viewed without employing any auxiliary apparatuses. For while there are an overwhelming number of African-Americans (and others across the African diaspora) associated with the movement, they are often marginalized, ignored, and subtly encouraged to worship separately. A prominent United Pentecostal Church in Alexandria, Louisiana, is a prime example of this; the leaders organized an outreach church, installing an African-American pastor, within the confines of a predominately African-American community, ostensibly to reach the lost. However, the actual reason for this move—many have concluded (and it can certainly be argued)—was the intolerance of Black cultural religiosity within the main, predominantly Caucasian assembly. There is also the recent case involving an interracial couple, Adam, and Dawn Medina (Dawn is Black, Adam's not), the pastors of New Destiny Apostolic Church in Maplewood, Missouri. They reluctantly defected due to pressure (e.g., often subtle, and occasionally conspicuous racial overtones) from some within the ranks of the United Pentecostal movement. Adam and Dawn renamed their assembly. There are other examples, much too numerous to list within these confines.

Lastly, to the UPCI and other cults within its confederacy that have butchered the scriptures and subsequently led tens of thousands (possibly millions) astray, the following must be reiterated: *solae scriptura*, *solae gratia*, *solae fide*, *solus Christus*, and in *Christus tetelestai*. That is to say, let scripture alone be the source of correct doctrine. Let grace alone be the determining factor of one's salvation. Let faith alone be the source of one's justification. Salvation is by faith in Christ alone, and as a result of his atonement at Calvary, it (i.e., God's plan of salvation) is *tetelestai*, or finished (see John 19:30 and Eph. 2:8–9).

Suggested Readings:

(1) Bass, Diana B. 2006. *Christianity for the Rest of Us*. HarperCollins Publishers.

(2) Beisner, E C.1998. *Jesus Only Churches*. Zondervan Publishing House.

(3) Burgos Jr., Michael R. 2016. *Against Oneness Pentecostalism: An Exegetical-Theological Critique*. Second edition. Church Militant Publications.

(4) Durall, Michael. 2004. *The Almost Church: Redefining Unitarian Universalism for a New Era*. Jenkin Lloyd Jones Press.

(5) Welchel, Tommy, and Griffith, Michelle P. 2013. *True Stories of the Miracles of Azusa Street and Beyond*. Destiny Image Publishers.

(6) Sumrall, Lester. 1982. *The Names of God*. Whitaker House.

(7) Sumrall, Lester. 1982. *The Gifts and Ministries of the Holy Spirit*. Whitaker House.

(8) Bruce, F. F. *Paul Apostle of the Heart Set Free*. The Paternoster Press Ltd. 1977.

(9) Bruce, F. F. 1979. *Peter, Stephen, James and John, Studies in Non-Pauline Christianity*. Paternoster Press, England.

Dr. A.J. Handy, Ph.D.

Section Ten

Rastafarianism

Founding/Brief History

Unlike Abakua, Santeria, Voodoo, and other cults that are the progenies of ancient African religions, Rastafarianism is not a derivative of African customs, per se. Its followers are nonetheless undeniably and unabashedly Afrocentric. Its progenitors, however, are rooted in Jamaica. Although the Jamaican-born Marcus Garvey had, some twenty or so years earlier (around 1915–16), provided and tilled the proverbial soil for the development of the Rastafarian movement, it would not come to fruition until nearly two decades thereafter (1935–36). The alchemy by which Rastafarianism was hatched was social unrest in the major cities of Jamaica (i.e., Kingston, Montego Bay). The tension and dissatisfaction was precipitated by mass unemployment and police harassment. The disadvantaged, however, were emboldened by the historic appointment of Haile Selassie I (formally known as Rastafari Makonnen) as king of Ethiopia. Prophetically, several years prior to his death, Garvey insisted that Black people should focus on Africa, for when a Black man is appointed king or emperor of Ethiopia, Black peoples (those dispersed throughout the Western Hemisphere), he alleged, would shortly be emancipated from White rule. Those who so desired, he continued, would be given passage provided by the emperor to ports of call in Africa. In 1935, Benito Mussolini of Italy ordered his deputies to marshal their forces against Ethiopia's capital, Addis Ababa. Mack

(1999) explained that after being denied military support against the Italian forces in 1936 from the League of Nations, Emperor Haile Selassie I more or less prophesied that those present at the assembly would live to regret their decision. Moreover, as is well documented in the annals of history, two years later in 1938, Mussolini would join forces with Adolf Hitler of Germany to unleash their forces upon the allied powers, plunging them into the second of the world wars. These two events—(1) the crowning of Rastafari Makonnen (as Haile Selassie I) as King of Ethiopia (attended by Indo-Europeans whose progenitors had, at one point or another, previously occupied every nation on the African continent except Ethiopia), and (2) the fulfillment of the emperor's prophecy—left no doubt in the minds and hearts of Black Jamaicans (originally called Xyamaicans) that Emperor Haile Selassie I was, without a shadow of doubt, the chosen one, the Lion of the tribe of Judah, the Messiah. The faithful allege that the two episodes listed above were a fulfillment of prophecy as punctuated in the book of Revelations, chapter seventeen in particular. Lastly, according to Lewis (2005), it was one Leipold Howell who would first espouse the Rastafarian beliefs from 1960 to 1976. Those beliefs expressed doctrines that included the concept that, phenotypically, Black peoples are the actual progeny of the ancient Israelites. However, Erskine (2004) argued that while it was indeed Howell who founded the Rastafarian movement, the founding was nearly thirty years earlier than that determined by Lewis (2005). Erskine (2004) insisted that Howell conducted his initial public gathering concerning Rastafarianism in the winter of 1933 in Jamaica's capital city.

Basic Beliefs and Rituals

The most pivotal tenet of this sect is the belief that Blacks (not only those of Jamaica) throughout the African diaspora are the true Israelites; however, because of their copious sins, God has relegated and delivered them to the oppression of White rule. However, they will, the fundamentalists maintain, eventually be liberated, return to Africa, and exercise hegemony over the White race (Doniger, 1999). The nexus between this belief and redemption, the Rastafarians assert, is the Messiah, Haile Selassie I, because it is he who is the proponent and deliverer of the Black race. The faithful believe that Jesus Christ is the incarnate God, or Jah, as God is commonly known. Moreover, Benedict (2008) reveals that the followers of Rastafarianism are certain that their physical bodies are the dwelling place of Jah. Subsequently, it is unnecessary to resort to a church building or an assembly in order to worship Jah.

Parallels to Orthodox Christianity

Because of the Elizabethan and Anglican Church's influence on the island of Jamaica (for up until August 6, 1962, Jamaica answered to the crown of Britain), the Rastafarians study and refer to the King James Bible. Not unlike orthodox Christians, the Rastafarians embrace many of the social mores and behaviors espoused by the bible. Like Christians, they are to avoid the consumption of alcohol, and adultery and fornication are unacceptable. Paradoxically, the inhalation of genja (marijuana) is a central aspect of the religion; the adherents insist that it increases one's spiritual awareness. The use of marijuana for nonmedicinal purposes, however, does not conform to the Christian quintessence.

Contrasts to Orthodox Christianity

The contrasts between Christianity and Rastafarianism are not quite as dichotomous as the differences between Christianity and those cults steeped in ancient African precepts (i.e., Voodoo, Santeria, Abakua). Fundamentally, there are no potions, profound bewilderments, or blood sacrifices of any kind. Absent is the abject grandiosity and perfectly choreographed drumming that are the hallmarks of Santeria or Voodoo. Nor does Rastafarianism comport with removing spells or unleashing them. It remains a cult, nonetheless, for it introduces polemics, arguments, and antitheses denouncing the deity and lordship of Jesus Christ. Moreover, it assigns lordship to Emperor Haile Selassie I.

The etiology of this biblical dissonance can perhaps be traced to and is deeply rooted in hundreds of years of chattel slavery and its various facets. This etiology is further compounded by a quest for self-actualization and the hierarchy of needs (Maslow, 1976). Herein lie the issues and probable causes or etiologies: Of the millions of African slaves who passed through the Middle Passage en route to distant and foreign lands, most, up until their second or third decade of captivity, could not read nor write the language of their slaveholders. The Haitians, of course, are an exception for they were under French rule in Africa prior to being removed to the French colony of Haiti. Colloquially, they knew the language already. In most instances, even among the Haitians, reading was forbidden. Those who had the audacity to learn were told to interpret the scriptures and the gospels according to the overlords' interpretation. The true meaning of salvation and how to acquire it was, of course, not to be shared—and seemed a waste of time—with those who were considered less than human.

      During the early stages of the nineteenth century, the London-based evangelical group known as Society for the Conversion of Negro Slaves made a bold attempt in 1807 to teach the Bible to the enslaved of the British West Indies. This would, of course, include those of Jamaica, the birthplace of the Rastafarian movement. However, the slaveholders insisted upon a compromise. The Society had to redact portions of the Old Testament—the exodus story in particular—that might have emboldened the slaves to seek their freedom. Approximately 80 to 90 percent of the Old Covenant scriptures were eliminated and half of the New. Scholars and others have colloquially referred to the text as "the Slave Bible." Scriptures such as Gal. 3:28 ("there is neither bond nor free…ye are all one in Christ Jesus") were, of course, eliminated, whereas those scriptures that referred to slavery and appeared to support the institution (that is to say, Eph. 6:5: "Servants be obedient to them that are your masters," Col. 3:22: "Servants, obey in all things your masters," etc.) were not only untouched but heavily exaggerated and enforced. So then, the Rastafarians believe the scriptures to be somewhat true but not holistically inerrant. They've been duped in the past, and now they're understandably skeptical.

The Deity of Emperor Haile Selassie I

In the preceding paragraphs, under the topic Contrasts to Orthodox Christianity, the Rastafarians concepts of Bible scripture were examined; we learned that the followers, unlike the adherents to Christianity, do not believe the scriptures to be without flaw. Rather, the Rastafarians accept the scriptures only as they relate to and promote the deity of Haile Selassie I. Subsequently, when encountering the passages of scriptures that seek to imply and single out Christ as Messiah, the Rastafarians begin their divergence. Unfortunately, the juncture at which they diverge from scripture is the most crucial for they have denied that Jesus Christ is the Messiah, the Christ, the savior of mankind. Rather, the faithful cling to the notion that Haile Selassie I (whom was also known as Ras Tafari) is the Lion of the tribe of Judah, the Root of David, the Messiah. This precept is predicated upon the narratives of Gen. 49:8–10 and Rev. 5:5. Of course, Christians maintain that those scriptures imply that Christ is the Lion of the tribe of Judah. Moreover, if indeed the lineage of King David was constructed to include the Emperor Haile Selassie I, that in and of itself, even when coupled with Selassie's alleged prophecies, would not elevate him to the level of Messiah. Surely the Messiah would embrace and change the lives of all mankind. It is difficult to conceive that the Messiah would regard one's phenotype, position, or life's status. The feats, the lineage, and accomplishments of the great emperor are well documented, but, as far as Messiah and deliverer, he is yet to be substantiated. It is not at all unreasonable to perceive of Selassie as possessing the status of a mere mortal. This conclusion was not arrived at arbitrarily, prejudicially, or without much research. The opposite is true. The emperor's final resting place can be found in Ethiopia's capital city, Addis Ababa.

Jesus Christ's lineage, feats, and accomplishments are also well documented. However, his lineage, feats, and accomplishments, unlike any other, are indisputable. His grave cannot be found in any of the great cities of the world (the Shroud of Turin's examinations notwithstanding)—not in Jerusalem, not in Mecca, not in Egypt, nor anywhere throughout the Fertile Crescent for his final resting place, for all practical purposes, is in heaven at the right hand of God (Acts 7:55–56, Rom. 8:34, Eph. 1:20, and Col. 3:1).

Soteriological Views

While the Rastas, as the faithful are commonly known, believe that Christ was the manifestation of God (Jah), they adamantly contend that it is Haile Selassie I who is the savior, redeemer, deliverer, and Messiah. All true Rastas, they insist, are uncombed; Blacks who comb their hair, they maintain, are legitimizing or ratifying the oppression of the African peoples.

Eschatological Perspectives

The Rastas do not perceive of heaven and hell in the same context as their Protestant Jamaican counterparts conceive the two. According to the Jamaican-born Junique (2004), who at one time lived in an area of the island nation where nearly 75 percent of the inhabitants were Rastafarians, Rastas do not comport with the belief that Jah will assign some people to heaven and others to hell. Conversely, they insist that Ethiopia is the holy land, heaven, the place where all true Rastafarians will go after death. However, death, they contend, is a misnomer for they have concluded that their bodies will undergo a period of adaptation and realignment; theirs, the adherents maintain, will nonetheless remain a physical body, immortal. Their conception of an afterlife, therefore, does not comport with the heaven/hell, second coming, rapture/Armageddon position promulgated by Judeo-Christianity.

Concerns and Implications for the Orthodox Christian

Rastafarianism has not risen to the point where it should be considered an existential threat to Christianity or any of the world's major, more sophisticated religions. It is of little concern. There is no charter, there isn't any ecclesiastical hierarchy or body to answer to, and there's no centralization of authority. They draw heavily from and rely primarily upon *The Holy Piby* (The Black Man's Bible); otherwise, its adherents do not manufacture any periodicals. There are no sufficient chronicles—that is to say, Rastafarianism offers no equivalence to, let's say, Joseph Smith Jr.'s *The Pearl of Great Price*, Jesus's "Sermon on the Mount," Confucius's *The Analects*, or the Hindu's *Bhagavad Gita*. Moreover, unlike the major religions of the world (i.e., Christianity, Mormonism, Islam, Catholicism), there aren't any aggressive, prolific proselytization methods. The cult continues to be popularized, animated, and kept alive only via the urban subculture. It will fade.

As the reader may have noticed, Rastafarianism is not profoundly diabolical, although it remains a cult nonetheless and is therefore to be rejected like those sects that include ancient African religious rituals (that is to say, Santeria, Abakua, Voodoo, and many others). There are, however, probing questions that the fundamentalists must ask themselves; among the most pressing are (1) If Haile Selassie I is their messiah, could he have been ousted by a band of low-ranking, ill-disciplined conscripts and young lieutenants in 1974? (2) If Selassie were truly the messiah, could the eighty-two-year-old be strangled to death, as he was in late summer of 1975? That was, of course, a very sad period; it engendered much grief throughout the globe. For although most around the world thought of him not as divine or anything of the sort, it was his accomplishments and persona that commanded respect. Lastly, (3) would a messiah—not unlike the deity of the Abakua construct—favor one population over all others?

      After the demise of the emperor, many of the disillusioned turned to Catholicism, not the syncretic type amalgamated with Santeria, but the Roman papal brand. Paradoxically, many went to various sects of Protestantism, a large amount to Candomble and Palo. The fundamentalists, of course, remained unperturbed. As of this date, the nearly one million Rastafarians worldwide still await the return of their messiah, Emperor Haile Selassie I.

Suggested Readings:

(1) Ayearst, Morley. *The British West Indies*. New York: New York University Press, 1960.

(2) Brisbane, Robert H. *The Black Vanguard*. Valley Forge, Pennsylvania: Judson Press, 1970.

(3) Gardner, W. J. *History of Jamaica*. London: T. Fisher Unwin, 1909.

(4) Hendriques, Fernando. *Jamaica, Land of Wood, and Water*. London: MacGibbon and Kee, 1957.

(5) Lee, Helene. *The First Rasta, Leonard Howell, and the Rise of Rastafarianism*. Lawrence Hill Books, 2003.

(6) Patterson, William. *The Man Who Cried Genocide*. New York: International Publishers, 1971.

Dr. A.J. Handy, Ph.D.

Section Eleven

Santeria

Founding/Brief History

Much will be discussed in this commentary concerning the papacy's unwitting contribution to the development of the cult Santeria. Also, for the purposes of this account—unless the author specifies differently—the Roman Catholic Church will be thought of as Christian, albeit heterodox. Of the exact date of the founding of this syncretic cult, historians are not specific, nor is Santeria attributed to any particular founder. Kirby (1985), however, argued that those who spoke Yoruba may have arrived in Cuba as chattel slaves as early as 1512 CE. Kirby's analysis is very credible for further research corroborates Kirby's findings.

    A vast number of the Yoruba peoples were taken from their West African homelands of Nigeria and other border nations that share a border with Benin (known as Dahomey before its independence). Many of the Yoruba-speaking peoples were also detained and forced to abandon their homeland of Senegal and its southern border nation of Guinea. The Bantus of Cameroon, Nigeria's eastern neighbor, were also enslaved by Spanish conquistadors and carted off to the sugarcane fields in a new world—Cuba. Many of the Bantus, Yorubas, and others would also disembark at Brazilian ports. The Yorubas and Bantus were treated not unlike the enslaved peoples of former and future voyages within the Middle and Transatlantic passages. They were snatched away from loved ones; they braved the gales of the unforgiving

Atlantic while enduring the inhumane treatment of their captors. Life was uncertain, perilous, and quite existential aboard the Guineamens. The voyage to Cuba would involve brutal and subhuman treatment for the cargo confined on vessels with hardly enough room to fidget. Not unlike sardines in a can, they were crammed into the smallest of spaces. The chattel could be seen wallowing in their feces and in the regurgitation and excrements of others. Stench, flies, and pesky mosquitoes—these all conspired with excessive heat and oppressive humidity to create a proverbial Petri dish aboard the vessels. None were safe for death was not the monopoly of the African phenotypes; crew members also often fell fatally ill during or shortly after some of those voyages. Nonetheless, the shipmasters were determined to document their records with the highest numbers possible. They were, after all, incentivized by their profit motive. Paradoxically, however, the slaves who became ill, frail, and the chattel who appeared unable to continue the odyssey were forced into the abyss of the Atlantic. To escape the crucible that awaited them, many would summarily plunge themselves quietly overboard. The remainder would arrive in Cuba, where a strange phenotype, an unfamiliar speech, and dire circumstances awaited them. Some were reduced from the privileged status of sons and daughters of kings and queens to mere laborers tied to the soil. Nonetheless, all were destined for life in the fields and the torment of harsh and unrelenting taskmasters.

However, unlike the slaves taken further north to, let's say, New Orleans, Tampa, Vicksburg, Jamestown, Charleston, or Galveston, the enslaved peoples of Cuba didn't marginalize or abandon their religious rituals.

Rather, the subjugated peoples, the Lucumi of Cuba, would acculturate many aspects of Romanism and amalgamate several of those precepts with their previous beliefs and practices. The Lucumi (the name indicating all West African slaves in Cuba whose progenitors once communicated in the Yoruba or Bantu languages) saw no sense in abandoning their practice of polytheism when their overlords and Catholic priests, who promulgated monotheism, were paradoxically and unwitting exponents of polytheism. It would appear, for example, to a people predisposed to polytheism that a priest and congregation praying the rosary to the mantra of "Hail, Mary, full of grace, Hail, Mary, full of grace" were in fact invoking the powers of the virgin Mary, equating her to a deity somehow.

      The papacy's position on transubstantiation also played a pivotal role in the development of Santeria. For if one considers the sacraments, the bread and wine, to be the actual blood and body of Christ, then as far as the enslaved peoples were concerned, there couldn't possibly be any offense in sacrificing animals, tasting the blood, and offering it to one or more of the seven main Orishas (gods) of their pantheon. This learning, although misguided, was undoubtedly the catalyst which provided the crescendo to and normalization of the Santeria cult. From the preceding thesis, it is apparent that the nexus between Santeria and many of its practices is Catholicism itself. The roots of Santeria have not ventured far from their source—popery. Subsequently, the Roman Catholic Church must be indicted as being complicit (unwittingly or no) in the development of Santeria. We shall illuminate more of this in our discussion (and comparison with Catholicism) of what is known as the seven main Orishas (for there are many) or Seven African Powers. Such a collation will be delineated under the heading Parallels to Orthodox Christianity.

Basic Beliefs and Rituals

Upon attending a Santeria ceremony, regardless of the occasion, onlookers can expect to see extremely well-choreographed ceremonial dances, props (i.e., plants, animals, or animal fragments), and music, which is almost invariably in the form of drumbeats. Occasionally, however (that is to say, during certain rituals), some of the actions employed can be quite eccentric, if not profoundly bizarre. The particular dance, music, drumbeats, props, and even the attire and colors worn by those invoking the Orishas depend upon which Orisha is being petitioned, for the Orishas are said to have different personalities. In some ceremonies during which a number of Orishas are invoked in succession, paradigm shifts are necessary during the ceremony in order to accommodate the particular desires of the Orisha. For example, Obatala prefers the color white. He can be invoked by displaying yams, pieces of coconuts, and white doves. Chango is satisfied with either white or red. He can be lured with red chickens, bananas, or apples. Yemaya insists upon either blue or white, and he can be appeased by means of hens, cane syrup, or portions of watermelon.

The followers of the Santeria cult purport that the universe is split into two separate and opposing forces: (1) Orishas, or forces that are virtuous and good, and (2) Ajogun, or forces that are volatile or malignant. So, to get an understanding of this cult, it is important to note that the faithful believe that the Orishas are anthropomorphic, viz., they tend to behave like humans and are assigned to control various forces of nature and human interactions. For example, the Orisha Oggun is assigned as the deity of soldiers or warriors; Chango is believed to be involved in the intensity of lightning and thunder. As such, the Orishas are to be propitiated and invoked, the adherents maintain, in order to ward off the forces of Ajogun. The believers also argue that the Orishas can be invoked for other reasons as well. For such reasons as: wealth, healing, the avoidance of hidden dangers, attracting a mate, and so forth. According to Murphy (1988), the main avenues by which the Orishas are approached are through trances, divination, sacrifices, or by an initiation. Because the Orishas are believed to be in control of the many functions of nature, when the Santero (priest) or Santera (priestess) consult the Orisha on behalf of him or herself or on behalf of another, they are poised and prepared to offer the Orisha its desired offering. The greater the petition, the greater the offering must be. Aside from the offering, onlookers (if they are allowed) will notice several plants, herbs, and spices; the practitioners assert that these will facilitate the arrival of the Orisha. Each Santero/Santera can only invoke the Orisha into whose order he or she was initiated, that is to say, one initiated into the order of Obatala, for example, can only invoke Obatala; the initiates of Oshun invoke Oshun, and so forth.

Parallels to Orthodox Christianity

Aside from the fact that both orthodox Christianity and Santeria champion a higher power and both promulgate that God is omnipotent, omnipresent, and omniscient, there are few other explicit resemblances. One of those few explicit resemblances is the fact that the cult Santeria (vis-à-vis its pantheon of deities) is actually monotheistic. It would be a faulty comparison, and subsequent inaccuracies would arise to attempt to conceptualize this concept (monotheistic but yet paying homage to other deities) in the context of the Christian tradition. In Christianity, it is asserted that God the Father, God the Son, and God the Holy Ghost are just that—one and the same (Deut. 6:4, 14–15 and Mark 12:29). In the Santeria/Yoruba pantheon, however, this is not so. For, as the table below delineates, Oloddumare/God and the lesser deities or Orishas are all separate and distinct entities. They are also all identified with, and share the role of, one or more of the Catholic saints, or Jesus Christ. The practitioners of this cult purport that while the Orishas are paid homage to, it is God only, known as Oloddumare, who is to be worshipped. Oloddumare, they allege, is not only the creator of all the universe, but the creator of all the Orishas as well. This universe creator is said to have endowed the Orishas with certain powers; for example: even though Oloddumare is alleged to be the creator of the Universe, the deity Obatala – as noted in section four of the following table - is given the authority to create human bodies. After being created the bodies are believed to be animated by Oloddumare. Let's be clear; such beliefs, and practices does not lend themselves to the liturgy, and convictions of the Papacy. Nevertheless, Santeria does, because of its incorporation of papal icons and Catholic saints, share many similarities with heterodox Catholicism. The table below codifies and reveals how the seven main African powers and Catholicism are, as they relate to venerations and deities, interrelated. The Catholics saints are venerated and will have a *V* located prior to their name; the deified Christ is annotated with the letter *D*. All the Santeria and Yoruba spirit entities are considered deified. The reader will also notice under the middle column of the table (Function) that the Catholic saint(s) with whom the Santeria deity is associated or syncretized is given that deity's power and authority. For example, as shown in section two (2) of the table, Oggun is Santeria's warrior deity who watches over soldiers; so too, is the function of St. Peter and Joan of Arc. As can be imagined—although it will be of no surprise to born again Christians—there are a plethora of differences between the Santeria cult and Orthodox Christianity. In the section which follows the table, Contrasts to Orthodox Christianity, we shall examine some of the more poignant of those distinctions.

Venerated/Catholicism___Function___ Deified/Santeria

(1) (V) St. Camillus de Lellis---Care of the sick------------Babalu-Aye
    (V) St. Lazarus

(2) (V) Joan of Arc-------------Watches over soldiers-------------Oggun
    (V) St. Peter

(3) (V) Virgin Mary,---Communicates with the Orishas--Olurun/Eshu
    (D) Christ,
    (V) St. Anthony of Padua

(4) (D) Christ-----------------Creator of humans-----------Obatala/Olofi

(5) (V) St. Monica--------Watches over motherhood-----------Yemaya
    (V) St. Gerard

(V) Our Lady of Regla	
(6) (V) St. Dwynwen-----Sensual love, wealth, marriages-------Oshun (V) St. Valentine	
(7) (V) St. Barbara-------Controls thunder and lightning--------Chango	

Table 1. The relationship between the seven main African powers and Catholicism.

Contrasts to Orthodox Christianity

Blood Sacrifices and Offerings

The dichotomies that exist between Christianity and Santeria are enormous and extremely profound; indeed of all the cults/sects examined in this inquiry, Santeria—as far as its contrast to Christianity is concerned—can only be rivaled by the art of Voodoo, another derivative of ancient African rituals. Moreover, as has been explored elsewhere in this corpus, blood sacrifices and offerings play an essential role in the religion of Santeria for blood sacrifices are often used as a propitiation to the Orishas when the petitions are major. The blood sacrifice could be selected from, let's say, among one's backyard chickens or even from a cattle ranch. The sacrifice that's offered depends upon the value of the petition or what's at stake. This concept (i.e., blood sacrifices and offerings) may have been adopted from the papacy's doctrine of transubstantiation, the belief that the Eucharist is actually the blood and body of Christ. This is not orthodoxy. Rather, in orthodox Christianity, the Eucharist is only symbolic.

Moreover, blood sacrifices and offerings as avenues of propitiations have no place and are not recognized in traditional Christianity. For Christians believe that as Jesus mumbled (a result of much excruciating pain at Golgotha), all sacrifices, including blood, for sins were supplanted by or finished with the atoning blood of Christ (John 19:30). See also Heb. 7:27, 9:14, 10:5, 10, 12, 26, 13:12, 1 Pet. 1:2, 18–19, and 1 John 1:7.

Divination (Diloggun) and Exorcism

The acts of divinations and exorcism do not comport with the practices or the liturgy of orthodox Protestantism. Nonetheless, they are long-held religious traditions of the Lucumi ethos. These traditions were conceived and cultivated long before the transatlantic slave trade. They would distill, however, in their new land. The practices were sustained by secretly combining them with aspects of popery. The Lucumi's best practices of divination is the arrangement of the seashells. It is from this, many insist, that fortune or misfortune can be foretold.

Christianity in its orthodox status, however, does not lend itself or its practices or liturgy to occultism for its practices are the very antithesis of divination. Orthodox Christianity, therefore, is not recognized by members of the occult; hence, its tenets are of no value to those who dabble in the occult. Christian orthodoxy and occultism cannot be syncretized with one another. The former denounces all aspects of occultism, divinations, and oracles. Occultism, reciprocally, offers no value to orthodox Christianity. The two are diametrically opposed.

The Bible offers a plethora of scriptures warning of the dangers and consequences of dabbling in the dark world of divination. These deterrents that the Bible explains concerning divination—consorting with soothsayers and those with familiar spirits—were addressed in our discussion of Mormonism. Therefore, no attempt will be made at this point in the corpus to elaborate on them. However, because of the diabolical nature of the Santeria cult, it is necessary at this juncture to reiterate, albeit briefly.

Scriptures that Warn against Divination:

(1) Lev. 19:31 reminds us to "Regard not them that have familiar spirits, neither seek after wizards."

(2) Deut. 18:10 commands, "There shall not be found among you...that useth divination...or an enchanter."

(3) 1 Chron. 10:13 reminds us that "Saul died for his transgressions which he committed...even against the word of the Lord...for asking counsel of one that had a familiar spirit."

(4) 2 Chron. 33:6 cautions us with the narrative, "He caused his children to pass through the fire...and used enchantments...and dealt with a familiar spirit...to provoke him to anger."

(5) Turning our attention to the New Testament we find Acts 8:9. It reminds us that "a certain man called Simon...used sorcery, and bewitched the people of Samaria."

(6) Finally, Gal. 3:1 is quite revealing. In his diatribe (Gal. 3:1–5) the Apostle Paul asked the question, "Who hath bewitched you, that ye should not obey the truth?"

The commanding of demons by Jesus and his

followers to release the possessed or to flee from an area was not considered to be an act of exorcism. Rather, it was a display of the power of the name Jesus, or *solus Christus*. Before we explore the etymology of the term "exorcism," we shall remind ourselves that Jesus insisted after his resurrection, "All power is given unto me [him] in heaven and in earth" (Matt. 28:18, emphasis added). Subsequently, when demons were commanded, they obeyed. This obedience was either due to Jesus's presence or as a result of his name being employed by his followers. When the name of Jesus or Christ is presented by the truly born again, no crosses, props, or prerequisites are necessary to acquire the devil's attention. None will argue that perhaps the most telling exemplification of this is found in Matt. 10:1, 5–10. The alert reader will notice that in verses nine and ten, the disciples, unlike those who practice divination, are commanded to avoid carrying any ancillary or supplementary devices on their journeys. Hence, all that was required to accomplish their tasks (healing the sick, raising the dead, casting out demons, etc.) was the name Jesus, or Christ. Those who insist that the power/*dunamis* (authority) to cast out demons, heal the sick, etc., was only given by Jesus to the original twelve disciples will have to decide how to suppress, ignore, and devalue Luke's prose as outlined in Luke 10:1, 4, 9, 17. A Herculean task.

    The term "exorcist" is translated from the Greek lexicon as *exorkismos*. It connotes a person who casts out demons by using formulas or incantations. However, after searching the New Testament, we find no episodes in which the Devil was cast out by followers of Christ employing incantations, mantras, etc. The following is a list of scriptures by which this premise and *solus Christus* (salvation by faith in Christ alone) have nexus: Matt. 8:28–33, Mark 1:23–27, Acts 5:15–16, 16:16–18, 19:11–12. Now, after considering those scriptures, the reader is advised to compare them to Acts 19:1–16. That was an episode in which several unsaved persons (exorcists or otherwise) could not command the Devil for they lacked the born again experience. For many (the uninitiated in particular), the mere thought of a person possessing power, or *dunamis*, greater than that of Satan is inconceivable. The scriptures assure those who are born again, however, that "greater is he that is in you, than he that is in the world" (1 John 4:4). See also John 14:12.

Priests and High Priests

The premise or concept of priesthood as it is currently touted and practiced in the Santeria religion evolved as a result of the Yoruba contact with and observance of the traditions of the popery. It was not totally novel for a resemblance of it was ritualized in Nigeria and its border states prior to the transatlantic slave trade. The Yoruba observed and learned that the Catholic Church employed many priests and that there was one priest to whom they were all accountable, the pope. Subsequently, in the Yoruba tradition, the pope's position was akin to that of a high priest. This presented the opportunity for the enslaved to disguise their practices by incorporating them with Catholicism. As has been explained elsewhere in this volume, the papacy's unwitting contributions were instrumental in fashioning Santeria into the form that it so proudly flaunts today.

The priesthood, however, as it is conceptualized by the adherents of Santeria and Romanism, is incongruent with Christian orthodoxy. Rather, Protestantism aligns with the concept of the priesthood of the believer, for Jesus's last words gasped on Mt. Calvary as he anguished there, covered with blood, were three: "It is finished." This indicated that, among other things, after him there would be no other priests in or of themselves. However, being redeemed by Christ, the believer has the royal priesthood of Christ within. 1 Peter 2:5–9 and Rev. 5:10 elucidate this view perfectly. See also Heb. 7:11–28, 8:1–5.

Reincarnation

Gonzalez-Wipper (2001) remarked that the initiates of the Santeria/Lucumi tradition are convinced that humans are born (predestined) to accomplish specific duties or tasks. The faithful in Panama City, Panama, with whom the author has discussed this topic were initially somewhat reluctant to converse about reincarnation, predestination, and other aspects of the cult. After the author won their trust, however, some shared their insights, and the details that they revealed corroborate Gonzalez-Wipper's thesis. They also shared their belief that if death arrives prior to the accomplishment of those predetermined duties, the individual must be reincarnated until those chores are completed. This concept is much like the Buddhist and Hindu premise of samsara whereby one experiences cycles of reincarnation until finally being released from desire, which is, allegedly, the cause of suffering. This, of course, is foreign to Christian orthodoxy. For further awareness concerning the orthodox Christian's antithesis to reincarnation, see section two, Buddhism, and section five, Hinduism.

Pantheon

Contrary to Santeria's stance and belief concerning a conglomerate of deities, Christianity (e.g., Protestants and Catholics) recognizes only one God—hence a monotheistic concept. Orthodox Christians maintain that the idea of the Trinity (i.e., God the Father, God the Son, and God the Holy Ghost) is not a misnomer or contradiction but that the three are all one. Matt. 3:16–17 and John 1:1–2 are very telling.

Surreptitiousness

The intricacies of Santeria are heavily guarded and veiled with secrecy. That which is written on the subject is almost invariably told by Westerners who, although they may have obtained high status within the cult, are almost without exception lacking cultural familiarity. Westerners who have adopted Santeria may have been sold a more benevolent form of the cult. The Yoruba themselves (perhaps those who have denounced Santeria and converted to Christianity) can reveal the true idiosyncrasies of the Santeria sect. They've lived it. As pertaining to secrecy, however, it is as though many of the adherents of Santeria are either not sure of its veracity or they regret having adopted it. The cult leaders' apprehension to discuss the religion could possibly be based in the premise of nonacceptance. More plausible conjecture, however, is that the leaders realize that the cult is diabolical in nature. Subsequently, when juxtaposed with more sophisticated religions such as: Christianity, Islam, or Mormonism, its inferiority is clearly exposed.

Christianity, however, is well promulgated far beyond western shores; contrary to the Santeria cult, Christians do not desire a clandestine form of worship. Instead, Christians are mandated to ensure that the doctrine of Christ remains ubiquitous (See Matt. 28:19–20). Christianity can even be found in the most unlikely domains: North Korea, mainland China, Yemen, the squares of old Havana, etc. Even in Haiti and its contiguous Dominican Republic, where Voodoo is the champion, Christianity is there. It's in Nigeria itself, the Lucumi's former homeland. Because of the Christian's Great Commission (Matt. 28:19–20), it can be found at the far reaches of the globe. Pursuant to the Protestant ethos and its blueprint, the Bible, the faithful are well aware from the examples given in scripture that Christianity will not be accepted by all. Nonetheless, being true to the creed, the faithful continue to evangelize, preach, teach, write, publish, and deploy missionaries to the most unwelcoming enclaves on the globe. Why such measures and risks? Because the gospel is true, it crosses all cultural, social, and economic demarcations; there is no nepotism, nor are there any forced confessions or total submission (as in the Islamic context). One can accept or reject the gospel by his or her own volition. The evangelist or missionary will not be offended. One of Christianity's greatest appeals is that when one accepts the persuasion, no offerings or propitiations are required. There is no baggage or props to bring, no mantras or chants to exude—such are not required. *Solus Christus* (faith in Christ alone) is the nexus between God and mankind. The prolific Apostle John explains in 1 John 2:2 that Christ has already propitiated for our sins. Hence, one's works, altruism, or theological or academic prowess can never supplant the atonement of Christ (see Rom. 3:24–27, Eph. 2:8). Moreover, for the true Christians, not the mere professors, there is of necessity the born again experience, an inexplicable, transforming experience akin to none other (see John 3:3–7). Moreover, unlike the Santeros, Santeras, and Babalawos (high priests, traditionally men) who officiate during Santeria rituals, the bishops, evangelists, pastors, and others who officiate during Christian worship do not wish to disguise their practices. Quite the contrary. Indeed, the renowned, ubiquitous Apostle Paul vociferously pontificated that he was not ashamed of the gospel (see Rom. 1:16).

Soteriological Views

Initiation into the Santeria cult is utterly profound; a ceremony known as Asiento is held during which time the Orisha enters the individual, and positions or seats itself in the head of the worshipper. At that moment, a bonding process is said to take place; subsequently, there is a rebirth of the neophyte. This rebirth is known among the faithful as salvation, or "making the saint." During this process, one is initiated into one of the orders of the Orishas (i.e., Eleggua, Chango, Obatala, etc.). After the confirmation, the devotee is said to have received *ashe* (the power to affect change). There is also a mutual devotion or symbiotic relationship between the convert and the Orisha. The individual is obligated to the Orisha; reciprocally, the Orisha looks after the person forever. After making the saint, he or she is known as either a Santera (female) or a Santero (male). Many of the nonconformists are persuaded that it is possible to proceed and make the saint in other Orisha orders as well.

Eschatological Perspectives

The Lucumi, or followers of Santeria, do not recognize a heaven or hell (that is to say, not as the two are acknowledged within the Christian ethos). Rather, they are of the belief that after death their *ashe* (life force/ability to affect change), which was received after making the saint, does not simply die. The *ashe* is believed to be repositioned and recycled back into the universe. The body, then, after death, becomes insignificant. It has no value. The deceased is now called an *egun*, a spirit that lives on. Their spirits are believed to offer guidance and warnings to surviving family members. The faithful maintain that these spirits must be fed, entertained, and conversed with as though they were still alive. The fundamentalists will position a table within the home on which are placed foodstuffs, perhaps the deceased's favorite drink, dessert, or meal. Articles of clothing formerly worn by the deceased are also placed on or near the table.

Concerns and Implications for the Orthodox Christian

Many African-Americans, Canadians of African descent, the progenies of the Windrush Generation (Blacks who migrated to Great Britain from the British tributaries in the Caribbean), and Africans across the diaspora have been erroneously convinced that the practices of Santeria, Candomble, Abakua, and other religions rooted in African traditions are means of regaining or connecting with their African culture. Very few assumptions can be further from the truth. Like all other populations, African peoples have never been monolithic—religiously, culturally, socially, or otherwise. Africa is a vast continent with some fifty-four countries; there are a mixture of over two thousand languages and dialects. It would be nonsensical, therefore, to assume that one's phenotype is a nexus that ties him or her to a particular religion, albeit heavily rooted in and transported from African traditions. One should also remain cognizant of the fact that Christianity, Islam, and Zoroastrianism all flourished on the subcontinent of Africa centuries prior to the advent of the transatlantic slave trade. This fact alone belies the notion that Africans across the diaspora can only truly relate to religions rooted in African rituals (i.e., Santeria, Voodoo, Abakua, etc.). Nonetheless, many have continued to chuckle and say, "But Christianity is not a Black man's religion." That, too, despite the language and contextual curvatures of Rogers's (1924) work, *The Holy Piby*, has been painstakingly denuded and proven false. Rogers's work is quite interesting and is widely read, however. Nevertheless, even though phenotypes, race, and God-given gender types are insignificant, there are those—whether Black, White, Hispanic, or otherwise—who continue to insists that Jesus Christ, to put it colloquially, "looks just like them." Even the learned, prolific scholar and author W. E. B. Du Bois (1980), in his short work titled *Prayers For Dark People*, is uncharacteristically ethnocentric (I've read all his non-fiction works). He implies that dark people are the reflection of God. However, as explained through a plethora of scriptures throughout the Bible, neither genotype nor one's outward appearance can be considered as a condition for salvation. The Apostle Paul pontificates this unequivocally in his rendering to the Galatians (3:28). Jesus's hypostatic union was not meant to simply court and save a specific group of people. Rather, the revelation of himself to mankind as simultaneously "fully God and fully man" was so that he might position himself to understand human infirmities, temptations, and imperfections (see Heb. 4:15). Subsequently, he was worthy of becoming a ransom for many, not just a few (see Matt. 20:28 and Heb. 2:9). As concerning the skeptics who continue to cling to and promulgate the narrative that Christianity is not a Black person's religion, it is advisable to view Christianity not only from a purely biblical perspective, but to some degree through ethnological lenses as well. Some Christians, of course, will disagree with this premise; that's because they're "all in" (that is to say, they adhere to the gospel), or so they allege. The naysayers, of course, make no such assertions; therefore, it is incumbent upon evangelists, missionaries, and pastors to point them in the right direction. That direction may sometimes mean a requisite history lesson along with, and perhaps initially in lieu of, the Bible. As a Christian, one must not think it inappropriate to court the unsaved. Rather, the zealots and sanctimonious should remain cognizant of the fact that at some point in their lives they, too, were in the very throes of Satan. Jesus explains this practice in the gospel according to Mark 2:15–17: "As Jesus sat at meat in his house, many…sinners sat also together with Jesus…for there were many, and they followed him…when the…Pharisees saw him eat with publicans and sinners, they said…'How is it that he eateth and drinketh with…sinners?' Jesus…saith unto them, 'They that are whole have no need of the physician, but they that are sick.'"

Structural constraints will betray us, and it would certainly make for a separate volume to elaborate upon the events of the Hebrews and Israelites of the Old Testament (e.g., Moses, Abraham, Isaac, Jacob, the Queen of Sheba, Esther, Ruth, and their progenies) who were Black people (Windsor, 2003). Moreover, from many of the aforementioned patriarchs and matriarchs would come the birth of Jesus Christ. One can also rightly conclude—if preconceived ideas can be momentarily silenced and the mind kept slightly ajar—from the book *From Babylon to Timbuktu* (Windsor, 2003) that the reason why Moses's siblings (who, along with Moses, were phenotypically and unmistakably Black) disapproved of his marriage to the Ethiopian woman (Num. 12:1) was not because they (e.g., Moses, Miriam, and Aaron) were of a White race and the bride Black. After tracing the lineage of both groups, it becomes quite evident, however, that they objected to the union because the Ethiopian woman was of a different culture than theirs. As alluded to elsewhere in this corpus, those of the African continent have always been diverse culturally, ethnically, linguistically, and in all other areas. So if one is of African ancestry and thinks himself or herself to be Gentile, think again, for such a nomenclature could possibly be false. Perhaps (and it will take a bit of research) a more accurate description would be that such a person is Jewish. Again, one would have to investigate for with investigation, we find solid evidence; without investigating, we're left to settle for and flounder in mere ignorance predicated upon conjecture, guesswork, and speculation. Moreover, Windsor (2003) argued that there were Black Jews in Jerusalem as far back as at least the year 331 BCE when Alexander the Great attacked the

Persian Empire. Windsor also explained that these Black Jews fled Jerusalem to escape persecution and settled in portions of North Africa (i.e., Egypt, Libya, and Ethiopia).

We shall now leap forward approximately fifteen hundred years into the New Covenant, exploring episodes, geography, conditions, and circumstances that may dispel the notion often harbored among many across the African diaspora that Christianity is specifically a White person's religion. The reader is now encouraged to follow the narrative's logos ethnologically, that is to say, try to investigate the backgrounds of those who were there in Jerusalem on the day of Pentecost. For it was on the day of Pentecost that Christianity or the church (the body of believers) had its infancy. Now, from a preponderance of biblical evidence along with other sources, the author shall show undeniable proof that there was at least one person (although there were many) who was not phenotypically Caucasoid attending the Shavuot, or Pentecost, festival.

During Pentecost, ten days after Jesus ascended into heaven (for he was with his disciples for forty days after his resurrection, Acts 1:3), there was a great ten-day gathering in Jerusalem. This congregation was not far from Mt. Calvary (the place of Jesus's crucifixion). When reading Acts 2:7–11, one will notice that there were in Jerusalem during the "birth of the church" Jews and illustrious or devout men. The scripture tells us that these men were "out of every nation under heaven" (Acts 2:5). Among those nations or areas listed were Egypt, Libya, Cyrene (an area of Libya), and Arabia. The inhabitants of those areas—particularly Egypt, Libya, and Cyrene— were (vis-à-vis their phenotypical differences) predominantly and descriptively Black.

Luke's prose (Acts 8:26–39) concerning the steward of Queen Candace of the Ethiopians is also quite telling. Hopefully, the information provided in the preceding narratives will help to resolve any enigma of whether Black people should be associated with Christianity. Note, however, that God (Yahweh/Jehovah) is not concerned with one's phenotype, ethnicity, nor background. *Sola fide*, or faith alone, matters. Nothing else.

Those who will continue to harbor the question of whether Blacks have a role in Christianity (and many will despite the plethora of information and circumstances that suggest that they most certainly do) should consider reflecting upon the works of post first-century Black theologians, those who appeared hundreds of years prior to the arrival of Luther, Jerome, Huss, Wycliffe, and the Reformation era. Bishop Cyprian of Carthage (North Africa) was one such theologian. It was he who, among other feats, would lead his flock through the prosecutorial period of Emperor Decius (250 CE). For not unlike the prophet Daniel (ch. 6) and those who we refer to as the Three Hebrew Boys, or Shadrach, Meshach, and Abednego (Dan. 3), Cyprian refused to obey the emperor's edict, an edict that insisted that the subjects pay homage to gods other than Jehovah. As it is with all faithful people of God, his position was *soli Deo gloria*, or "glory to God alone." Sadly, however, martyrdom would await him.

This narrative would be demonstratively unacceptable without at least briefly mentioning the venerable St. Augustine (Aurelius Augustinus Hipponensis) and the sage's brilliant and captivating prose (i.e., *City of God* (426 CE), *Confessions* (399 CE), *On Christian Doctrine* (397–426 CE). While his works are not quite as copious as some others, Augustine's *City of God* is not at all lightweight. This Black theologian from North Africa had arguably the greatest influence on Christianity (other than, of course, the Bible itself) than any other volumes ever written (as it relates to repentance, Augustine's *Confessions*, in particular). They're a rare breed who, after reading the ubiquitous, acclaimed, and highly sought-after *Confessions*, do not come away from it for the better. *Confessions* is likely to bring even the most pious to tears and could easily prompt repentance. Conversely, Clement of Alexandria's *Stromata* and *Christ the Educator*, St. Jerome's *Against Jovinianus* and *Dialogue against The Luciferians*, and Martin Luther's *Ninety-Five Theses* are all great media. However, when critically analyzed, many biblical theologians will agree that those works flounder in inferiority when juxtaposed with the exquisite and heartfelt prose of Augustine.

      Consider, also, Athanasius of Alexandria (Egypt), who was extremely instrumental in the decision-making process at the Nicean Council (CE 325). And one mustn't discount or ignore the sage Origen of Alexandria (Egypt), who, even though he maintained a position of modalism (The belief that the Son/Jesus and the Holy Ghost are not distinct persons but only aspects of God) concerning the triune Godhead, was quite a prolific writer. He highly promoted Christianity in many of his works, the most notable of which is arguably *On First Principles*. Lastly (for it would certainly make for a separate volume to laud the many others), we mustn't be remiss and terminate this topic without at least briefly mentioning Tertullian of Carthage (Tunisia). This sage was one of the premier, quintessential, and highly celebrated writers of Christian literature of his day. Time and confines would betray us if we attempted to elaborate upon the feats of Polycarp (Bishop of Smyrna), the Apostle Peter and his brother Andrew, Judas Iscariot, St. Benedict the Moor, and the plethora of other early Black Christian leaders. Catholics, for the most part, tend to be cognizant of the works of these celebrated men; my fellow Protestants, I regret, are almost invariably not so well informed, for busying themselves with erroneously vilifying and indicting the Catholic Church as the etiology of all the sins of the world, Protestants have neglected to teach early church history. Lastly, those across the African diaspora who have adamantly concluded that Christianity is not a Black person's religion should seriously consider sending misconceptions, stereotypes, and confirmation biases into retirement and giving the Black theologians mentioned in this volume further review.

Suggested Readings:

(1) Andrews, George R., 2004. *Afro-Latin America*, 1800-2000. New York, NY. Oxford University Press.

(2) Apter, Andrew, 1992. *Black Critics and Kings, the Hermeneutics of Power In Yoruba Society*. Chicago: University of Chicago Press.

(3) Barnes, Sandra T., 1989. *Africa's Ogun, Old World and New*. Bloomington, Indiana. Indiana University Press.

(4) Beliso-De Jesus, Aisha M., 2015. *Electric Santeria, Racial and Sexual Assemblages of Transnational Religion*. Columbia University Press, New York.

(5) Berger, Peter L., 1967, 1990. *The Sacred Canopy, Elements of a Sociological Theory of Religion*. New York: Anchor Books.

(6) Carr, C. Lynn. 2015. *A Year in White, Cultural Newcomers to Lukumi in the United States*. Rutgers University Press, New Brunswick, New Jersey, and London.

(7) Chang, Heewon. 2008. *Autoethnography as Method*. Walnut Creek, California. Left Press.

(8) Farrow, Stephen S., 1926. *Faith Fancies and Fetish; or Yoruba Paganism*. London Society for Promoting Christian Knowledge.

(9) Handy, Adam J., 2019. *Comprehending the Pauline Epistles, A Study Guide*. Lighthouse Publishing, Buford, Ga.

(10) McClelland, E.M., 1982. *The Cult of Ifa among the Yoruba*. Volume 1. London: Ethnographica.

(11) Prince, Raymond. 1996. *Ifa: Yoruba*

Divination and Sacrifice. Ibadan: I badan University Press.

(12) Thomas, Robert Farris., 1976. *Black Gods and Kings*. Bloomington: Indiana Press.

(13) Wenger, Susanne, and Chesi, Gert., 1983. *A Life with the Gods: In Their Yoruba Homeland*. Worgl: Perlinger.

Dr. A.J. Handy, Ph.D.

Section Twelve

Voodoo (Vodou) (Vodun—West Africa, Vodou—Haiti, Voodoo— Louisiana)

Founding/Brief History

There are several brands and splinter sects of the Voodoo cult; it is best, therefore, as with any exegesis, to explicate the founding of this cult from the position of those who were its first practitioners. Therefore, this narrative is intended to portray the cult from the Dahomey and Haitian perspective. This cult is believed to have originated in the West African kingdom of Dahomey during the eighteenth century, the country now known as Benin since the French withdrew its occupation and granted its subjects independence in 1960. The odysseys and calamities experienced by the Dahomeian/Fon peoples while they were forced to embark upon their journey as chattel to the Middle Passage and finally to Haiti can be seen as a duplicate of that braved by the Yoruba (mostly Nigerians) who were shackled, branded, carted off to Cuba, and paraded - to the delight and anticipation of the bidders - to the auction blocks. Not unlike the merchants who displaced the Yoruba and brought them to Cuba, the shipmasters bound for Haiti would hoist Spain's ensign. For further insight concerning the calamities while aboard the Guineamens, refer to section eleven, Santeria (Founding/Brief History).

For several years and periodically after the arrival of the slaves to Haiti, the island was devoid of papal influence and European clergy. According to Nichols, et al. (2006), to fill the vacuum, the pope signed an agreement in 1860 that allowed Haiti to have presbyters who commanded the French language. By that time, however, the Dahomeyan people were far along in the continuation of their native rituals. However, not unlike Santeria, which is often misidentified as Voodoo, this cult borrows much from and is syncretic with Catholicism, for in accordance with the beliefs of Catholics, in Voodoo the Supreme Being is the Judeo-Christian God Jehovah. There is a caveat, though. The caveat is that Jehovah is known as Bondye. Moreover, as of this date (Nov. 2020), because of Haiti's close proximity to the U.S. and the papacy's ubiquitous influence, a great majority of Haitians identify as Roman Catholics. A large portion—nearly 30 percent—subscribe to a form of Protestantism. Most, however, are not exclusively Catholic nor Protestant, for clandestinely they dabble in Voodoo. In fact, Tann (2012) reveals on page three of the introduction that the practice of Voodoo is endemic within the culture of the Haitian populous even though there are many who do not practice the craft. Tann, who is also known as Tamara L. Siuda, also insists that it is not unusual for applicants who are secluded within the *djevo* (a room where those seeking initiation into the Voodoo cult are lodged) to venture out of seclusion to attend Mass.

Basic Beliefs and Rituals

Deeply ingrained within the psyche of Voodoo practitioners is the belief that man's soul is dualistic, performing two functions: (1) those of the Gros bon Ange, and (2) those of the Petit bon Ange (Nichols, et. al. 2006). The Gros bon Ange is said to be the big (hence the term *gros*) good angel or guardian. It is asserted that all of one's basic life functions (i.e., heart rate, pulse rate, blood flow, etc.) are reliant upon this aspect of the soul. The Hungans and Mambos, male priests, and female priestesses respectively, maintain that once a person enters or falls into a deep sleep, the Gros bon Ange is not static. Rather, it is at this time during sleep that this soul is at liberty to leave the body. If the Gros bon Ange does not return to the individual, death is said to have occurred. The practitioners declare that the Gros bon Ange remains in close proximity of the corpse until such time as the Hungan or Mambo disposes of it. The Petit bon Ange is alleged to be the little (hence the term *petit* or small) good angel, or guardian. This lesser of the two souls does not provide for biological functioning; however, it is alleged that the Petit bon Ange gives personality to the individual. The priests and priestesses assert that, in most instances, after death the Petit bon Ange must be captured and placed into a container. The followers maintain that this will prevent it from acting out or harming estranged and neglectful relatives. These ceremonies are normally performed in the gloom of darkness at night.

  Abakua has its Famba, Santeria its altar, and Voodoo has its temple around which all worship and ceremonies takes place. Upon attending a Voodoo ceremony, one can expect to witness a decorative pole in the middle (Poteau-Mitan) of the temple. The Poteau-Mitan will be embellished with icons such as pictures of the Virgin Mary, Jesus, crosses, etc. This pole in the middle, as the Poteau-Mitan is often termed, is considered to be the point of attention in Voodoo ceremonies. For it is there, the adherents maintain, that the Loas (gods) will begin to reveal themselves to the individuals. Ritual sacrifices, including drumming and dances, are pivotal aspect of any Voodoo ceremony; these are conducted near the pole in the center of the temple. On the floor of the temple, one will notice a plethora of Vevers. These drawings or designs formed by sprinkling cornmeal or flour on the floor and creating a peristyle are placed there to attract the attention of one or more of the gods within the Voodoo pantheon. In this respect, Voodoo is much like Santeria, for the adherents of Santeria invoke the presence of their gods through food, drinks, or by the colors of the drawings. There is a Vever for each Loa in the Voodoo collections of gods, although all are not necessarily employed in every ceremony. Blood sacrifices are performed, and food items are offered and displayed on the Vever(s) to the Loa(s) that are being invoked. Also, not unlike the gods of the Santeria pantheon, the gods of the Voodoo cult allegedly possess personality traits, proclivities, and wants and needs which must be catered to. If these needs are not seen to, the Loas are said to become very hostile, agitated, and will often have a conniption.

    Voodoo is said to be a form of magic, with good magic and bad. Even though prima facie all of Voodoo's tenets appear to be "bad" magic, the Hungans and Mambos are alleged to be the practitioners of the good (that is to say, healing, prosperity, attracting a mate, etc.). Any Voodooist, however, can practice good or bad magic. To realize their goals, they employ a form of divination known as a Wanga; this is a puppet or doll which is stuffed with various items. These items and substances are carefully amalgamated and placed in the appropriate area in order to accomplish the Voodooist's desired outcome.

Unlike the Hungans and Mambos, who primarily practice what the faithful term good magic, the Caplata (Bokor) is known for the workings of evil. To accomplish his or her goals, a Wanga can be used; however, the Paquet, another method of divination, is said to be the Bokor's favorite tool. The Paquet is simply a compilation of various constituents such as soil, chicken heads or feet, herbs, apple skins, etc., which are all folded in a cloth and embellished with colorful cords or string. The feathers of a chicken or bird are usually attached. When the Paquet is presented to the Loas (gods), the Voodooist employs esoteric potions, mantras, and incantations to usher death or harm upon an individual. There is a plethora of diabolical elements within the repertoire of this cult; all, not even a fifth, of them cannot be delineated within this narrative. A separate volume would be necessary. However, one, the Anvwa Mo, in particular (arguably the most diabolical) will be delineated within the parameters of this corpus.

The most feared tactic within the repertoire of Voodooism is believed to be the Anvwa Mo, translated "sending the dead." During this ritual, the client goes before a priest (Hungan) or priestess (Mambo) to seek the death of someone. The priest/priestess goes into a trance and is possessed by the deity Baron Samedi. He is said to be the caretaker or guardian of cemeteries. Allegedly, he gives directions to the client via the Mambo or Hungan. Subsequently, the customer is told to visit a cemetery, normally around midnight, with certain food items. Upon arrival, he or she is to scoop up a certain amount of soil, usually about a handful, for each individual who is to be killed. After this, the soil is spread along a trail or path frequented by his or her targeted individual(s). Or, in lieu of gathering soil from the graveyard, the patron is advised to locate a stone within the confines of the graveyard, which will transform itself into an evil spirit. The customer is instructed to launch this missile against the doorway of the victim's dwelling; the victim will slowly become extremely emaciated, adopt an abnormal gait (usually a shuffle), experience episodes of rapid breathing, exude blood from one or more of the portals, and lose stamina.

The victims, once they become symptomatic with two or more of those incessant comorbidities (i.e., lack of stamina, rapid breathing,), realize that they've been hexed. They must now seek for a reputable Hungan or Mambo who can relieve him or her of the deleterious and existential effects of the curse. If none can be found or if the shaman's services are unaffordable, it is alleged that the footsteps of death will soon arrive. Although nonpractitioners, most Haitians living on the island and in other areas where Voodoo is prevalent (that is to say southeast Florida around Miami; the Hispanic neighborhoods of New York City, Chicago, and Los Angeles; and in the Black and Creole neighborhoods of New Orleans, Louisiana) are quite familiar with the Voodoo cult. They have observed such symptoms before in others.

Parallels to Orthodox Christianity

Paradoxically (that is to say, in spite of its abject diabolical and polytheistic ethos), this cult lauds the Judeo-Christian God as the Supreme Being. Nevertheless, the adherent does not refer to this God, nor invoke him, in the context that orthodox Christians would. The followers maintain that he (the Christian God) is the highest among the plethora of the gods of the Voodoo pantheon. However, because of Voodoo's nature, it cannot amalgamate or position itself with the orthodoxy or the orthopraxy of Christianity. Moreover, even the tyro Christian, after briefly studying the Bible, will conclude that the Voodoo cult's practices and beliefs bear not a modicum of resemblance to Protestantism. Rather, for the same warnings given against dabbling in the Santeria cult, Voodoo practices are to be avoided for they do not comport with Christian ideology.

Contrasts to Orthodox Christianity

The Santeria motifs and ceremonies are remarkably similar to those of the Voodoo cult; in some instances, they nearly mirror one another. For example, their pantheistic gods are each associated with one of the Catholic saints or with some aspect of Catholicism. Both cults also present sacrifices (often blood) to the gods. There are other striking similarities as well. Subsequently, that which were described as the dichotomies between Santeria and orthodox Christianity can be referred to when contrasting Voodoo to orthodox Christianity. When Santeria and Voodoo are both juxtaposed with orthodox Christianity, their differences are almost symmetrical. Therefore, to avoid redundancy, the reader is advised to see Contrasts to Orthodox Christianity under section eleven, Santeria.

Other dichotomies between Santeria and Orthodox Christianity, located in section eleven, Santeria, that mirror those between Voodoo and Orthodox Christianity are as follows:

(1) Blood sacrifices and offerings
(2) Divination and exorcism
(3) Priests and priestesses
(4) Reincarnation
(5) Surreptitiousness/esotericism
(6) Pantheon of deities and polytheism

Not unlike the Santeria cult, Voodoo also has its collection of prominent deities. Of course, in Christianity, monotheism is the ethos, for the scriptures say, "The Lord our God is one Lord" (Deut. 6:4, Mark 12:29). The table below depicts the functions of the more prominent deities of the Voodoo tradition.

Deity	**Function**
(1) Agwe	God of those at sea
(2) Aida Wedo	God of rainbows
(3) Ayza	God that protects
(4) Baron Samedi	Caretaker of cemeteries and graves
(5) Damballah Wedo	God (Serpent) of the waters/rivers.
(6) Ezili	Goddess of eros/passion
(7) Mawu Lisa	God of creation
(8) Ogu Bodagris	God of war
(9) Zaka	God of husbandry/agriculture

Table 2. Prominent deities and functions within the Voodoo pantheon.[2]

---

[2] Source: Nichols, et al. (2006)

Dr. A.J. Handy, Ph.D.

Soteriological Views

As expressed elsewhere in this work, those who adhere to the beliefs of Voodoo maintain that the universe consists of two forces: good and evil. Therefore, in hopes of gaining protectorate status, the faithful insist that they must appease the Loas (deities). They allege that this appeasement and subsequent protection from evil forces is gained by performing rituals, gesticulations, divinations, and sacrifices to one or more of the Loas. The Christian ethos of worshipping and having faith in a monotheistic God, living a holy life, altruism, loving one's neighbor, seeking to one day abide in heaven, and doing unto others as one wishes to be done unto them, is, of course, foreign to Voodoo practitioners.

Eschatological Perspectives

Tann (2012), a Mambo (priestess) of the Voodoo tradition, maintained that if the deceased was of a Voodoo persuasion prior to death, there are two ceremonies which are held: one soon after the demise of the individual and the other during what is known as "pot-breaking." This procedure is said to bring the person's spirit from beneath the water, where the individual's soul lies peacefully with one of the deities for a period of 366 days or so. Afterward, the person's soul is believed to be raised from the waters to join the souls of his or her deceased ancestors. In contrast, the souls of many of the deceased who were not of the Voodoo persuasion are alleged to go underwater forever. Others, it is maintained, are collected by one of the deities and assigned new opportunities. Some Voodooists, however, purport that after death, the inferior soul, known as the Petit bon Ange (little good angel), is eventually reincarnated if not captured and contained.

Concerns and Implications for the Orthodox Christian

Voodoo practitioners have been known to piece together and stage quite a mind-boggling and diabolical montage, the effects of which can be quite deleterious. The superfluity of gesticulations, coupled with seemingly uninhibited frenzies and dances, can be quite profound. The Christian neophyte, therefore, should not rush to convert members of this population. Only those Christian evangelists who are truly born again, astute, and extremely sagacious should attempt such a feat. Moreover, those orthodox Christians with a long history of evangelism should be more concerned with proselytizing among this group than with the effects that the cult can have on him or her. Prior to being censured and banished to the island called Patmos, the Apostle John pontificated, "Greater is he that is in you, than he that is in the world" (1 Jn. 4:4). John 15: 4-5 is also worthy of note. Consider, however, that those to whom he (John) pontificated were born again Christians (not the mere professors of Christianity). They were also well versed in the Apostles' doctrine. The critical reader will recall that the necessity of the born again experience has been addressed copiously throughout this volume. That is consistent with Jesus' mandate; see John 3: 3-7. To further exemplify the importance of the experience and remove much of the enigma, we shall, at this juncture, turn our attention to an episode in which some, whom lacked the transformation, sought to command Satan. One will discover the following in Acts 19: 13-16: "Then certain of the vagabond Jews, exorcists, took upon them to call over them which had evil spirits the name of the Lord Jesus, saying, we adjure you by Jesus whom Paul preacheth…the evil spirit answered and said, Jesus I know, and Paul I know; but who are ye?...the evil spirit…leaped on them,…and overcame them,…they fled out of that house naked and wounded."

Both France, the country that gave the Haitians their language and the use of its coinage (the livre), and Spain, the country which christened and provided the vessels which brought the Africans to Haiti, have been miserable failures in their (eighteenth through the twentieth centuries) attempt to bring salvation to the islanders. Rodman (1954) reasoned that the failed attempts to convert the islanders to Christianity stemmed from the fact that Haitian Voodoo absorbed and subsequently amalgamated all of the tenets, patron saints, and ceremonies of the papacy. Water baptism (a ritual practiced by the progenitors of the Haitian slaves prior to the slaves' arrival in Haiti), the crucifix, and even the Holy Trinity are of no exceptions. Moreover, in Voodoo, the cross of Christ, or the crucifix, is seen as a symbol of Baron Samedi, one of the cult's most feared deities. Water baptism, Rodman (1954) alleges, was a ritual endemic to most West Africa peoples not only prior to the advent of the transatlantic slave trade but long before the advent of Christianity. Haitians, therefore, were predisposed to this aspect of Christianity. The Trinity is said to be the representation of the three primal authorities, which are summoned to all Voodoo ceremonies (Rodman, 1954, pg. 64). Perhaps popery (which is to say Roman Catholicism) was the wrong design. Nevertheless, given the slaves' profound ritual predispositions, one may ask if Protestantism would have been accepted by the islanders as a more viable alternative. Rodman (1954) answers this question. In his *Haiti: The Black Republic*, the author reveals some amazing statistics (pgs. 75–76). Those data, of course, are reflective of the era in which he accounts, the early to mid-twentieth century. Nevertheless, according to Rodman's algebra, there were at that time several Protestant groups operating within the island nation. Collectively, those groups (i.e., Methodist, Baptist, Wesleyan, Episcopal) are to be lauded for contributing to the conversion of 10 percent (400,000) of Haiti's population, a populous, which was at that time around 4,000,000 (Rodman, 1954). Orthodox Christianity (although a latecomer to the island when juxtaposed with Catholicism), therefore, in its proper context, appears to be the only purely Western-devised religious dogma in Haiti that has rivaled popery within the arena of religious conversions. The table below is a numeration of more recent demographics. It is based on data compiled in July of 2018 by the United States government, which estimated Haiti's population to have been approximately 10.8 million.

Dr. A.J. Handy, Ph.D.

A Numeration of Haiti's Religious Demographics in 2018

Religion   **Percentage of population**

Religion	Percentage
Catholic	55%
Protestant (All)	29%
(1) Baptist Protestants	15%
(2) Pentecostal Protestants	8%
(3) Adventist Protestants	3%
(4) Methodist Protestants	1.5%
(5) Other Protestants	0.7%
Voodoo/Vodun	2.1%
Other	4.6%
Non-Affiliated	10%

Table 3. Religious Demographics of Haiti as of July 2018.[3]

Those data released by the United States Department of State, revealing a religion vacuum of 10 percent and converts to Protestantism to be at 29 percent, gives no reason to celebrate or to rest upon laurels for they are not at all impressive. As revealed elsewhere in this section, Rodman (1954) calculated the percentage of Protestant conversions in Haiti to have been at 10 percent; that was some sixty-six years ago. Subsequently, if Protestant evangelism continues along its trajectory of the

---

[3] Source: International Religious Freedom Report (2018), United States Department of State.

past, Haiti will remain predominantly under Romanism for the next, say, several hundred years. Evangelicals/Protestants must do more. It would help to lay aside and ignore insignificant denominational differences, the minutiae. For the Apostle Paul insisted, "I have planted, Apollos watered; but God gave the increase." The sage continued, "Neither is he that planteth any thing, neither he that watereth…he that planteth and he that watereth are one" (1 Cor. 3:6–8).

Suggested Readings:

(1) Elkins, W. F. *Street Preachers, Faith Healers, and Herb Doctors in Jamaica 1890–1925*. New York: Revisionist Press, 1977.

(2) Fauset, Arthur H. *Black Gods of the Metropolis, Negro Religious Cults of The Urban North*. University of Pennsylvania Press, 2020.

(3) Filan, Kenaz (2007). *The Haitian Vodou Handbook*.

(4) Hughes, Langston, *The Big Sea*. New York, Thunder's Mouth Press, 1986.

(5) Rigaud, Milo (1969). *Secrets of Voodoo*.

(6) Tann, Mambo C. (2012). *An Introduction to Haiti's Indigenous Spiritual Tradition*. Llewellyn Publications.

Summary and Avoiding the Lure of the Devil's Advocates

The philosophies, beliefs, and rituals of twelve cults and sects, which the author has termed Devil's advocates and counterfeits, were investigated, exposed, and annotated within this corpus. All of the cults/sects subjected to this inquiry were found to be either illusory or profoundly ritualistic in practice—illusory in that the practices and rituals are not sustaining and consequently have to be often repeated and profoundly ritualistic in that the practices (unlike those of Christianity) require various types of performances as a necessity for propitiation. Some, with their emphasis upon blood sacrifices, priesthoods, and offerings (i.e., Santeria, Voodoo, Mormonism), are briefly reminiscent of and analogous to Judaism. The first several chapters of the book of Hebrews (that is to say, chapters 1–10) let us know that these practices could never take away sin for they were only shadows or types of that which the truly born again now realizes.

    The conspicuous practice and positive portrayal of orthodox Christianity is extremely suppressed (if not completely banned) in many countries (i.e., N. Korea, Cuba, China, Yemen, Afghanistan, and Somalia, just to mention a fraction). The leaders of these regions fear that Christianity will usurp the authority of their theocracy or their regime. However, at the very core of Christianity is the requisite of the born again experience; this exposure does not comport with conspiracies to overthrow nations, sovereign or otherwise.

    Christianity requires a person to acquire a personal relationship—not simply adhering to vague, nepotistic, or congenital religious practices—with the God that Christians refer to as Jehovah, Yahweh, El Elyon, Jehovah-Jireh, Jehovah-nissi, etc. As such (for there are many even within the ranks of Christianity who have only a form of godliness—2 Tim. 3:5), even many Christian loyalists professing Christianity have not acquired the born again experience (John 3:3–7, Rom. 8:5–10, 1 Cor. 2:14). Their brand of Christianity is vain, a misnomer, for without the born again experience, one is a Christian in name only. Moreover, unlike the cults and sects that were investigated, Christianity is a religion not founded in the quagmire of uncertainty but was inaugurated on the day of Pentecost and consummated on that day by the outpouring of the Holy Ghost. Christians make no claims of being cognizant of all the details and minutiae associated with the born again experience. However, they make no apologies for the experience for it aligns and comports with Old and New Testament scripture. There is no other religion, sect, cult, nor any other assembly that can truthfully profess a similar experience. What is this grip and mind-altering effect, then, that Satan has on those of the occult, and why do the numbers continue to swell? I shall attempt to bring closure to these questions and resolve these enigmas in the succeeding narratives.

Many contemporary liberal Christian writers have narrated to the effect that all sincere seekers of God are on the same trajectory. One would be ill advised by such liberal theology. Such a premise resonates slightly with Taoism or Buddhism, of which much has been denuded and applauded within this volume. It does not, however, comport with the tenets of orthodox Christianity, Islam, Judaism, or Catholicism. Subsequently, the uninitiated must not be sold on the misconception that all major religions in essence lead to the same god vis-à-vis a vast dichotomy of nomenclatures, for within the Apostle Paul's homily (Eph. 4:4–5), he insisted that there is "one Lord, one faith, one baptism." Not all religions and seekers of the truth, however, subscribe to the apostle's doctrine. Subsequently, not all those who are seeking God's truth are on the correct path. Moreover, the dichotomies that exist between orthodox Christianity and other religions are vast and compelling. They're not as dismissive or insignificant as, say, one Christian denomination squabbling about the minutiae of another; they are consequential differences, dichotomies drenched with existential overtures and implications. Lastly, as concerning whether all religions lead one to God, the venerable Apostle Paul pontificated (Gal. 1:13–23, Phil. 3:4–14) that as a result of his initial encounter with Christ (Acts 9), he was compelled to abandon his former erroneous religion, Judaism. When the apostle announced that "all scripture is given by inspiration of God, and is profitable for doctrine...for instruction in righteousness" (2 Tim 3:16), he was not espousing that one should borrow from, let's say, the *Quran*, the Aryan/Hindu Vedas and *Bhagavad Gita*, the *Book of Mormon*, etc. For those sources—or any other—have no confluence with orthodox Christianity. The ubiquitous Apostle Paul was not led to salvation by an encounter with Buddha, Confucius, Moroni, or Allah. Rather, it was to the Incarnate Word, Jesus of Nazareth, to whom he would surrender (Acts 9).

The Mormons must ask themselves, among other things, were Joseph Smith's alleged visions and revelations actually from God, or were they mere illusions brought on by his copious acts of divinations? Similarly, the conundrum that the Jehovah's Witnesses must resolve is why there is such a dichotomy between the early metamorphosis stages of their religion as promulgated by C. T. Russell and much of the later literature and concepts perpetuated by Russell's successors, Judge Rutherford in particular. They must also continue to wrestle with the mystifications and glaringly unsubstantiated claims of Russell and Rutherford, allegations that can be found even among Mormon repositories. Many of those indictments were exposed elsewhere in this text.

More importantly, however, the two questions that the Muslims, Mormons, and Jehovah's Witnesses must ask themselves are the following: (1) Am I willing to entrust my eternal fate to concepts espoused by Muhammad, Smith, and Russell (purports that cannot be substantiated nor corroborated)? and (2) Is there a more substantiated religion to which I can subscribe? There is indeed—Christianity offers a more holistic alternative for it changes the whole individual. In Christianity, there's no need for the props and baggage that are quite compulsory for other sects. One must be vigilant, however, and able to differentiate the biblical brand of Christianity from the charlatan's facade. The scripture says, "Beware of false prophets…by their fruits ye shall know them" (Matt. 7:15–20).

Whereas John the Baptist (Matt. 3:11–17), the Apostles Peter, James, and John (Matt. 8:24–27, 16:13–16, 17:1–6, John 11:11–14, 41–44), and even Jesus's enemies (Matt. 2:3–8, 16, 27:54, John 9:6–25) can corroborate the deity and works of Jesus Christ, there is absolutely no one who can attest to any eyewitness accounts of God's encounters with Russell (JW's), Smith (Mormons), or Muhammad (Islam).

The biblical scriptures are by far the ultimate agency with which one must confer in order to determine how to be set free from occultism; Jesus insisted that "If the Son therefore shall make you free, ye shall be free indeed" (John 8:36). Whereas other religions employ various types of performances, rituals, props, contortions, etc., Christianity, contrastingly, is that which is predicated upon faith and faith alone (Rom. 4:16). This predicate always results in grace (Greek=*chari*, or unmerited favor). Hence, although many have been introduced and adopted, there are no prerequisites or rituals required by Christianity. Nepotism also, as the Apostle Paul asserted, is a foreign concept within Christianity (See Acts 10:34–35, Phil. 3:4–7). The venerable and legendary Apostle Paul, after fruitlessly pursuing God through the concepts of his progenitors (i.e., in accordance with the Levitical law), finally conceded that "by grace are ye saved through faith; and not of yourselves: it is the gift of God: Not of works" (Eph. 2:8–9).

Students of the Protestant Reformation will recall that Martin Luther harbored somewhat similar reservations concerning the ideal of salvation for he, after matriculating at the University of Erfurt (Germany) would discover the Latin Bible. Filled with wonder, amazement, and confusion, Luther felt that in order to please God, he was required to lead the life of a pious, lowly pauper. He sought to fulfill this requirement by entering a monastic order. However, the thoughts of sin would continue to pepper and haunt him. To relieve himself of such ideations, he would whip or scourge himself to drive out the sinful notions that permeated and darkened his mind. Despite the monk's fruitless self-afflictions, sin simply refused to take a holiday, nor would it seek an armistice.

Rather—as it always does—it would continue its onslaught. Disillusioned by the fact that he could not go it alone, absolve himself of sin, or at the very least assist God in providing his salvation, Luther's life would be thrown into a proverbial tailspin. Each passing day, he would spiral further and further into the doldrums. Eventually, he would entertain the perception that his situation was a colossal quagmire; this precipitated a bitter resentment toward God. White (1911), however, purported that when it seemed as though there was no hope, God sent a trusted colleague to Luther; this was Johann Von Staupitz. Professor Staupitz would eventually convince Luther to cease punishing himself, simply throw himself to the mercy and forgiveness of God, and trust in God alone to relieve him of his sins. The professor was only reiterating what the Apostle Peter proclaimed centuries earlier: "Casting all your care upon him; for he careth for you" (1 Pet. 5:7). At that juncture, Luther's life would be forever changed; hence, his capitulation to the grace of God would—while resulting in his excommunication—catapult him to the forefront of the Protestant Reformation. Such is the case with everyone, religious persuasions notwithstanding, who comes to God by Jesus Christ (see John 6:37, 10:7–15, 14:3–6, 2 Cor. 5:17, Heb. 7:25, 2 Pet. 3:9); one's life is forever changed.

Many readers, prior to studying this text, could've only imagined and were completely unaware of much of the demonic dogmas practiced and espoused by non-Christian sects. The information is available now; the reader will have to decide how to proceed with it. The choices are (1) repudiate the apostate who has strayed from the gospel, (2) remain indifferent at the expense of a soul being lost, or (3) become emboldened and, where and when possible, share the gospel with someone. The truly born again will, of course, choose the latter, for she or he realizes that it isn't the individual who is rejecting the gospel but the demonic forces that are manipulating the person. This is, of course, exemplified throughout the scriptures; however, it is nowhere better explicated than in the book of Mark (5:1–19). Moreover, the Apostle Paul pontificated that "we wrestle not against flesh and blood [the person himself or herself], but…against powers, against the rulers of the darkness of this world, against spiritual wickedness in high places" (Ephesians 6:12, emphasis added).

Moreover, when anyone came to Jesus requesting to be delivered from demonic influences, Jesus never resorted to ridicule or satire; none were rejected, regardless of stripe or circumstances (see Matt. 4:24, 17:14–18, 20:30–34). Pasquinades serve no purpose for they only serve to further alienate the reluctant and the vacillators. Moreover, despite the egregiousness of one's sins, he or she is secure or sealed until the day of redemption after accepting Jesus Christ as Lord and Savior (Eph. 4:30 and John 6:37). For those so intertwined with the diabolical forces of darkness, breaking free from the occult can be quite a daunting task; therefore, as it was in the view of Professor Staupitz and Martin Luther (White, 1911), it is incumbent upon the missionary/evangelist to remain cognizant of the facts that no one, regardless of their status within the occult, is inextricably meshed, for truth can always be realized via the gospels. As the scriptures reveal, and perhaps more importantly than all that has been annotated within this summary, those who reject Christ and attempt to enter the sheepfold by ignoring the door (Jesus) and climbing up some other way (see John 10:1–2, 7–10) will find disappointment, disillusionment, and failure inevitably awaiting them.

This mode of research should, perhaps, not be undertaken by those who are not truly born again and fully led by the Spirit of God. To obtain an accurate assessment of and properly treat any topics, one would have to go where the research leads, documenting as it unfolds. Some of the rituals and contagions, however that were investigated and annotated within the corpus of this commentary are quite animated, persuasive, and compelling. Subsequently, the novice, when venturing into such proverbial uncharted waters could, allegorically, be pulled in. Furthermore, the devil's advocates' counterfeit measures—as were mentioned in the introduction—crosses all social, economic, and phenotypic strata. Hence, when investigating such topics as those that have been treated in this work, one's academic standing should never be relied upon. For in this model of research, a zeal and bravado predicated exclusively upon one's academic or theological prowess would only lead to betrayal, uncertainty, and miserable failure. It is advised in the book of Proverbs (3:5–6) to "lean not unto thine own understanding…and he shall direct thy paths." Jesus also reiterated, "He that abideth in me…the same bringeth forth much fruit…without me ye can do nothing" (John 15:5). Lastly, as mentioned elsewhere within this corpus, the Apostle Paul pontificated that "All scripture is given by inspiration of God, and is profitable for doctrine…for instruction in righteousness" (2 Tim. 3:16). Secondary sources, although having much to lend, can often be misleading; unreliable; improperly referenced to Greek, Latin, or

Hebrew; and sprinkled with deceit. Therefore, one should rely totally upon the scriptures; addendums and redactions are to be rejected. As Martin Luther would advise, *solus scriptura*, or consider the scriptures alone as the source of correct doctrine.

Suggested Churches/Denominations:

The list that follows is, certainly, not meant to be a remedy for all the ills of Protestantism, nor are the denominations listed in any order of preference. For example, even though my beloved Church of God In Christ (COGIC) - into which I was first ordained as a minister - is first on the list, those of us who are very familiar with the late Bishop C. H. Mason's (the founder) dogma can attest that his exact theology is not being promulgated, or exuded, within a great majority of COGIC assemblies today. Suffice it to say, colloquially, that it's not your great grandfather's COGIC. Nevertheless, this largest Pentecostal denomination in North America, currently piloted by J. D. Sheard Sr. became such by maintaining much of the venerable Bishop Mason's philosophies. Therefore the Church of God In Christ in the main – as it relates to the exposal of biblical scriptures, and the adherence to the founder's precepts – is highly recommended.

Also, as it is with any church or assembly where there are fundamentalists—that is to say, those who abide strictly by the tenets of the movement—there are also charlatans as well as skeptics within most assemblies. Therefore, the groups and assemblies that are suggested are only recommended to the extent to which they've maintained and adhered to their fundamentals, the premises upon which they were originally founded. One is encouraged to be prayerful and to immerse himself or herself in the scriptures when deciding which church or denomination to become affiliated with for there are many members of the clergy—irrespective of affiliations—who are not as genuine as many were back in the day. Falling prey to a capricious ethos and an iniquitous social climate, a great number of preachers have succumbed to their salacious proclivities and the lure and deceptions of financial gain. Beware of the ministers who are reluctant to confront those who are obviously engaged in sinful activities. Those are the clergy who vacillate out of fear of offending and subsequently losing the culprit's membership. Many ecclesiastics believe that with a dwindling membership, the church's coffers—and the lining of their own pockets with much of the funds—will become too severely hampered. This will help to explain (and the readers will surely wonder) why the list that I have formulated is quite brief. It was originally comprised of several other suggested denominations; however, after much prayer and consideration, I was compelled to abbreviate the list. Perhaps your church or affiliation is not included in the compilation; exclusions were not meant to slight or bring an indictment against any congregation. Your church might be almost flawless, and you're happy with it; nonetheless, each of us must take the responsibility for seeking out the denomination that we believe best reflects biblical doctrine. It is important to remain leery and suspicious of those churches/denominations whose requisites for membership are an application fee, monthly or annual fees to remain a member, and classes of indoctrination. Those ministers who can barely finish their sermons without badgering for a supplemental donation or insisting that the congregants or listeners make a purchase should also be kept at bay. Such continued practices are not scriptural; rather, they run counter to orthodox Christianity. The observant reader will find that there were only six (seven for those who insist on including 1 John 3:17) occasions during which the apostles elicited a supplemental offering. Those six were for dire circumstances (see Acts 5:1–2, Rom. 15:26, 1 Cor. 16:1–2, 2 Cor. 8:1–5, 9:12–15, and Gal. 6:10). Consequently, those denominations/assemblies that support such inclinations listed above (i.e., annual membership fees, classes of indoctrination, etc.) will not be suggested by this author as places to fellowship. Moreover, those assemblies listed below are only suggestions; they are not listed because they are perfect, nor should they be thought of as panaceas. Sadly, there aren't any.

List of Suggested Churches and Denominations:

(1) Church of God in Christ (Bishop C. H. Mason)
www.cogic.org
930 Mason St.
Memphis, TN 38126
(901) 947-9358

(2) Jimmy Swaggart Ministries www.Jsm.org
8919 World Ministry Ave.
Baton Rouge, LA 70810
(225) 768-8300

(3) The Potter's House of Dallas (T. D. Jakes)

www.thepottershouse.org
6777 W. Kiest Blvd.
Dallas, TX 75236
(214) 331-0954

(4) Creflo Dollar Ministries/World Changers Church International
www.creflodollarministries.org
P.O. Box 490124 College Park, GA 30349
(770) 210-5730

(5) Assemblies of God www.ag.org
1445 N. Boonville Ave.
Springfield, MO 65802-1894
(417) 862-2781

(6) National Baptist Convention
www.nationalbaptist.com
5202 Watkins Dr.
Jackson, MS 39206
(601) 362-6265

(7) Southern Baptist Convention www.sbc.net
Nashville, TN (615) 244-2355

(8) The Lutheran Church (Orthodox)
www.infocenter@lcms.org
St. Louis, MO
1-888-843-5267

(9) Church of the Nazarene (Orthodox)
www.info@nazarene.org
17001 Prairie Star Parkway

Lenexa, KS 66220
(913) 577-0500

(10) The Episcopal Church (Orthodox)
www.episcopalchurch.org
815 Second Ave. New York, NY 10017
(212) 716-6000), (800)334-7626)

(11) AME/African Methodist-Episcopal
www.cio@ame-church.com
500 8th Ave. South
Nashville, TN 37203
(615) 254-0911

(12) American Baptist Association
www.abaptist.org
P.O. Box 1050
Texarkana, TX 75504-1050
(903) 792-2312

(13) The Oral Roberts Evangelistic Association
www.oralroberts.com
6355 E. Skelly Dr. #74135
Tulsa, OK 74135
(918) 591-2000

(14) Lester Sumrall Evangelistic Association
www.lesea
530 E. Ireland Rd.
South Bend, IN 46614-6614
(574) 291-8200

(15) Jessie Duplantis Ministries www.jdm.org

1973 Ormond Blvd.
Destrehand, LA 70047
(985) 764-2000

(16) John Hagee Ministries www.jhm.org
239 N. Loop 1604 W.
San Antonio, TX 78232
(210) 494-3900

(17) The United Methodist Church (Orthodox)
www.umc.org
304 S. Perimeter Park Dr.
Nashville, TN 37202-0320
(615) 329-1177

References:

Aland, K., and Aland, B. (1987). *The Text of the New Testament*. Grand Rapids, Michigan: Williams B. Eerdman's Publishing.

American Psychiatric Association: Diagnostic and Statistical Manual of Mental Disorders, Fourth Edition. Washington, DC, American Psychiatric Association, 1994.

Ankerberg, J., Weldon, J., and Buroughs, D. (1998, 2008). *Facts on Jehovah's Witnesses*. Eugene, Oregon: Harvest House Publishers.

Armstrong, K. (2000). *Islam, a Short History*. New York: Random House, Inc.

Arya, V. (2003). *The Book of the Vedas, Timeless Wisdom from Indian Tradition*. New York: Barron's Educational Series.

Barkun, M. (1994). *Religion and the Racist Right, the Origins of the Christian Identity Movement*. Chapel Hill, NC: University Of North Carolina Press.

Benedict, G. (2008). *The Watkins Dictionary of Religious and Secular Faiths*. London: Watkins Publishing.

Brock, E. J. (2001). *Images of America, Shreveport Faces of the Past*. Charleston, SC: Arcadia Publishing.

Brown, D. H. (2003). *The Light Inside: Abakua Society Arts and Cuban Cultural History*. Philadelphia,

Melbourne, New Delhi, Singapore, Beijing, UK.: Routledge Revivals.

Butler-Bowdown, T. (2006). *Fifty Spiritual Classics*. (on M-P-3). Boston, MA: Gilden Media Corp.

Calvin, J. (1961, 1977). *Concerning the Eternal Predestination of God.* Louisville, KY: John Knox Press. Catholic Biblical Association (1970). *The New American Bible: The Confraternity of Christian Doctrine.*

Cochrant, H., and Howard, H. (1961). Song: I Fall To Pieces.

Deissmann, G. A. (1910, 1911). *Light from the Ancient East*. New York, Toronto: Hodder And Stoughton.

Doniger, W. (1999). *Merriam-Webster's Encyclopedia of Religions*. Merriam-Webster, Inc.

Du Bois, W. E. B. (1980). *Prayers for Dark People.* Amherst: University Of Massachusetts Press.

Erskine, N. L. (2004). *From Garvey to Marley, Rastafari Theology*. Gainesville: University Press of Florida.

Esposito, J. L. (1988). *Islam the Straight Path*. Oxford: University Press.

Ferrell, V. (2019). *Down through the Centuries, Little Known Facts from Church History*. Altamont, TN: Harvestime Books.

Freud, S. (1923). *The Ego & the Id*. Vienna: International Psycho-Analytischer. Norton & Company.

Freud, S. (1961). *Civilization and Its Discontents*. New York: Norton & Company.

Gonzalez-Wipper, M. (2001). *Santeria, the Religion*. St. Paul, MN: Llewellyn Publications.

Hall, T. L. (2003). *American Religious Leaders*. New York: Facts On File, Inc.

Handy, A. J. (2019). *Comprehending the Pauline Epistles, A Study Guide*. Savage, MN: Lighthouse Christian Publishing.

Hazelton, L. (2013). *The First Muslim, a Story of Muhammad*. New York: Riverhead Books.

Joiner, G. D., and Prime, J. A. (2016). *Legendary Locals of Shreveport*. Charleston, SC: Arcadia Publishing.
Joiner, J. (2013) *Badge of Dishonor: A True Story of Police Racism, Brutality, and Murder in a Deep South City*. Louisiana: Morris Publishing.

Jung, C. G. (1961, 1962, 1963). *Memories, Dreams, and Reflections*. New York: Vintage Books, A Division of Random House.

Junique, K. (2004). *Rastafari? Rasta for You, Rastafarianism Explained*. London: Athena Press.

Khattab, M. (2016). *The Clear Quran, A Thematic*

English Translation of the Message of the Final Revelation. Lombard, IL: Book of Signs Foundation.

Kirby, D. H. G. (1985) *Santeria: African Influences on Religion in Cuba*. Negro History Bulletin. 48, 39–44.
Knipe, D. M. (1991). *Hinduism, Experiment in the Sacred*. Long Grove, IL: Waveland Press, Inc.

Langone, M. D. (2015). "Characteristics Associated with Cultic Groups—Revised." *International Cultic Studies Association (ICSA) Today*, Vol. 6, No. 3, 2015, 10.

Lau, D. C. (1979). *Confucius, The Analects*. New York: Penguin Books.

Lee, N. H. (1960). *To Kill A Mockingbird*. Philadelphia, PA: J. B. Lippincott & Company.

Lennon, J. W., and Ono, Y. (1971). Song: Imagine. London: Apple Records.

Lewis, J. R. (2005). *Cults: A Reference Handbook*. (2nd ed.). Santa Barbara, CA: ABC-CLIO, Inc.

Lloyd-Jones, H. (1991). *Greek in A Cold Climate*. Salvage, MD: Barnes and Noble.

MacArthur, J. (2010). *The MacArthur Study Bible, English Standard Version*. Wheaton, IL: Crossway.

Mack, D. (1999). *From Babylon to Rastafari: Origin and History of the Rastafarian Movement*. Chicago, Jamaica, London, Republic Of Trinidad and Tobago: Research

Associates; School Times Publications.

Martin, W. (2003). *The Kingdom of the Cults.* Bloomington, MN: Bethany House.

Maslow, A. H. (1954). *Motivation and Personality.* New York: Harper & Brothers.

Maslow, A. H. (1976). *The Far Reaches of Human Nature.* London: Penguin Publishing.

Millman, D. (2000). *Way of the Peaceful Warrior.* (New Revised ed.). Novato, CA: H. J. Kramer, New World Library.

Molloy, M. V. (2002). *Experiencing the World's Religions: Traditions, Challenge, And Change.* (2nd ed.). London, Toronto: Mayfield Publishing Co.

Murphy, J. M. (1998). *Santeria, an African Religion In America.* Boston, MA: Bacon Press.

Nichols, L. A., Mather, G. A., and Schmidt, A. J. (2006). *Encyclopedic Dictionary of Cults, Sects, and World Religions.* Grand Rapids, MI: Zondervan.

Patterson, E., and Rybarczyk, E. J. (2007, pp. 123–124). *The Future of Pentecostalism in the United States.* New York: Lexington Books.

Pfeiffer, C. F. (1974). *Works of Josephus, the War of The Jews.* Grand Rapids, MI: Baker Book House.

Prabhavananda, S., and Isherwood, C. (1944, 51, 87, 95). *Bhagavad-Gita*. New York: Barnes & Noble Books.

Renard, J. (2012). *The Handy Religion Answer Book*. (2nd ed.). Canton, MI: Visible Ink Press.

Roberts, J. (2004). *Chinese Mythology, A-to-Z*. New York: Facts On File Inc.

Rodman, S. (1954). *Haiti: The Black Republic*. New York: The Devin-Adair Company.

Rogers, R. (1924). *The Holy Piby, The Blackman's Bible*. New York: Robert Rogers, Publisher.

Rummel, R. J. (1994). *Death by Government*. New Brunswick (U.S.), London (UK):Transaction Publishers.
Rushdie, S. (1988). *The Satanic Verses*. New York: Random House.

Schucman, H., and Thetford, W. T. (1976). *A Course in Miracles*. New York: Viking, The Foundation For Inner Peace.

Scofield, C. I. (2015). *The Classic King James Bible*. Uhrichsville, OH: Barbour Publishing.

Smith, J., Jr. *The Book of Mormon, Another Testament of Jesus Christ*. (1981, 2013). Salt Lake City, Utah: Intellectual Research, Inc. The Church Of Jesus Christ Of Latter-Day Saints.

Smith, J., Jr. (1951). *The Pearl of Great Price*. Salt Lake

City, Utah: The Church Of Jesus Christ Of Latter-Day Saints.

Tann, M. C. (2012). *Haitian Vodou, an Introduction to Haiti's Indigenous Spiritual Tradition.* Woodbury, MN: Llewellyn Publication.

United States Department of State. (2018). *International Religious Freedom Report.* Washington, DC: Bureau of Democracy, Human Rights And Labor.

Velez, M. T. (2000). *Drumming for the Gods, the Life and Times of Felipe Garcia Villamil: Santeria, Palero, and Abakua.* Philadelphia, Pennsylvania: Temple University Press.

Vlastos, G. (1994, 95). *Socratic Studies.* New York, Melbourne: Press Syndicate of the University of Cambridge.

Watchtower Bible and Tract Society. (1961). *The New World Translation Bible.* Warwick, NY: Watchtower Bible and Tract Society.

Watchtower Bible and Tract Society. (2018). *Country and Territory Report.* Warwick, NY: Watchtower Bible and Tract Society.

White, E. G. (1911). *The Great Controversy of The Great Protestant Reformation.* Altamont, TN: Harvestime Books.

Windsor, R. R. (2003). *From Babylon to Timbuktu, A*

History Of Ancient Black Races, Including the Black Hebrews. Atlanta, GA: Windsor's Golden Series.

Wright, C. (1955). *The Beginnings of Unitarianism in America*. Boston, MA: Starr King Press.

Wright, C. (1975, 1989). *A Stream Of Light, A Short History Of American Unitarianism*. (2 ed.). Boston, MA: Skinner House Books.

Zodhiates, S. (1993). *The Epistles of John, an Exegetical Commentary*. Chattanooga, TN: Amg Publishers.

Further Suggested Literature:

Beliso-DeJesus, A. M. (2015). *Electric Santeria, Racial and Sexual Assemblages of Transnational Religion.*

Blaut, J. M. (1992). *1492, The Debate on Colonialism, Eurocentrism, and History.*

Brodie, F. M. (1971, 1979). 2nd ed. *No Man Knows My History; the Life of Joseph Smith the Mormon Prophet.*

Brown, R. E., Fitzmyer, J. A., and Murphy, R. E. (1990). *The New Jerome Biblical Commentary.*

Bruce, F. F. (1977). *Paul Apostle of the Heart Set Free.*
Bruce, F. F. (1979). *Peter, Stephen, James, and John; Studies in Non-Pauline Christianity.*

Carr, L. (2015). *A Year in White, Cultural New Comers to Lukumi and Santeria in the United States.*

Davidson, B. (1991). *African Civilization Revisited.*
Du Bois, W. E. B. (1896, 1965). *The Suppression of the African Slave Trade to the United States of America, 1638–1870.*

Filan, K. (2007). *The Haitian Vodou Handbook, Protocols for Riding With The Lwa.*

Godet, F. L. (1977). *Commentary on Romans.*
Handy, A. J. (1999). *Ethnocentrism and Black Students with Disabilities, Bridging the Cultural Gap. Vol. 1.*

Latourette, K. S. (1953). *A History of Christianity*.

Laurence, R. (2000). *The Book of Enoch the Prophet*.
Pfeiffer, C. F. (1979). *The Works of Flavius Josephus. Vol. 1–4*.

Redfield, J. (1993). *The Celestine Prophecy, an Adventure*.

Rice, J. R. (1963). *Filled with the Spirit, a Verse-by-Verse Commentary on Acts of the Apostles*.

Smith, D., (1920). *The Life and Letters of St. Paul*.

Smith, J. Jr. (1984). *Joseph Smith and the Beginnings of Mormonism*.

Sumrall, L. F. (1982). *The Names of God*. (Updated ed.).
Wise, M., Abegg, M. Jr., and Cook, E. (1996). *The Dead Sea Scrolls*.

Wright, D. C. (2011). *The History of China*.

Zanini, R. I. (2013). *Bakhita, from Slave to Saint*.

Evangelist A. J. Handy, PhD (11/1/2020)

Other works by Dr. A. J. Handy:

(1) *Ethnocentrism and Black Students with Disabilities: Bridging the Cultural Gap*

(2) *Comprehending the Pauline Epistles: A Study Guide*

The picture of the Stranger (in the acknowledgement) drawn by Victoria Skye English, a senior at Alexandria Senior High, Alexandria, Louisiana (12/25/2020).

Dr. A.J. Handy, Ph.D.

For comments, questions, or to borrow from these narratives, contact the author: ahandy1951@gmail.com, or adamhandy1@icloud.com

www.ingramcontent.com/pod-product-compliance
Lightning Source LLC
Chambersburg PA
CBHW071400160426
42811CB00115B/2434/J